# Bibliography of Nonsexist Supplementary Books (K-12)

# Bibliography of Nonsexist Supplementary Books (K-12)

Developed by
Northwest Regional Educational Laboratory
Center for Sex Equity

Karen Stone, Developer
Barbara K. Berard
Lillian Dixson
Janice Druian
Joan Goforth
Ginger Denecke Hackett
Barbara Hutchison, Director

ORYX PRESS
1984

The rare Arabian Oryx is believed to have inspired the myth of the unicorn. This desert antelope became virtually extinct in the early 1960s. At that time several groups of international conservationists arranged to have 9 animals sent to the Phoenix Zoo to be the nucleus of a captive breeding herd. Today the Oryx population is over 400 and herds have been returned to reserves in Israel, Jordan, and Oman.

*Bibliography of Nonsexist Supplementary Books (K–12)* was first published as *BIAS (Building Instruction Around Sex Equity): Bibliography of Non-Sexist Supplementary Books (K–12)* by Northwest Regional Educational Laboratory in 1982.

Copyright © 1984 by The Oryx Press
2214 North Central at Encanto
Phoenix, AZ 85004

Published simultaneously in Canada

Printed and Bound in the United States of America.

Library of Congress Cataloging in Publication Data
Main entry under title:

Bibliography of nonsexist supplementary books (K–12)

   Includes indexes.
   1. Children's literature—Bibliography.   2. Sex role in literature—Bibliography.   3. Women in literature—Bibliography.   4. Sexism in literature—Bibliography.   I. Northwest Regional Educational Laboratory. Center for Sex Equity.
Z1037.B578     1983     011'.62     83-42838
[PN1009.A1]
ISBN 0-89774-101-3

# Contents

**Preface**        vii

**Acknowledgements**        ix

**Introduction**        xi

**Bibliography**

Reading Grade Level  1        1

Reading Grade Level  2        3

Reading Grade Level  3        11

Reading Grade Level  4        19

Reading Grade Level  5        29

Reading Grade Level  6        37

Reading Grade Level  7        49

Reading Grade Level  8        59

Reading Grade Level  9        65

Reading Grade Level 10        69

Reading Grade Level 11        71

Reading Grade Level 12        73

**Appendixes**

Appendix 1: Resource Bibliographies        75

Appendix 2: Analysis Procedures        77

Appendix 3: Readability        81

Appendix 4: Subject Definitions        83

**Indexes**

Title Index        85

Author Index        91

Subject Index        95

# Preface

This bibliography was developed by the Center for Sex Equity Program at the Northwest Regional Educational Laboratory to provide teachers with materials to offset the influence of sex-biased texts. We believe that it can be used in conjunction with current textbooks to provide a balanced reading experience for students.

We have found that many books portray girls and women in only a few careers. Therefore, we have attempted to select books that promote sex equity and present a wide range of careers and interests for both girls and boys. We hope that in the future more books will be available that portray women in a wider variety of careers.

Some of the books included in the bibliography, especially biographies, were found to contain some forms of language bias or to portray secondary characters in stereotyped ways. However, we have included them because they do present major female characters in positive roles.

If a book is not included on our list, it does not mean we discourage its use in the classroom. For example, some books are not included merely because we did not know about them. Other books, especially historical and cross-cultural works may present accurate portrayals of people in other times and in other places but did not meet our criteria for sex-fair materials. (See Appendix 2: "Analysis Procedures" for a complete description of the criteria and procedures used in making selections for the bibliography.) Under the guidance of skillful teachers, these still present valuable reading for students.

This list, compiled during the last three years, is for K–12 students and will provide classroom teachers and librarians with a full range of books for use in promoting equitable education for all students. We suggest teachers use this bibliography in conjunction with the *Guide to Nonsexist Teaching Activities K–12* (published by Oryx Press).

This work was made possible by a grant from the Women's Educational Equity Act Program of the U.S. Education Department.

*Barbara Hutchison, Director*

# Acknowledgements

The development of this bibliography has been a collaborative effort requiring the cooperation of many people. The Center for Sex Equity Program staff would like to thank the following people for their assistance in this effort:

Gwyneth Britton and Margaret Lumpkin, Britton and Associates, Oregon State University, Corvallis, Oregon, for their research and development of the initial analysis instrument and readability assessment program, as well as their endless encouragement in this endeavor.

Sharon Sherner, Sally Gay, Nance O'Dell, Lynn Brown, Janis Hallinan, Deborah Kernan, Barbara Vanslow, Joy Wallace, and Ann Wehbring for their assistance in reading and analyzing the books included in the bibliography.

Judy Davis, Sharon Mallen and Geri Canfield for their assistance in readying the bibliography for production.

Patricia Goins and Doris Shakin, our program monitors, Women's Program Staff of the U.S. Education Department, for their advice and support of this work.

# Introduction

## WHY THE BIBLIOGRAPHY WAS COMPILED

Many of the texts and supplementary books available in schools today are

| | |
|---|---|
| Sex-Biased and/or | They contain a disproportionate number of stories or biographies with males as major characters |
| Sex-Role Stereotyped | They depict males as having a common set of abilities, interests, values and roles that are different from the abilities, interests, values and roles of females |

For teachers to teach in an equitable manner and in a way which offers the maximum career choices and role models for students, they must have access to books that do not promote sex bias or stereotyping. Therefore, this bibliography was compiled after a thorough and systematic analysis for sex, race and career bias of many of the supplementary, nonsexist books currently available.

## WHO CAN USE THE BIBLIOGRAPHY

This list is for K–12 classroom teachers and librarians who seek alternatives to the books they currently use. Books on the list are either

| | |
|---|---|
| Nonsexist or | They present both females and males as major characters with equal skills or competencies |
| Compensatory | They feature females as leading characters with skills and competencies that so often have only been allocated to male characters |

## HOW THE BIBLIOGRAPHY WAS COMPILED

Staff from the Center for Sex Equity Program selected books for review and analysis from several existing nonsexist bibliographies and from publishers' recommendations. Books chosen for inclusion on this list were then analyzed for

| | |
|---|---|
| Sex, Race and Career Bias and | Using a quantifiable analysis instrument |
| Grade Level Readability | Using a multitest computerized readability formula |

## HOW THE BIBLIOGRAPHY IS ORGANIZED

The bibliography is organized by reading level for grades one through 12. In addition to the main bibliography, author, title and subject indexes have been provided to facilitate its use.

Each book has an identification number with the first digit indicating its grade level readability and the subsequent digits indicating its numerical sequence within the grade level. For example, 4.56 would indicate the 56th book listed in the fourth grade reading level section.

## WHAT INFORMATION IS PROVIDED

The citation for each book includes bibliographic data, an annotation, career count and subject descriptors. The symbol "X" by the number for each title indicates the book may be inappropriate for the grade level at which it is written because of its format or subject matter.

Bibliographic data for each book include the title, author or editor, name and place of publisher, date of publication, number of pages, price (if available), and original publisher (if applicable). Books available in paperback are so noted. Prices were obtained from the 1978–79 *Books in Print*

(R.R. Bowker) or from the edition of the book reviewed and should be considered approximations.

Each annotation contains a brief description of the content of the book and the gender, ethnicity or nationality of the major character. Also included is qualitative information to aid educators in selecting appropriate books for their students. The annotations indicate particularly positive or, in some cases, controversial aspects about books of which teachers should be aware. Following the annotation is the number of female, male and neutral careers mentioned in the book. Because books are not always written or published with reading levels appropriate to their content, it is important that users of this bibliography do not rely solely on the designated reading grade level but refer also to the annotation for information regarding the appropriate audience for the book.

It should also be noted that the books included in the bibliography have not been assessed for cultural or racial authenticity. Such an assessment was beyond the scope of the project and expertise of the staff. If a book appeared to a reviewer as blatantly unauthentic, it was not included in the bibliography.

The major subject categories covered in the book are listed to enable teachers to easily match the subject of a book to an individual student's interest or to a particular lesson the teacher is planning. The following categories are used:

American Ethnic Minority
Animals
Autobiography/Biography
Behavioral Science
Careers
Contemporary Issues/Current Events
Cultural Heritage
Families/Friendship
Fine Arts
Foreign Countries
The Handicapped
Health/Human Development
History
Information Book

Language Arts
   Anthologies
   Drama
   Essays/Short Stories
   Fantasy, Folk & Fairy Tales
   Literature by Women
   Poetry/Rhyme
Mystery/Adventure
Picture Book
Religion/Mythology
Science/Technology
Science Fiction
Sports
Women's Studies

Users of the bibliography are particularly encouraged to refer to the subject index to facilitate finding books appropriate to the interests of students.

## FOR MORE DETAILED INFORMATION

Appendixes provide more detailed information about the bibliography and how it was compiled.

*Appendix 1: Resource Bibliographies*—provides a list of bibliographies used to identify books for analysis

*Appendix 2: Analysis Procedures*—provides a description of procedures and instruments used to analyze books for sex, race and career bias

*Appendix 3: Readability*—provides a description of the computerized readability assessment used to determine grade level readability

*Appendix 4: Subject Definitions*—provides definitions of subject descriptors

For more information about the project, contact Ms. Barbara Hutchison, Director, Center for Sex Equity, Northwest Regional Educational Laboratory, 300 S.W. Sixth Avenue, Portland, Oregon 97204, (503) 248-6800.

# Reading Grade Level 1–Spache Formula

**1.1 The Train.** Robert Welber. New York: Pantheon, 1972. 46 p. $4.99.

Elizabeth is afraid of the wide meadow she must cross in order to see the trains go by. But with support from her family, she finds the courage to cross the unknown meadow and realizes she enjoys the adventure. Book breaks stereotypes in that the illustrations show an interracial family.

*Careers:* Female = 1 Male = 3 Neutral = 0
*Subject Categories:* American Ethnic Minority; Families/Friendship; Health/Human Development

**1.2 And I Mean It, Stanley.** Crosby Bonsall. New York: Harper & Row, 1974. 32 p. $4.95.

Delightful story of a little girl who is creating a junk sculpture while talking to Stanley, who is behind the fence. But *who* is Stanley? Story shows female actively making/building something.

*Careers:* None shown
*Subject Categories:* Picture Book

**1.3 I Can Help Too.** Ilon Wikland. New York: Random House, 1974. 20 p. $1.95.

This is an excellent book that shows a young boy's success with household tasks.

*Careers:* None shown
*Subject Categories:* Families/Friendship; Picture Book

**1.4 A Hole Is to Dig.** Ruth Krauss. New York: Harper & Row, 1952. 46 p. $3.95.

With words and pictures, children give their definitions of eyebrows, love, a party and more. Delightful illustrations show little girls and boys sharing activities together, including building things, holding hands, rolling in mud and climbing mountains. Sentences are not punctuated and type size ranges from primary to intermediate.

*Careers:* Female = 0 Male = 1 Neutral = 0
*Subject Categories:* Families/Friendship; Picture Book

**1.5 Ann Can Fly.** Fred Phleger. New York: Beginner Books, 1959. 63 p. $2.95.

Ann flies with her father to summer camp in his plane. On the way, she learns how to fly and gets the chance to pilot the plane herself. The book breaks stereotypes by showing a positive father-daughter relationship in which the two are engaged in nontraditional activities. Illustrations are rather dated.

*Careers:* Female = 0 Male = 4 Neutral = 0
*Subject Categories:* Families/Friendship; Picture Book

**1.6 Snow.** Roy McKie and P.D. Eastman. New York: Beginner Books, 1962. 61 p. $3.50.

This rhyming story shows two children playing in the snow—skiing, sledding and throwing snowballs.

*Careers:* None shown
*Subject Categories:* Families/Friendship; Picture Book; Poetry/Rhyme

**1.7 Rabbit Finds a Way.** Judy Delton. New York: Crown, 1975. 28 p. $4.95.

Rabbit learns how to bake his own carrot cake instead of depending on Bear to make the cake.

*Careers:* None shown
*Subject Categories:* Animals; Fantasy, Folk & Fairy Tales

**1.8 What Is a Girl? What Is a Boy?** Stephanie Waxman. Culver City, CA: Peace Press, 1976. 40 p. $3.95. Paper.

A book for parents and teachers to read together with young children. Black and white photographs and simple text point out the differences between the bodies of girls and boys; women and men. The book also points out that girls and boys can have the same names, enjoy the same activities and feel the same emotions. Children from a variety of ethnic minority groups are portrayed in the photographs.

*Careers:* None shown
*Subject Categories:* Health/Human Development; Picture Book

**1.9 Sunshine.** Jan Ormerod. New York: Lothrop, Lee & Shepard, 1981. 24 p. $7.95.

Without words, this picture book tells a charming story of a young girl awakening with the sun and taking charge of herself and her day—including getting everyone out the door in time for work and school. Conveys a sense of family closeness without being cloying.

*Careers:* Female = 1 Male = 1 Neutral = 0
*Subject Categories:* Families/Friendship; Picture Book

# Reading Grade Level 2–Spache Formula

**2.1 Why Am I Different?** Norma Simon. Chicago: Albert Whitman, 1976. 31 p. $5.25.

This book portrays everyday situations in which children see themselves as "different" in family life, preferences and attitudes. It shows children that *everyone* is different and that being different is all right! Book is an honest attempt at portraying children and adults in nonstereotyped sex and ethnic roles.

*Careers:* Female = 8 Male = 13 Neutral = 0
*Subject Categories:* American Ethnic Minority; Families/ Friendship; Health/Human Development; Picture Book

**2.2 Max.** Rachel Isadora. New York: Macmillan, 1976. 26 p. $4.95.

Max has a new way to warm up for his baseball game on Saturday—he goes to his sister's ballet class. This is a delightful story with amusing illustrations throughout.

*Careers:* Female = 1 Male = 1 Neutral = 0
*Subject Categories:* Fine Arts; Picture Book; Sports

**2.3 Mary Jo's Grandmother.** Janice May Udry. Chicago: Albert Whitman, 1976. 26 p. $4.75.

Mary Jo, a young black girl, shows courage when her grandmother goes through a crisis. Although females are stereotypically portrayed only as grandmothers/mothers, and families are the typical mother/father, sister/brother configuration, the sensitivity shown throughout the story is particularly appealing.

*Careers:* Female = 2 Male = 3 Neutral = 0
*Subject Categories:* American Ethnic Minority; Families/ Friendship

**2.4 Bodies.** Barbara Brenner. New York: E.P. Dutton, 1973. 43 p. $6.95.

A picture book of bodies—every size, shape, color, sex and age—with a simple text that praises the uniqueness of each individual.

*Careers:* Male = 2
*Subject Categories:* Health/Human Development; Picture Book

**2.5 Oh Lord, I Wish I Was a Buzzard.** Polly Greenberg. New York: Macmillan, 1968. 28 p. $6.95.

This is a warm story about a young black girl who picks cotton in the fields with her family under the hot sun and wishes she were somewhere else—a buzzard in the sky, a dog lying under a bush. But at the end of the day as she walks home with her daddy, she is content.

*Careers:* Female = 1 Male = 1

*Subject Categories:* American Ethnic Minority; Families/ Friendship; Picture Book

**2.6 Granny's Fish Story.** Phyllis LaFarge. New York: Parents' Magazine Press, 1975. 35 p. $5.95.

Julie and Sarah visit Julie's grandmother who lives in the country. Granny is a positive role model of a brave, independent, likeable person.

*Careers:* Female = 2 Male = 0 Neutral = 0
*Subject Categories:* Families/Friendship

**2.7 Becky and the Bear.** Dorothy Van Woerkom. New York: G.P. Putnam's Sons, 1975. 44 p. $4.69.

This is a story of life in colonial Maine, where winters are hard and food is scarce. Eight-year-old Becky catches a bear which provides her family with food, a warm rug and fat to burn in the lamps.

*Careers:* Female = 1 Male = 1 Neutral = 0
*Subject Categories:* Families/Friendship; History; Mystery/ Adventure

**2.8 Black Is Brown Is Tan.** Arnold Adoff. New York: Harper & Row, 1973. 32 p. $4.95.

A story-poem about an interracial family—people of all colors, happily living and growing up in a house of love.

*Careers:* Female = 2 Male = 1 Neutral = 0
*Subject Categories:* American Ethnic Minority; Families/ Friendship; Picture Book; Poetry/Rhyme

**2.9 Don't You Remember?** Lucille Clifton. New York: E.P. Dutton, 1973. 25 p. $6.50.

Tate is a four-year-old black girl who becomes discouraged when her family keeps putting off doing some things they have promised to her. One morning, however, she wakes up to a nice surprise.

*Careers:* Female = 1 Male = 1 Neutral = 0
*Subject Categories:* American Ethnic Minority; Families/ Friendship; Picture Book

**2.10 Harriet and the Promised Land.** Jacob Lawrence. New York: Windmill Books (Simon & Schuster), 1968. 28 p. $6.73.

With powerful illustrations and rhyming verse, this book tells the story of Harriet Tubman, a courageous black woman who led her fellow slaves to freedom in the North.

*Careers:* Female = 1 Male = 2 Neutral = 1

*Subject Categories:* American Ethnic Minority; Biography; History; Mystery/Adventure; Picture Book; Poetry/Rhyme

**2.11 The Girl Who Would Rather Climb Trees.** Miriam Schlein. New York: Harcourt, Brace, Jovanovich, 1975. 24 p. $4.95.

Melissa is given a doll to play with, but she would rather climb trees, play ball or ride a bike. After all, what can you do with a doll but carry it? Shows girls engaged in nonstereotypic activities.

*Careers:* Female = 2 Male = 0 Neutral = 0
*Subject Categories:* Families/Friendship; Health/Human Development; Picture Book

**2.12 Will I Have a Friend?** Miriam Cohen. New York: Macmillan, 1967. 26 p. $1.25. Paper.

After his father takes him to his first day of nursery school, a young boy deals with the uncertainties of making new friends. Illustrations show children of different races and boys and girls playing together.

*Careers:* Female = 2 Male = 2 Neutral = 0
*Subject Categories:* Families/Friendship; Picture Book

**2.13 Pippa Mouse.** Betty Boegehold. New York: Alfred A. Knopf, 1973. 62 p. $3.95.

Six read-aloud/read-alone stories about Pippa, a very active and inventive young mouse, with delightful illustrations throughout the book.

*Careers:* Female = 1 Male = 1 Neutral = 0
*Subject Categories:* Animals; Families/Friendship; Fantasy, Folk & Fairy Tales

**2.14 Marian Anderson.** Tobi Tobias. New York: Thomas Y. Crowell, 1972. 40 p. $4.50.

This is a simply written and beautifully illustrated biography of a very talented black opera singer who had to gain recognition in Europe before her own country would accept her.

*Careers:* Female = 6 Male = 12 Neutral = 11
*Subject Categories:* American Ethnic Minority; Biography; Families/Friendship; Fine Arts

**2.15 Dorothea L. Dix: Hospital Founder.** Mary Malone. Champaign, IL: Garrard, 1968. 80 p. $3.96.

Biography of Dorothea L. Dix, who in the early 1800s devoted her life to improving the treatment of the mentally ill.

*Careers:* Female = 7 Male = 19 Neutral = 6
*Subject Categories:* Biography; The Handicapped; Health/Human Development; History

**2.16ˣ  The Good Morrow.** Gunilla B. Norris. New York: Atheneum, 1969. 92 p. $5.25.

Josie, a young black girl from the city and Nancy, a young white girl from the city, meet at camp. Josie expects to be rejected because of her race, and Nancy acts out her hostility against her mother on Josie. At the end of the story, each girl has a better understanding of herself and the other person. Because of the subject matter, small print and lack of illustrations, this book appears to be more appropriate for intermediate-grade readers.

*Careers:* Female = 3 Male = 2 Neutral = 1

*Subject Categories:* American Ethnic Minority; Families/Friendship; Health/Human Development

**2.17 The Sunshine Family and the Pony.** Sharron Loree. New York: Seabury Press, 1972. 56 p. $5.95.

A group of families move to a house in the country. Together they share the work and get a pony.

*Careers:* None shown
*Subject Categories:* Animals; Families/Friendship; Picture Book

**2.18ˣ  Nobody's Family Is Going to Change.** Louise Fitzhugh. New York: Dell, 1976. 221 p. $1.50. Paper. (Originally published by Farrar, Straus & Giroux, 1974.)

Eleven-year-old Emma Sheridan, who wants to be a lawyer, and her seven-year-old brother Willie, who wants to dance, are middle-class black children. Their father, an attorney, and their mother have dreams about their children's future which have little to do with what Emma and Willie want. The story will hold the reader spellbound as it encompasses black rights, women's rights, children's rights and interfamily relationships which all children can recognize. Because of the subject matter, small print and lack of pictures, this book appears more appropriate for intermediate-grade readers.

*Careers:* Female = 11 Male = 26 Neutral = 6
*Subject Categories:* American Ethnic Minority; Cont. Issues/Curr. Events; Families/Friendship

**2.19 Noisy Nora.** Rosemary Wells. New York: Dial Press, 1973. 34 p. $4.58.

This charmingly illustrated picture book is about noisy Nora, a mouse who makes noise to get attention when her parents pay more attention to her brothers and sisters.

*Careers:* Female = 1 Male = 1 Neutral = 0
*Subject Categories:* Animals; Families/Friendship; Picture Book; Poetry/Rhyme

**2.20 I Was So Mad!** Norma Simon. Chicago: Albert Whitman, 1974. 34 p. $4.75.

This book helps young readers deal with their own anger by showing what makes other boys and girls angry.

*Careers:* Female = 5 Male = 3 Neutral = 0
*Subject Categories:* Families/Friendship; Health/Human Development; Picture Book

**2.21 Rachel Carson: Who Loved the Sea.** Jean Lee Latham. Champaign, IL: Garrard, 1973. 80 p. $3.96.

Story of how Rachel Carson's love for the sea and biology led her to become a scientist and how her gift for writing allowed her to write about the work she loved. She helped awaken the world to the destructiveness of pesticides.

*Careers:* Female = 10 Male = 7 Neutral = 9
*Subject Categories:* Biography; Science

**2.22 Blue Trees, Red Sky.** Norma Klein. New York: Pantheon Books, 1975. 57 p. $5.99.

Eight-year-old Valerie learns that her mother works because she loves it, not just because her father died, and that her working doesn't interfere with her love for Valerie.

*Careers:* Female = 7 Male = 3 Neutral = 2

*Subject Categories:* Families/Friendship; Health/Human Development

**2.23 Sidewalk Story.** Sharon Bell Mathis. New York: Viking Press, 1971. 72 p. $5.95.

This is a moving story of a young black girl named Lilly Etta who comes up with a plan to keep her friend Tanya and her family from being evicted from their apartment. A beautiful story of friendship; a positive portrayal of a young girl who isn't afraid to try something different to help a friend.

*Careers:* Female = 2 Male = 8 Neutral = 4
*Subject Categories:* American Ethnic Minority; Families/Friendship

**2.24 Lucille.** Arnold Lobel. New York: Harper & Row, 1964. 64 p. $4.79.

A farm couple took their horse Lucille to town dressed up in "lady-like" finery. But Lucille decided she'd rather be a "plain, happy horse" than a lady.

*Careers:* Female = 3 Male = 2 Neutral = 0
*Subject Categories:* Animals; Fantasy, Folk & Fairy Tales; Picture Book

**2.25 Howie Helps Himself.** Joan Fassler. Chicago: Albert Whitman, 1975. 28 p. $4.50.

Although Howie, a physically handicapped child, is dependent on others to help him with basic everyday tasks, he discovers his individuality and knows that how he feels deep inside is what really counts. Ethnic minorities and females are portrayed nonstereotypically in illustrations.

*Careers:* Female = 4 Male = 3 Neutral = 0
*Subject Categories:* Families/Friendship; The Handicapped; Health/Human Development; Picture Book

**2.26ˣ Grandma Didn't Wave Back.** Rose Blue. New York: Dell, 1972. 62 p. $.95. Paper.

Ten-year-old Debbie is upset by her grandmother's failing health and the changes that will have to come. Subject matter may be more appropriate for intermediate-grade readers.

*Careers:* Female = 6 Male = 2 Neutral = 0
*Subject Categories:* Families/Friendship; Health/Human Development

**2.27 Plants in Winter.** Joanna Cole. New York: Thomas Y. Crowell, 1973. 32 p. $4.50.

A botanist tells her young friend how various plants survive the winter. This book is very informative, with good descriptive drawings.

*Careers:* Female = 1 Male = 0 Neutral = 0
*Subject Categories:* Picture Book; Science

**2.28 Shoeshine Girl.** Clyde Robert Bulla. New York: Thomas Y. Crowell, 1975. 84 p. $6.95.

While staying with her aunt for the summer, an independent 10-year-old gets a job as a shoeshine girl because she likes to have some money in her pocket. What she learns is worth more than the money she earns.

*Careers:* Female = 5 Male = 6 Neutral = 1
*Subject Categories:* Families/Friendship; Health/Human Development

**2.29 Delilah.** Carole Hart. New York: Harper & Row, 1973. 63 p. $4.79.

Ten-year-old Delilah plays drums in the rain and wants to grow tall enough to play basketball with the New York Knicks. Good story of a young girl growing up in a nonsexist/androgynous environment.

*Careers:* Female = 4 Male = 6 Neutral = 5
*Subject Categories:* Families/Friendship

**2.30 Joshua's Day.** Sandra Lucas Surowiecki. Chapel Hill, NC: Lollipop Power, 1972. 27 p. $1.75. Paper.

This stereotype-breaking story is about a day in the life of Joshua, who goes to a day care center while his mother goes to work as a photographer. Illustrations show ethnic minorities, girls playing with trucks, girls playing doctor and cowgirl and boys in nurturing roles.

*Careers:* Female = 2 Male = 1 Neutral = 0
*Subject Categories:* Families/Friendship; Picture Book

**2.31 Mothers Can Do Anything.** Joe Lasker. Chicago: Albert Whitman, 1976. 35 p. $4.75.

Simple narrative and pictures showing mothers in a variety of different careers, many of them nontraditional.

*Careers:* Female = 33 Male = 11 Neutral = 2
*Subject Categories:* Careers; Picture Book

**2.32 Grownups Cry Too.** Nancy Hazen. Chapel Hill, NC: Lollipop Power, 1973. 23 p. $1.75. Paper.

Young Stanley, who used to think that only little kids cry, learns that everybody cries sometimes. This is a sensitive story with illustrations showing a racially mixed marriage.

*Careers:* Female = 2 Male = 1 Neutral = 1
*Subject Categories:* American Ethnic Minority; Families/Friendship; Health/Human Development

**2.33 Umbrella.** Taro Yashima. New York: Penguin, 1977. 32 p. $1.75. Paper. (Originally published by Viking Press, 1958.)

Momo eagerly waits for a rainy day so she can use the new umbrella she received for her third birthday.

*Careers:* Female = 1 Male = 1 Neutral = 0
*Subject Categories:* American Ethnic Minority; Picture Book

**2.34 Evan's Corner.** Elizabeth Starr Hill. New York: Holt, Rinehart & Winston, 1967. 40 p. $1.45. Paper.

Evan, a young black child growing up in a crowded apartment in the city, needs a place he can call his own. This story is simply told, with warmth and sensitivity, and has good illustrations.

*Careers:* Female = 2 Male = 6 Neutral = 0
*Subject Categories:* American Ethnic Minority; Families/Friendship; Health/Human Development; Picture Book

**2.35 Jane Addams.** Gail Faithfull Keller. New York: Thomas Y. Crowell, 1971. 41 p. $4.50.

This biography of Jane Addams tells how she established Hull House, a community center in Chicago, to help impoverished immigrants in the city. As a result of her efforts with the poor and in the international peace movement during World War I, she received the Nobel Peace Prize.

*Careers:* Female = 5 Male = 8 Neutral = 12
*Subject Categories:* Biography; History

**2.36 Just Think!** Joan Blos and Betty Miles. New York: Alfred A. Knopf, 1971. 40 p. $5.39.

This book contains pictures, poems, sayings and words for young readers to think about—including a myriad of working mothers, nurturing fathers and a full-fledged, well-functioning day care center. Women and ethnic minorities are well represented and portrayed nonstereotypically in the illustrations.

*Careers:* Female = 3 Male = 4 Neutral = 0
*Subject Categories:* Families/Friendship; Picture Book

**2.37 A Birthday for Frances.** Russell Hoban. New York: Harper & Row, 1968. 31 p. $4.95.

Frances the Badger becomes jealous when her sister has a birthday.

*Careers:* Female = 1 Male = 1 Neutral = 0
*Subject Categories:* Animals; Families/Friendship; Picture Book

**2.38 Don't Ride the Bus on Monday: The Rosa Parks Story.** Louise Meriweather. Englewood Cliffs, NJ: Prentice-Hall, 1973. 29 p.

Biography of Rosa Parks whose refusal to give her seat on a bus to a white person marked the beginning of the civil rights movement in the South.

*Careers:* Female = 8 Male = 12 Neutral = 4
*Subject Categories:* American Ethnic Minority; Biography; Cont. Issues/Curr. Events; Picture Book

**2.39 All Kinds of Families.** Norma Simon. Chicago: Albert Whitman, 1976. 34 p. $3.56.

Different kinds of families are shown through pictures and descriptions. The book acknowledges that families vary in makeup and lifestyles and are not always composed of two parents and their children. Ethnic minorities are well represented in the illustrations of this picture book.

*Careers:* Female = 1 Male = 4 Neutral = 0
*Subject Categories:* Families/Friendship; Picture Book

**2.40 Best Friends for Frances.** Russell Hoban. New York: Harper & Row, 1969. 31 p. $5.95.

Albert and Frances learn the value of friendship after first trying to exclude each other from one another's play. This is a good book for a class discussion about "no girls allowed" and "no boys allowed."

*Careers:* Female = 1 Male = 0 Neutral = 0
*Subject Categories:* Animals; Families/Friendship; Picture Book

**2.41 I Love Gram.** Ruth A. Sonneborn. New York: Viking Press, 1971. 25 p. $4.95.

Ellie, a young black girl, fears her grandmother will die when she has to go to the hospital. The story depicts three generations of women living happily and lovingly together.

*Careers:* Female = 3 Male = 1 Neutral = 0
*Subject Categories:* American Ethnic Minority; Families/Friendship; Picture Book

**2.42 Rosa Parks.** Eloise Greenfield. New York: Thomas Y. Crowell, 1973. 32 p. $4.50.

By refusing to give her seat on a bus to a white person, Rosa Parks helped initiate the fight in 1955 for desegregation of buses in Montgomery, Alabama. Her action became an important first step in the civil rights movement.

*Careers:* Female = 7 Male = 8 Neutral = 5
*Subject Categories:* American Ethnic Minority; Biography; Cont. Issues/Curr. Events

**2.43ˣ Rod-N-Reel Trouble.** Bobbi Katz. Chicago: Albert Whitman, 1974. 64 p. $4.00.

Lori, a sixth grader who loves to fish, is the only girl to enter the Annual Fishing Contest. Not only does she win a prize in the contest, more importantly, she saves the life of a friend when he falls in the creek and bumps his head. Subject matter and lack of illustrations may make this book more appropriate for older readers.

*Careers:* Female = 5 Male = 8 Neutral = 2
*Subject Categories:* Families/Friendship; Mystery/Adventure

**2.44 Quiet on Account of Dinosaur.** Jane Thayer. New York: William Morrow, 1964. 30 p. $6.01.

In this delightful story, a young girl named Mary Ann finds a dinosaur in a cave. She takes him home and to school, but Dandy, the dinosaur, is unhappy. A famous doctor is called in, and together he and Mary Ann discover the problem—Dandy doesn't like noise! Because of her interest in dinosaurs, Mary Ann becomes a scientist and becomes famous.

*Careers:* Female = 3 Male = 6 Neutral = 0
*Subject Categories:* Animals; Fantasy, Folk & Fairy Tales; Picture Book

**2.45 Nice Little Girls.** Elizabeth Levy. New York: Delacorte Press, 1974. 46 p. $5.47.

When Jackie shows up at a new school, her teacher tries to make her behave like a "nice little girl." But Jackie wants to build boxes and do the things boys get to do. This delightfully illustrated picture book is light and entertaining, yet makes an important point about sex role stereotyping.

*Careers:* Female = 2 Male = 1 Neutral = 0
*Subject Categories:* Families/Friendship; Picture Book

**2.46 He Bear, She Bear.** Stan and Jan Berenstain. New York: Random House, 1974. 34 p. $2.95.

This is a cute story about a she bear and a he bear who can do anything they want to do and be anything they want to be. Illustrations and text show boy and girl bears in a variety of careers, many of them nontraditional.

*Careers:* Female = 24 Male = 20 Neutral = 0
*Subject Categories:* Animals; Careers; Fantasy, Folk & Fairy Tales; Picture Book

**2.47 Amigo.** Byrd Baylor Schweitzer. New York: Collier Books, 1973. 41 p. $.95. Paper. (Originally published by Macmillan, 1963.)

A sensitive and gentle Mexican boy wants a pet, but his parents can't afford one. He succeeds in making friends with a prairie dog who wants to have a human for a friend. This tale is written in verse and is charmingly illustrated.

*Careers:* Female = 1 Male = 1 Neutral = 0
*Subject Categories:* American Ethnic Minority; Animals; Families/Friendship; Fantasy, Folk & Fairy Tales; Poetry/Rhyme

**2.48 Try and Catch Me.** Nancy Jewell. New York: Harper & Row, 1972. 32 p. $5.79.

In this lovely picture book, an enthusiastic little girl explores the outdoors by herself and with a boy. The accompanying text is simply written.

*Careers:* Female = 1 Male = 0 Neutral = 0
*Subject Categories:* Families/Friendship; Picture Book

**2.49 Jellybeans for Breakfast.** Miriam Young. New York: Parent's Magazine Press, 1968. 37 p. $5.41.

Two little girls imagine all the fantastic things they will do someday—including being "space men" and going to the moon.

*Careers:* Female = 4 Male = 4 Neutral = 0
*Subject Categories:* Families/Friendship; Fantasy, Folk & Fairy Tales

**2.50 Annie Sullivan.** Mary Malone. New York: G.P. Putnam's Sons, 1971. 61 p. $3.96.

This is a story of Annie Sullivan, a woman of courage and intelligence who became Helen Keller's teacher.

*Careers:* Female = 3 Male = 5 Neutral = 2
*Subject Categories:* Biography; The Handicapped; History; Picture Book

**2.51 Clowning Around.** Beverley Allinson and Judith Lawrence. Toronto, ON: D.C. Heath, Canada Ltd., 1976. 32 p.

The activities of a clown and her two children are vividly portrayed with color photographs and simple text.

*Careers:* Female = 1 Male = 0 Neutral = 0
*Subject Categories:* Picture Book

**2.52 A Pony for Linda.** C.W. Anderson. New York: Macmillan, 1951. 52 p. $5.95.

Linda, who comes from a family of horse lovers, makes a friend at a horse show.

*Careers:* Female = 1 Male = 1 Neutral = 0
*Subject Categories:* Animals; Families/Friendship; Picture Book

**2.53ˣ Heroines of '76.** Elizabeth Anticaglia. New York: Walker, 1975. 109 p. $5.95.

This book chronicles the contributions of 14 outstanding women to the fight for independence during the American Revolution. Because of the small print and lack of illustrations, this book may be more appropriate for older readers.

*Careers:* Female = 10 Male = 14 Neutral = 0
*Subject Categories:* American Ethnic Minority; Biography; History; Mystery/Adventure

**2.54 What Mary Jo Wanted.** Janice May Udry. Chicago: Albert Whitman, 1968. 26 p. $4.75.

Mary Jo, a young black girl, gets what she wanted—a puppy, but she soon discovers that being responsible is a 24-hour job.

*Careers:* Female = 1 Male = 1 Neutral = 0
*Subject Categories:* American Ethnic Minority; Animals; Families/Friendship; Picture Book

**2.55 Amelia Earhart.** John Parlin. Champaign, IL: Garrard, 1962. 80 p. $3.96.

A simply written biography of Amelia Earhart, the first woman to fly a plane across the Atlantic Ocean.

*Careers:* Female = 8 Male = 8 Neutral = 3
*Subject Categories:* Biography; Mystery/Adventure

**2.56 Helen Keller: Toward the Light.** Stewart and Polly Anne Graff. Champaign, IL: Garrard, 1965. 80 p. $3.96.

A simply written biography of Helen Keller, blind and deaf from an early age, and her teacher Anne Sullivan Macy, who taught her to communicate.

*Careers:* Female = 3 Male = 6 Neutral = 3
*Subject Categories:* Biography; The Handicapped

**2.57 Eleanor Roosevelt: First Lady of the World.** Charles P. Graves. Champaign, IL: Garrard, 1966. 80 p. $3.96.

A biography of Eleanor Roosevelt, who as First Lady traveled about the country reporting on conditions and doing all she could to help the poor during the depression. She worked tirelessly for peace and became a delegate to the United Nations.

*Careers:* Female = 4 Male = 11 Neutral = 2
*Subject Categories:* Biography; History

**2.58 Steffie and Me.** Phyllis Hoffman. New York: Harper & Row, 1970. 32 p. $5.79.

In this picture book, a little girl describes a day in her life, including school and her friendship with a classmate named Steffie. Although the major character is portrayed as a spirited child, she and Steffie want to "marry Brucie" when they grow up; her brother wants to be a lawyer and a garbage collector.

*Careers:* Female = 2 Male = 4 Neutral = 1
*Subject Categories:* American Ethnic Minority; Families/Friendship; Picture Book

**2.59 Linda Richards: First American Trained Nurse.** David R. Collins. Champaign, IL: Garrard, 1973. 80 p. $3.96.

An easy-to-read biography of Linda Richards, whose concern for the sick led her to become the first professional nurse in the United States in 1873.

*Careers:* Female = 10 Male = 3 Neutral = 3
*Subject Categories:* Biography; Health/Human Development; History

**2.60ˣ Nancy Ward, Cherokee.** Harold W. Felton. New York: Dodd, Mead, 1975. 86 p. $4.95.

Biography of Nancy Ward, who became a Ghigan (Beloved Woman) of her people and whose voice was heard in important tribal council decisions. She was a respected leader and helped bring temporary peace among the Cherokees and the white settlers. Her relationship to the historical events of her time, including the Revolutionary War, is depicted from a white perspective. Small print size makes this book appropriate for older readers.

*Careers:* Female = 7 Male = 14 Neutral = 8
*Subject Categories:* American Ethnic Minority; Biography; History

**2.61 Women Who Dared to Be Different.** Wayne Bennett (ed.). Champaign, IL: Garrard, 1973. 162 p. $4.95.

Simply written biographical sketches of women who dared to be different, including Nellie Bly, Annie Oakley, Maria Mitchell and Amelia Earhart.

*Careers:* Female = 35 Male = 32 Neutral = 0
*Subject Categories:* Biography; History

**2.62ˣ It's Not the End of the World.** Judy Blume. New York: Bantam Books, 1972. 167 p. $1.75. Paper. (Originally published by Bradbury Press, 1972.)

A very realistic story about the end of a marriage told from the point of view of a sixth grade daughter. Preteens and teenagers whose parents are divorcing should find this book particularly helpful. Without being preachy, it will let preteens and teenagers know that fantasies of their parents getting back together are often unrealistic, yet understandable. They also should be able to relate to the different perspectives of the three children in the story, each of whom responds differently to their parents' separation. The parents in the story are characterized as being neither too good, nor just awful; but sometimes lonely, confused and powerless, and who at times take out their anger with each other on their children. Formatting makes this book more appropriate for intermediate-grade readers.

*Careers:* Female = 8 Male = 3 Neutral = 2
*Subject Categories:* Behavioral Science; Health/Human Development

**2.63 The Clock Book.** Donna Kelly. Racine, WI: Golden Press, 1978. 23 p.

A little girl describes her day in terms of clocks she sees at home, during the day and in the the clock shop owned by her mother and father. In the illustrations nontraditional family roles and children from various ethnic backgrounds are presented.

*Careers:* Female = 2 Male = 2 Neutral = 1
*Subject Categories:* Families/Friendship; Picture Book

**2.64 My Doctor Bag Book.** Kathleen Daly. Racine, WI: Golden Press, 1977. 24 p.

Cathy takes her doctor bag everywhere to cure the ills of her friends, their pets and dolls. She herself is treated by her own physician, a woman.

*Careers:* Female = 1 Male = 0 Neutral = 0
*Subject Categories:* Careers; Health/Human Development; Picture Book

**2.65 Dumb Old Casey Is a Fat Tree.** Barbara Bottner. New York: Harper & Row, 1979. 42 p. $6.95.

Eight-year old Casey overcomes her feelings about being too fat to be a dancer. With determination to practice in order "to show everyone," she discovers that dancing brings a wonderful free feeling. In fact, she practices so hard that she forgets her usual sweet treats. Her triumphant feelings at the performance are shared by the reader.

*Careers:* Female = 9 Male = 10 Neutral = 0
*Subject Categories:* Families/Friendship; Health/Human Development

**2.66 Monday I Was an Alligator.** Susan Pearson. Philadelphia, PA: J.B. Lippincott, 1979. 40 p. $6.95.

In this delightfully illustrated picture book, a high spirited girl pretends to be several animals, usually winding up in trouble. Finally, she decides to be just herself to the satisfaction of her family.

*Careers:* None shown
*Subject Categories:* Families/Friendship; Picture Book

**2.67 Where Is Daddy? The Story of a Divorce.** Beth Goff. Boston: Beacon Press, 1969. 27 p. $5.95.

Told from the point of view of a preschooler, this book is about the fears and guilt young Janey feels when her mother and father get a divorce.

*Careers:* Female = 2 Male = 2 Neutral = 0
*Subject Categories:* Families/Friendship; Health/Human Development; Picture Book

**2.68 Animal Daddies and My Daddy.** Barbara Hagen. Racine, WI: Western Publishing, 1976. 23 p.

Picture book of girls and boys comparing their daddies to animal daddies. Ethnic minority mix in the illustrations.

*Careers:* Female = 1 Male = 1 Neutral = 0
*Subject Categories:* Animals; Families/Friendship; Picture Book

**2.69ˣ Cold Feet.** Gen LeRoy. New York: Harper & Row, 1979. 217 p. $7.95.

Geneva Michillini, a high school girl, is a loner. Furthermore, she longs for excitement and something more than her small town can offer. Quite by accident, she gets a job as a "cleaning boy" at a penny arcade in a nearby city. Sexual stereotypes and the problems of growing up are combined with hilarious fun as Geneva copes with two identities; in getting "mixed up," she begins to find herself. Small print and subject matter make this book more appropriate for junior high readers.

*Careers:* Female = 8 Male = 20 Neutral = 8
*Subject Categories:* Families/Friendship; Health/Human Development

**2.70ˣ We Are Mesquakie We Are One.** Hadley Irwin. Old Westbury, NY: The Feminist Press, 1980. 117 p. $7.95.

Hidden Doe, a Mesquakie, grows from childhood to maturity during the time that her people are driven off their land in Iowa to a reservation in Kansas. The story depicts the intelligence, cohesiveness and courage of the Mesquakie in general and the sharing, love and integrity among Mesquakie women and between generations. The story is based on historical fact. Formatting and lack of illustrations may make this book more appropriate for the intermediate-grade reader.

*Careers:* Female = 3 Male = 8 Neutral = 2
*Subject Categories:* American Ethnic Minority; Cultural Heritage; Families/Friendship; History

**2.71 The Stubborn Old Woman.** Clyde Bulla. New York: Thomas Y. Crowell, 1980. 44 p. $7.95.

The story of an obstinate old woman who meets her match in a spirited, wise, very stubborn little girl. Even though the old woman's house was falling into the river, she would not leave it. Finally she went to live with the little girl and promised to be obstinate no longer.

*Careers:* Female = 2 Male = 2 Neutral = 0

*Subject Categories:* Families/Friendship; Health/Human Development; Picture Book

**2.72 That Is That.** Jeanne Whitehouse Peterson. New York: Harper & Row, 1979. 30 p. $7.95.

A perceptive book about a young Native American child's stormy and conflicting feelings when her father leaves home. Beautifully illustrated.

*Careers:* Female = 0 Male = 0 Neutral = 1
*Subject Categories:* American Ethnic Minority; Family/Friendship; Health/Human Development; Picture Book

**2.73 About Dying.** Sara Bonnett Stein. New York: Walker and Company, 1974. 47 p. $7.95.

This unique presentation creates a shared experience for adult and child by offering two texts. The author enables children to explain their feelings about death and prepares the adult for questions the children might ask. The presentation is well done and includes pictures of children of mixed races.

*Careers:* Female = 0 Male = 1 Neutral = 0
*Subject Categories:* Health/Human Development; Picture Book

**2.74 Through Grandpa's Eyes.** Patricia Maclachlan. New York: Harper & Row, 1979. 40 p. $8.95.

In this beautifully illustrated picture book, the author tells a tender story about a young boy who learns to see through his grandpa's eyes. Since Grandpa is blind, John learns to perceive his surroundings through sound, smell and taste.

*Careers:* None shown
*Subject Categories:* Families/Friendship; The Handicapped; Picture Book

**2.75 I Wish Laura's Mommy Was My Mommy.** Barbara Power. New York: J.B. Lippincott, 1979. 47 p. $7.95.

This picture book deals with a child's perceptions of homes with different lifestyles. It is a humorous approach to the role of full-time homemaker versus the working mother. Recommended as nonsexist literature.

*Careers:* Female = 2 Male = 0 Neutral = 0
*Subject Categories:* Families/Friendship; Health/Human Development; Picture Book

**2.76 My Daddy Don't Go to Work.** Madeena Spray Nolan. Minneapolis, MN: Carolrhoda Books, 1978. 27 p.

This simply written, beautifully illustrated picture book describes the feelings of a young black girl when her father can't find a job. The story portrays the love and tenderness between her mother, father and herself and how they come together as a family in a time of crisis.

*Careers:* Female = 1 Male = 1 Neutral = 0
*Subject Categories:* American Ethnic Minority; Families/Friendship; Picture Book

**2.77 The Rabbit Is Next.** Gladys Leithauser and Lois Breitmeyer. Racine, WI: Western Publishing, 1978. 26 p.

Jenny takes her stuffed rabbit to the veterinarian's office. There is a good deal of interaction among the patients. Finally, the vet cares for the "injured" rabbit with a needle and thread. Ethnic minorities are well represented in the illustrations.

*Careers:* Female = 1 Male = 0 Neutral = 0
*Subject Categories:* Animals; Careers; Picture Book

**2.78 Words in Our Hands.** Ada B. Litchfield. Chicago: Albert Whitman, 1980. 32 p.

This book portrays a family in which the parents are deaf. The coping mechanisms of parents and children are explored, including finger spelling, sign language, hearing ear dogs and special equipment for the deaf. Moving to a new town is difficult until the family becomes acquainted with other deaf people through the "National Theatre for the Deaf."

*Careers:* Female = 1 Male = 2 Neutral = 0
*Subject Categories:* Families/Friendship; The Handicapped; Health/Human Development

**2.79 Nick Joins In.** Joe Lasker. Chicago: Albert Whitman, 1980. 30 p.

This beautifully illustrated and thoughtfully presented book explores the feelings of Nick, a young boy confined to a wheelchair, as he enters public school for the first time. The illustrations portray a variety of ethnic groups.

*Careers:* Female = 3 Male = 2 Neutral = 0
*Subject Categories:* Families/Friendship; The Handicapped; Health/Human Development; Picture Book

**2.80 A Look at Divorce.** Margaret Sanford Pursell. Minneapolis: Lerner Publications, 1977. 30 p.

With black and white photographs and simple text, this book reassures children of their continuing relationships with their parents despite the problems a family faces when a divorce occurs. A mix of races is represented in the illustrations.

*Careers:* Female = 1 Male = 1 Neutral = 0
*Subject Categories:* Families/Friendship; Health/Human Development; Picture Book

**2.81 Jim Meets The Thing.** Miriam Cohen. New York: Greenwillow Books, 1981. 29 p. $7.95.

Jim watches The Thing on television, has nightmares and worries the next day at school that he is the only coward in first grade. At noon recess, the playground is full of super hero types, such as Gravity Girl and Captain Mighty, and Jim feels left out. However, when a praying mantis is discovered crawling on Danny's coat, Jim is the only one who dares remove it (and rejects the suggestion of squashing it as well). As the children talk, Jim realizes that everyone gets scared sometimes and that fears are overcome. Reflects a multiethnic classroom setting. The book's value is twofold: it shows boys acknowledging their fears, and it redefines "hero" as something less superhuman (and certainly less macho) than the traditional versions.

*Careers:* None shown
*Subject Categories:* Families/Friendship; Picture Book

**2.82 Darlene.** Eloise Greenfield. New York: Methuen, Inc., 1980. 26 p. $7.95.

Darlene, a young black girl, wants to go home, but her cousin Joanne matter-of-factly gets her to take part in a board game, playing catch and jump rope. Uncle Eddie also plays his guitar while they all sing. The illustrations warmly depict Darlene's changing mood. By the time Mama arrives to take her home, Darlene has cheered up and changed her mind about leaving. The fact that Darlene participates from a wheelchair is secondary to the common theme of a young child adjusting to her mother's absence and making up her own mind.

*Careers:* Female = 1 Male = 0 Neutral = 0

*Subject Categories:* American Ethnic Minority; Families/ Friendship; The Handicapped; Picture Book

**2.83 My Mom Travels a Lot.** Caroline Feller Bauer. New York: Frederick Warne, 1981. 34 p. $8.95.

A young girl contrasts the good points of having a mom who travels a lot ("we get to go to the airport,""sometimes I get to stay up late") with the bad points ("there's only one nightime kiss,""we miss her") and concludes that the *best* thing about it is "she always comes back." Colorful drawings add to the lightly humorous tone of this father and daughter carrying out their daily routine in a companionable fashion. Although some stereotyping is implicit in the text, the book is valuable for showing a close and nurturing father/daughter relationship.

*Careers:* Female = 1 Male = 3 Neutral = 1
*Subject Categories:* Families/Friendship; Picture Book

**2.84 Now One Foot, Now the Other.** Tomie de Paola. New York: G.P. Putnam's Sons, 1981. 44 p. $3.95. Paper.

A love story, told in soft blue and brown pictures, about Bobby and his grandfather Bob. They play together, and Bobby never tires of hearing how Bob taught him to walk—holding his hands and saying "now one foot, now the other." Their roles change when grandfather has a stroke. In spite of his first fears at Bob's strangeness, Bobby draws near and reaches out to his grandfather, helps him feed himself, and finally, by placing Bob's hands on his shoulders for balance, helps him learn to walk once more. The story emphasizes the nurturing relationship between grandfather and grandson.

*Careers:* Female = 1 Male = 1 Neutral = 1
*Subject Categories:* Families/Friendship; The Handicapped; Picture Book

**2.85 Daddy and Ben Together.** Miriam B. Stecher and Alice S. Kandell. New York: Lothrop, Lee & Shepard, 1981. 24 p. $7.95.

"Remember to laugh a lot," Ben's mother, a professional photographer, advises when her new job takes her away for a few days. Ben and his Daddy have their ups and downs until Ben figures out what's missing. He starts by making funny faces, and it works! By the time Mommy returns, Daddy and Ben are a team enjoying close times together. Provides a realistic example of a nurturing father, well illustrated with black and white photographs.

*Careers:* Female = 1 Male = 1 Neutral = 0

*Subject Categories:* Families/Friendship; Picture Book

**2.86 Aekyung's Dream.** Min Paek. San Francisco, CA: Children's Book Press, 1978. 24 p. $4.95. Paper.

A bilingual story (English/Korean) about Aekyung, who has been in the U.S. for six months and is losing her sense of self because of difficulty with English and the teasing of her classmates. In a dream, the fifteenth century leader, King Sejong (creator of the Korean alphabet) instructs her to develop strong roots so that cruel winds cannot shake her and her life will blossom. With this inspiration, she perseveres in her adopted country, learning English while maintaining her Korean heritage. Aekyung's courage comes from a male historical figure surrounded by female court dancers, rather than from Aunt Kim who has just traveled to Korea on her own.

*Careers:* Female = 2 Male = 2 Neutral = 0
*Subject Categories:* American Ethnic Minority; Cultural Heritage

**2.87 The Balancing Girl.** Berniece Rabe. New York: E.P. Dutton, 1981. 29 p. $10.25.

Margaret has a steady hand and is *very* good at balancing things: she can build block towers and balance herself on crutches when she's not gliding along in her wheelchair. Spunky Margaret puts these talents to good use, in spite of classmate Tommy's efforts to put down (literally) her accomplishments by building an elaborate city of dominoes for the school carnival. Tommy wins the opportunity to demolish her creation, without having to feel sorry about it, and Margaret has the pleasure of earning the most money for the school's new gym equipment. Both Tommy's jealousy and Margaret's pride are treated sensitively. No minorities are represented.

*Careers:* Female = 2 Male = 0 Neutral = 1
*Subject Categories:* The Handicapped; Picture Book

**2.88 A Chair for My Mother.** Vera B. Williams. New York: Greenwillow Books, 1982. 30 p. $9.50.

A young girl, her waitress mother and her grandmother pool their respective earnings, tips and savings in a big glass jar for the day when they will have enough money to buy a soft, "comfy" armchair for all three to enjoy. A heartwarming story about love, mutual support and sharing—illustrated with bright, colorful pictures.

*Careers:* Female = 4 Male = 2 Neutral = 1
*Subject Categories:* Families/Friendship; Picture Book

# Reading Grade Level 3–Harris-Jacobson Formula

**3.1 Ramona the Pest.** Beverly Cleary. New York: William Morrow, 1968. 192 p. $6.01.

This story depicts the delightful and humorous adventures of a spirited five-year-old girl whose entry into kindergarten is less than calm.

*Careers:* Female = 2 Male = 1 Neutral = 0
*Subject Categories:* Families/Friendship

**3.2 Animals Should Definitely *Not* Wear Clothing.** Judith Barrett. New York: Atheneum, 1970. 29 p. $1.95. Paper.

A humorous, read-aloud picture book showing what would happen to different animals if they wore clothes.

*Careers:* None shown
*Subject Categories:* Animals; Fantasy, Folk & Fairy Tales; Picture Book

**3.3 Curious Missie.** Virginia Sorensen. New York: Harcourt, Brace & World, 1953. 208 p. $5.50.

Missie, who's known in her rural Alabama town as the "girl who asks questions," fights hard to get a bookmobile for her county. Although the sex roles of the peripheral characters are stereotypic, Missie is positive, active and inquisitive.

*Careers:* Female = 9 Male = 14 Neutral = 3
*Subject Categories:* Families/Friendship

**3.4ˣ Island of the Blue Dolphins.** Scott O'Dell. New York: Dell, 1978. 189 p. $.95. Paper. (Originally published by Houghton Mifflin, 1960.)

This story is based on The Lost Woman of San Nicolas, who lived alone on the island of San Nicolas from 1835 to 1853. Story tells of the Indian girl, Karana, who is left behind on the Island of the Blue Dolphins when her people leave for the mainland. As she waits over the years for another ship to take her away, she keeps herself alive by building shelter, making weapons, finding food and fighting off wild dogs. Unusual and moving adventure of survival. Because of small print and subject matter, book may be more appropriate for intermediate-grade readers.

*Careers:* Female = 2 Male = 8 Neutral = 2
*Subject Categories:* American Ethnic Minority; History; Mystery/Adventure

**3.5 Harriet and the Runaway Book.** Johanna Johnston. New York: Harper & Row, 1977. 79 p. $5.79.

Biography of Harriet Beecher Stowe, whose book, *Uncle Tom's Cabin*, denounced slavery and helped start the Civil War. Because she felt the horror of slavery, Ms. Stowe wrote a story that made people really care about and understand what slavery meant.

*Careers:* Female = 7 Male = 22 Neutral = 6
*Subject Categories:* American Ethnic Minority: Biography; Families/Friendship; History

**3.6 Clara Barton: Soldier of Mercy.** Mary Catherine Rose. Champaign, IL: Garrard, 1960. 80 p. $3.96.

Biography of Clara Barton, a famous nurse during the Civil War who founded the American Red Cross.

*Careers:* Female = 6 Male = 11 Neutral = 6
*Subject Categories:* Biography; Health/Human Development; History

**3.7 Ira Sleeps Over.** Bernard Waber. Boston: Houghton Mifflin, 1972. 48 p. $1.95. Paper.

When Ira plans to sleep over at Reggie's house, he can't decide whether to take his teddy bear. He leaves "Tah Tah" at home, only to find out Reggie sleeps with *his* teddy.

*Careers:* Female = 1 Male = 2 Neutral = 0
*Subject Categories:* Families/Friendship; Picture Book

**3.8 Hello, Aurora.** Anne-Catherine Vestly. New York: Thomas Y. Crowell, 1974. 135 p. $6.50.

This story depicts the everyday activities of a family in which the mother is a lawyer and the father stays home and takes care of two children, one an eight-week-old baby. Their neighbors find this arrangement hard to understand. Book was translated from Norwegian; has few illustrations and small print.

*Careers:* Female = 6 Male = 5 Neutral = 2
*Subject Categories:* Families/Friendship; Foreign Countries

**3.9 Abigail Adams: "Dear Partner."** Helen Stone Peterson. Champaign, IL: Garrard, 1967. 80 p. $3.96.

Biography of Abigail Adams, whose letters to her husband during the Revolutionary War paint an accurate picture of life in the new nation.

*Careers:* Female = 5 Male = 19 Neutral = 5
*Subject Categories:* Biography; Families/Friendship; History

**3.10ˣ Over the Hills and Far Away.** Lavinia Russ. New York: Harcourt, Brace & World, 1968. 160 p. $5.50.

Set in 1910, this story depicts a growing girl who can emulate her traditionally "feminine" sister or her active mother who is involved in peace and labor movements. Because of small print and lack of pictures, this book appears to be more appropriate for intermediate-grade readers.

*Careers:* Female = 14 Male = 25 Neutral = 8
*Subject Categories:* Families/Friendship; Health/Human Development; History

**3.11 Nannabah's Friend.** Mary Perrine. Boston: Houghton Mifflin, 1970. 29 p. $3.40.

Story of a young Navajo Indian girl who lives with her grandmother and grandfather in the traditional way and how she deals with her loneliness as she watches over the sheep in the canyon.

*Careers:* Female = 2 Male = 2 Neutral = 0
*Subject Categories:* American Ethnic Minority; Families/Friendship

**3.12 Daddy.** Jeannette Caines. New York: Harper & Row, 1977. 32 p. $5.95.

Saturdays are special times with Daddy for a young black girl whose parents are separated. They play, shop and cook together.

*Careers:* Female = 0 Male = 1 Neutral = 0
*Subject Categories:* American Ethnic Minority; Families/Friendship

**3.13ˣ  Heart-of-Snowbird.** Carol Lee Lorenzo. New York: Harper & Row, 1975. 227 p. $5.95.

Twelve-year-old Laurel Ivy wants to leave her small Southern mountain town and become a dental hygienist after high school. However, as her friendship deepens with a young Native American boy who has just moved to town, she realizes that she belongs in Snowbird Gap and decides to become a soil and crop expert. This story warmly portrays friendship among girls and boys on an equal basis. Subject matter, small print and lack of illustrations make this book more appropriate for intermediate-grade or junior high readers.

*Careers:* Female = 12 Male = 15 Neutral = 11
*Subject Categories:* American Ethnic Minority; Families/Friendship; Health/Human Development

**3.14 Mandy and the Flying Map.** Beverley Allinson. Toronto, ON: The Women's Press, 1973. 30 p. $2.00. Paper.

One day Mandy sits on one of her maps, flies out the window and looks around the town where she sees a female firefighter, the mayor, town councilwomen and men and her friends.

*Careers:* Female = 3 Male = 6 Neutral = 0
*Subject Categories:* Fantasy, Folk & Fairy Tales; Picture Book

**3.15ˣ  A Promise Is a Promise.** Molly Cone. Boston: Houghton Mifflin, 1964. 153 p. $6.95.

Story of a young Jewish girl who is self-conscious about being Jewish because her faith and family customs are different from her friends. But, as she prepares for her *bas mitzvah*, she comes to realize that it's all right to be different, and it's important to know who you are in order to be what you want to be. Good portrayal of Jewish customs in context of the story. Subject matter, lack of illustrations and print size make this book more appropriate for intermediate-grade readers.

*Careers:* Female = 4 Male = 17 Neutral = 8
*Subject Categories:* Families/Friendship; Health/Human Development; Religion/Mythology

**3.16 Coleen, the Question Girl.** Arlie Hochschild. Old Westbury, NY: The Feminist Press, 1974. 32 p. $2.50. Paper.

This is an engaging story, illustrated with amusing photographs, of a young girl who asks many questions.

*Careers:* Female = 2 Male = 3 Neutral = 4
*Subject Categories:* Families/Friendship; Mystery/Adventure; Picture Book

**3.17 The Silver Whistle.** Jay Williams. New York: Parent's Magazine Press, 1971. 38 p. $5.41.

In this delightful fairy tale, bright, resourceful and good-hearted Prudence saves the Prince from marrying the beautiful but wicked witch and ends up marrying him herself. Although she is "chosen" by the prince, she has a strong character and a mind of her own.

*Careers:* Female = 4 Male = 3 Neutral = 0
*Subject Categories:* Fantasy, Folk & Fairy Tales; Picture Book

**3.18 Ikwa of the Temple Mounds.** Margaret Zehmer Searcy. University, AL: University of Alabama Press, 1974. 70 p. $5.50.

Sensitive portrayal of the fear, courage and strength of Ikwa, a Native American girl, as she struggles to become a young woman. The story is based on the culture of the Temple Mound people of Mississippi.

*Careers:* Female = 6 Male = 16 Neutral = 0
*Subject Categories:* American Ethnic Minority; Health/Human Development; History; Religion/Mythology

**3.19 Sue Ellen.** Edith Hunter. Boston: Houghton Mifflin, 1969. 170 p. $3.50.

Eight-year-old Sue Ellen, a slow learner from a large family with an invalid mother and father, has difficulty adjusting in a regular classroom. Going to a class for children with learning problems changes her self-concept and sheds a different light on her life experiences.

*Careers:* Female = 5 Male = 14 Neutral = 5
*Subject Categories:* Families/Friendship; The Handicapped; Health/Human Development

**3.20 Carlotta and the Scientist.** Patricia Riley Lenthall. Chapel Hill, NC: Lollipop Power, 1973. 47 p. $2.00. Paper.

Carlotta is a mother penguin who is so curious she has to see what's behind every ice flow. One day she finds a scientist with a broken leg and discovers a new world she never imagined. Women, ethnic minorities and careers are portrayed nonstereotypically.

*Careers:* Female = 3 Male = 3 Neutral = 2
*Subject Categories:* Animals; Families/Friendship; Fantasy, Folk & Fairy Tales; Picture Book; Science

**3.21 Eliza's Daddy.** Ianthe Thomas. New York: Harcourt, Brace, Jovanovich, 1976. 59 p. $4.95.

Eliza, a young black girl, is curious about her father's new family, especially his new stepdaughter. This story deals with divorce in a sensitive manner.

*Careers:* Female = 1 Male = 3 Neutral = 0
*Subject Categories:* American Ethnic Minority; Families/Friendship; Picture Book

**3.22 The Dragon and the Doctor.** Barbara Danish. Old Westbury, NY: The Feminist Press, 1971. 21 p. $2.00. Paper.

A dragon with a sore tail finds a little girl doctor. She solves his problem and they go off to a party together. This is a delightful story with charming illustrations.

*Careers:* Female = 3 Male = 1 Neutral = 0
*Subject Categories:* Animals; Fantasy, Folk & Fairy Tales; Picture Book

**3.23 Thunder at Gettysburg.** Patricia Lee Gauch. New York: Coward, McCann & Geoghegan, 1975. 46 p. $5.95.

This is an excellent story of a strong and brave little girl who is caught in the middle of the Battle of Gettysburg during the Civil War. Story portrays not only the girl's courage but also the horrible realities of war.

*Careers:* Female = 3 Male = 8 Neutral = 2
*Subject Categories:* History; Mystery/Adventure

**3.24 Blueberries for Sal.** Robert McCloskey. New York: Penguin Books, 1976. 57 p. $1.95. Paper. (Originally published by Viking Press, 1948.)

A bear cub and a little girl inadvertently exchange mothers while picking blueberries.

*Careers:* Female = 1 Male = 0 Neutral = 0
*Subject Categories:* Animals; Families/Friendship; Picture Book

**3.25ˣ The Mulberry Music.** Doris Orgel. New York: Harper & Row, 1971. 130 p. $5.79.

Twelve-year-old Libby struggles with the reality of her grandmother's illness and health. Warm, positive portrait of a girl's relationship with her nonconformist, mulberry sweatsuit-wearing grandmother. Subject matter, small print and lack of illustrations make this book more appropriate for intermediate-grade readers.

*Careers:* Female = 7 Male = 12 Neutral = 11
*Subject Categories:* Families/Friendship; Health/Human Development

**3.26ˣ Frankie and the Fawn.** Marcia Polese and Dorothea Wender. Nashville, TN: Abingdon, 1974. 126 p. $4.50.

This entertaining story is about a family who nurses an injured fawn back to health. With the help of her veterinarian mother, her teacher father and her brother, 12-year-old Frankie takes charge of the feeding and care of the injured animal. Excellent portrait of a loving, nonstereotypic family of equals who share work and support one another. Because of the subject matter and lack of illustrations, intermediate-grade readers should also enjoy this book.

*Careers:* Female = 4 Male = 4 Neutral = 5
*Subject Categories:* Animals; Families/Friendship; Science

**3.27 Four Women of Courage.** Wayne Bennett (ed.). Champaign, IL: Garrard, 1975. 167 p. $4.96.

The stories of four courageous American women—Dorothea Dix, Linda Richards, Helen Keller and Jacqueline Cochran—who reached their goals despite overwhelming obstacles.

*Careers:* Female = 29 Male = 34 Neutral = 15
*Subject Categories:* Biography; The Handicapped; Health/Human Development; History

**3.28 A Train for Jane.** Norma Klein. Old Westbury, NY: The Feminist Press, 1974. 28 p. $3.50. Paper.

Jane, a mischievous, winsome, cheerfully unkempt girl, has her heart set on getting an electric train for Christmas. Story is told in rhyming verse.

*Careers:* Female = 2 Male = 3 Neutral = 0
*Subject Categories:* Families/Friendship; Picture Book; Poetry/Rhyme

**3.29ˣ Harriet the Spy.** Louise Fitzhugh. New York: Dell, 1964. 298 p. $1.50. Paper. (Originally published by Harper & Row, 1964.)

Because Harriet wants to become a writer, she begins recording her candid observations of people in her New York neighborhood. After she is ostracized by two of her best friends who discover her writings, Harriet reexamines her needs against the feelings of others. Small print and lack of illustrations make this book more appropriate for intermediate-grade readers.

*Careers:* Female = 12 Male = 17 Neutral = 3
*Subject Categories:* Families/Friendship; Mystery/Adventure

**3.30ˣ The Real Me.** Betty Miles. New York: Avon Camelot Books, 1975. 122 p. $1.25. Paper. (Originally published by Alfred A. Knopf, 1974.)

Barbara Fisher, an independent 11-year-old, doesn't think it's fair that girls aren't allowed to have paper routes and that girls can't take tennis classes at her school. She is labeled a "nut" when she tries to change these rules by circulating petitions but learns that it's important to stand up for what she knows is fair and that all pioneers for change are labeled "nuts" at first. Because of the small print and lack of illustrations, this book is appropriate for intermediate-grade readers.

*Careers:* Female = 13 Male = 12 Neutral = 6
*Subject Categories:* Families/Friendship; Health/Human Development

**3.31ˣ Red Rock over the River.** Patricia Beatty. New York: William Morrow, 1973. 248 p. $6.94.

This colorful story is told through the eyes of 13-year-old Dorcas, who lived with her brother Charlie and her father at Fort Yuma in the Arizona Territory in 1881. It tells of her friendship with a young Native American woman, Hattie Lou Mercer, who is a crack shot but somewhat evasive about her past. Despite their friendship, Dorcas doesn't discover the real reason Hattie is at the fort until one day when her purpose is revealed in a wild and frightening escapade. Subject matter, small print and lack of illustrations make this book more appropriate for intermediate-grade or junior high readers.

*Careers:* Female = 12 Male = 33 Neutral = 22
*Subject Categories:* American Ethnic Minority; Families/Friendship; History; Mystery/Adventure

**3.32 Mary McLeod Bethune.** Ruby L. Radford. New York: G.P. Putnam's Sons, 1973. 61 p. $3.96.

Biography of Mary McLeod Bethune, one of 14 children of former slaves, who spent her life working for education and justice for blacks.

*Careers:* Female = 7 Male = 6 Neutral = 6
*Subject Categories:* American Ethnic Minority; Biography; History

**3.33 William's Doll.** Charlotte Zolotow. New York: Harper & Row, 1972. 30 p. $4.95.

Young William is teased by his family and friends because he wants a doll. His grandmother, however, gives him a doll so he can hug it, cradle it and practice being a father.

*Careers:* None shown
*Subject Categories:* Families/Friendship; Picture Book

**3.34 Sumi's Prize.** Yoshiko Uchida. New York: Charles Scribner's Sons, 1964. 40 p. $5.95.

Sumi enters the village kite flying contest because she has always wanted to win a prize. Although her kite crashes when she tries to rescue the mayor's hat which was blown away by the wind, Sumi gets a special prize. Story is set in a small Japanese village.

*Careers:* Female = 1 Male = 7 Neutral = 0
*Subject Categories:* Foreign Countries; Picture Book

**3.35 The Lancelot Closes at Five.** Marjorie Weinman Sharmat. New York: Macmillan, 1976. 120 p. $6.95.

Two nonconforming girls living in suburbia secretly spend the night in a model home and involve the neighborhood in a mystery.

*Careers:* Female = 4 Male = 14 Neutral = 13
*Subject Categories:* Families/Friendship; Mystery/Adventure

**3.36 Ann Aurelia and Dorothy.** Natalie Savage Carlson. New York: Harper & Row, 1968. 130 p. $4.95.

After her mother remarries, Ann Aurelia has many problems as she is sent from one foster home to another. At one home she makes friends with Dorothy, a black girl. They have fun together and Ann Aurelia learns to grow a bit more flexible. Because of the subject matter, this book would also be appropriate for intermediate-grade readers.

*Careers:* Female = 5 Male = 7 Neutral = 0
*Subject Categories:* American Ethnic Minority; Families/Friendship; Health/Human Development

**3.37ˣ Zia.** Scott O'Dell. Boston: Houghton Mifflin, 1976. 179 p. $7.95.

This sequel to *Island of the Blue Dolphins* tells of the final days of the Native American woman Karana through the eyes of her niece Zia as they live together at the Santa Barbara Mission. The story shows Zia caught between two worlds—the world of her mother's culture and the Native Americans. Subject matter and illustrations make this book more appropriate for intermediate-grade readers.

*Careers:* Female = 7 Male = 20 Neutral = 3
*Subject Categories:* American Ethnic Minority; Families/Friendship; History

**3.38 Charlotte's Web.** E.B. White. New York: Harper & Row, 1952. 184 p. $1.50. Paper.

A beautifully written animal fantasy story about a wise and clever spider who comes to the rescue of a friend in trouble.

*Careers:* Female = 0 Male = 4 Neutral = 1
*Subject Categories:* Animals; Families/Friendship; Fantasy, Folk & Fairy Tales

**3.39ˣ Never Jam Today.** Carole Bolton. New York: Atheneum, 1971. 241 p. $.95. Paper.

Seventeen-year-old Maddy Franklin becomes involved in the suffragist movement in America during the early 1900s. Despite objections from her family and boyfriend, she finds herself picketing the White House, for which she is arrested, put in prison and force-fed by harsh jailors when she refuses to eat. The reader sees Maddy mature from a young, somewhat romantic girl into a young woman determined to make a life for herself on her own terms. Formatting more appropriate for intermediate-grade and junior high readers.

*Careers:* Female = 20 Male = 26 Neutral = 17
*Subject Categories:* Families/Friendship; Health/Human Development; History; Women's Studies

**3.40ˣ The Amazing Miss Laura.** Hila Colman. New York: William Morrow, 1976. 192 p.

Seventeen-year-old Josie spends the summer working as a companion to Miss Laura, an 80-year-old eccentric widow of a well-known painter. Through her experience with the capricious, forgetful, frequently tyrannical, yet vigorous and zestful woman, Josie reexamines her relationship with her grandfather and gains a different idea about old age and herself. The story is rather traditional, yet provides a positive and warm portrait of a woman trying to grow old with dignity and in charge of her affairs. May be more appropriate for older readers.

*Careers:* Female = 6 Male = 7 Neutral = 15
*Subject Categories:* Families/Friendship; Health/Human Development

**3.41ˣ The Soul Brothers and Sister Lou.** Kristin Hunter. New York: Avon, 1969. 192 p. $1.50. Paper. (Originally published by Charles Scribner's Sons, 1968.)

A warmly positive yet unsentimental story of a young black girl growing up in the North. The book vividly and realistically describes the problems and sorrows, as well as the love and joy, of 14-year-old Lou and her family and friends as they cope with life in the ghetto. An excellent portrait of a young girl's growing awareness of her own worth and pride in her black heritage. Formatting makes this book more appropriate for junior high readers.

*Careers:* Female = 9 Male = 28 Neutral = 16
*Subject Categories:* American Ethnic Minority; Cultural Heritage; Families/Friendship; Health/Human Development

**3.42ˣ Marly the Kid.** Susan Beth Pfeffer. New York: Doubleday, 1975. 137 p. $5.95.

This is an amusing story about 15-year-old Marly, who runs away from home to live with her father and new stepmother. Peripheral characters are shown in a variety of nonstereotypic careers. Formatting makes this book more appropriate for older readers.

*Careers:* Female = 20 Male = 10 Neutral = 6

*Subject Categories:* Families/Friendship; Health/Human Development

**3.43ˣ Mixed Marriage Daughter.** Hila Colman. New York: William Morrow, 1968. 191 p.

When 17-year-old Sophie Barnes moves with her family from New York City to a small town in Massachusetts, she experiences anti-Semitism and confronts her mixed heritage for the first time. With a Jewish mother and Protestant father, she finds herself caught between two worlds and has her eyes opened to both the pain and pride of being an American Jew. Although the characters and careers portrayed are rather stereotypic, the book provides a thoughtful examination of a young woman discovering her cultural heritage and gaining a better understanding of herself. Formatting makes this book more appropriate for older readers.

*Careers:* Female = 7 Male = 14 Neutral = 12
*Subject Categories:* Cultural Heritage; Families/Friendship; Health/Human Development; Religion Mythology

**3.44ˣ Mom, the Wolfman and Me.** Norma Klein. New York: Avon, 1974. 156 p. $1.50. Paper. (Originally published by Pantheon Books, 1972.)

An entertaining story about soon to be 12-year-old Brett, who lives with her mother, a photographer, in New York City. The characterizations are wonderfully nonstereotypic: Brett's mother has never been married, sleeps in her blue jeans, occasionally has friends stay over, and sometimes doesn't wake up until noon after working all night in her darkroom. Brett is afraid their life will change if her mom marries the wolfman, a special education teacher who bakes bread and has a huge Irish wolfhound. But Brett finds out that marriage doesn't necessarily mean wearing dresses, having babies and eating dinner at six. Print size and formatting make this book more appropriate for intermediate-grade readers.

*Careers:* Female = 20 Male = 13 Neutral = 7
*Subject Categories:* Families/Friendship; Health/Human Development

**3.45ˣ Child of the Dark: The Diary of Carolina Maria de Jesus.** Carolina Maria de Jesus. New York: New American Library, 1962. 159 p. $1.50. Paper. (Originally published by E.P. Dutton, 1962.)

Originally written on scraps of paper picked from gutters, this is the raw, primitive journal of a young black woman who struggled for survival for herself and her three children in a squalid Brazilian favela. Despite a daily battle against hunger, disease and people grown callous and brutal from deprivation, Carolina Maria de Jesus managed to write a deeply disturbing, compassionate and moving chronicle. Print size, formatting and subject matter make this book more appropriate for junior high and secondary students.

*Careers:* Female = 29 Male = 62 Neutral = 33
*Subject Categories:* Autobiography; Behavioral Science; Cultural Heritage; Foreign Countries; Health/Human Development; Women's Studies

**3.46ˣ The Trouble with Thirteen.** Betty Miles. New York: Avon, 1979. 108 p. $1.95. Paper. (Originally published by Alfred A. Knopf, 1979.)

Annie and Rachel are best friends. Twelve years old and wanting life to stay as perfect as it is, both of them have trouble coping with unexpected changes: death, divorce and moving away from each other. This is a beautiful story about friendship, growing up and the importance of saying what you really feel. Subject matter makes this book more appropriate for junior high readers.

*Careers:* Female = 6 Male = 10 Neutral = 4
*Subject Categories:* Families/Friendship; Health/Human Development

**3.47ˣ Cross Fox.** Jane Scott. New York: Atheneum, 1980. 130 p. $7.95.

An involving story about a lonely 12-year-old boy who tries to protect a fox from hunters, only to learn that it is sometimes difficult to tell the hunter from the hunted. Formatting may make this book more appropriate for the intermediate-grade reader.

*Careers:* Animals; Families/Friendship; Health/Human Development
*Subject Categories:* Female = 4 Male = 6 Neutral = 2

**3.48ˣ Winter Wheat.** Mildred Walker. New York: Harcourt, Brace, Jovanovich, 1972. 341 p. $3.95. Paper. (Originally published by Harcourt, Brace, Jovanovich, 1944.)

This substantial novel tells the moving story of Ellen Welsk, her family and the Montana wheatland that is their home. Ellen, a college student and teacher in a one-room schoolhouse, has a deep and abiding love for the land as the story begins. She learns about other kinds of love and understanding and by the end of the book can compare true love to wheat, with its strong roots that endure the passage of storms and that always has its own kind of beauty. This book presents women in roles which require physical strength, endurance and courage. Subject matter and small print make this book more appropriate for secondary students.

*Careers:* Female = 17 Male = 34 Neutral = 8
*Subject Categories:* Cultural Heritage; Families/Friendship

**3.49 Don't Forget Tom.** Hanne Larsen. New York: Thomas Y. Crowell, 1972. 23 p. $5.79.

Tom is a mentally disabled six-year-old who can't do all the things other six-year-olds can do. Although he has difficulty with many things like eating and dressing, he is an integral part of his family. The photographs and text are straightforward and will assist children to have a fuller understanding of children who are different.

*Careers:* Female = 2 Male = 1 Neutral = 1
*Subject Categories:* Families/Friendship; The Handicapped; Health/Human Development; Picture Book

**3.50 A Book about Us.** New Seed Collective. Stanford, CA: New Seed Press, 1977. 30 p. Paper.

A group of children who do not identify with the children in their schoolbooks decides to print their own book. With the help of parent/printers, they are able to accomplish this. A light story showing children of mixed ethnic backgrounds and sexes actively working out a solution to a problem.

*Careers:* Female = 1 Male = 0 Neutral = 0
*Subject Categories:* American Ethnic Minority; Families/Friendship; Picture Book

**3.51 Rice Cakes and Paper Dragons.** Seymour Reit. New York: Dodd, Mead, 1973. 79 p.

Marie Chan is a young Chinese American girl living in New York City's Chinatown. In an entertaining combination of photographs and easy-to-read text, the reader is treated to a glimpse of Chinese life and the Chinese New Year celebration. Shows a close family structure and a warm, nurturing father-daughter relationship.

*Careers:* Female = 4 Male = 10 Neutral = 12
*Subject Categories:* American Ethnic Minority; Families/Friendship; Cultural Heritage

**3.52 Rachel Pushes Back.** Samantha Willow. Portland, OR: Samantha Willow, 1977. 11 p. $1.50. Paper.

When 11-year-old Rachel's mom and dad are divorced, she goes with her dad to meet his new wife and her son, Eddie. This book vividly describes Rachel's emotions and inner conflicts.

*Careers:* None shown
*Subject Categories:* Families/Friendship; Health/Human Development

**3.53ˣ  A House for Jonnie O.** Blossom Elfman. Boston: Houghton Mifflin, 1976. 175 p. $8.95.

Sixteen-year-old Jonnie is pregnant and unmarried. Her parents separated long ago, and she and her mother don't get along. Attending a "pregnant school" while waiting for her baby to be born, Jonnie feels misunderstood by everyone except her pregnant friends and longs for independence. The story is "real," and the difficult decisions Jonnie faces have no fairy tale endings. Subject matter and formatting make this book more appropriate for junior and senior high readers.

*Careers:* Female = 8 Male = 16 Neutral = 6
*Subject Categories:* Families/Friendship; Health/Human Development

**3.54 It Can't Hurt Forever.** Marilyn Singer. New York: Harper & Row, 1978. 186 p. $7.95.

Ellie Simon has a heart defect and is afraid of the operation she will need to repair it. The author carefully explains medical procedures and stresses the importance of honesty in dealing with young patients. Female and male doctors and medical technicians are depicted as equals.

*Careers:* Female = 8 Male = 3 Neutral = 5
*Subject Categories:* Families/Friendship; Health/Human Development

**3.55 Higher than the Arrow.** Judy Van der Veer. New York: Avon, 1969. 132 p. $1.50. Paper.

Francie is a 12-year-old Native American living on a reservation in California. Proud of her heritage and her artistic ability, Francie has a lot to learn about the *wrong* kind of pride, prejudice and friendship. An easy-to-read, sensitive story with special appeal for animal lovers.

*Careers:* Female = 3 Male = 7 Neutral = 3
*Subject Categories:* American Ethnic Minority; Animals; Families/Friendship; Cultural Heritage

**3.56 Star Ka'ats and the Plant People.** Andre Norton and Dorothy Madlee. New York: Walker, 1979. 122 p. $6.95.

With the help of the Ka'ats, super-intelligent feline beings from the Ka'at planet, two young earthlings save the plant people from vicious crabs. This intriguing science fiction story is nonsexist and nonracist in the portrayal of its two major characters, a young black girl and white boy who both exhibit ingenuity and courage.

*Careers:* Female = 0 Male = 0 Neutral = 2
*Subject Categories:* American Ethnic Minority; Science Fiction

**3.57 The Cry of the Crow.** Jean Craighead George. New York: Harper & Row, 1980. 149 p. $7.95.

There are really two protagonists in this story: Mandy, a teenager, and Nina Terrance, a crow. Mandy finds the helpless baby crow in the woods and tames her in secret. To Mandy's father and older brothers, crows are pests and must be shot. The crisis comes when Mandy must choose between her love for Nina Terrance and her little brother. An excellent story in many ways, with fascinating information about crows. Some subtle sex role stereotyping with males cast as hunters/predators and females as protectors.

*Careers:* Female = 5 Male = 13 Neutral = 6
*Subject Categories:* Animals; Families/Friendship; Health/Human Development

**3.58ˣ  Waiting for Johnny Miracle.** Alice Bach. New York: Harper & Row, 1980. 240 p. $8.95.

Becky and Theo are identical twins and seniors in high school when Becky gets bone cancer. The author tells an unflinchingly honest story based on her real-life experience with teenage cancer patients. The reader learns along with Becky and Theo that a life-threatening disease touches everyone involved with the patient and that the struggle for survival must be shared. Subject matter and formatting may make this book more appropriate for junior high students.

*Careers:* Female = 13 Male = 16 Neutral = 15
*Subject Categories:* Families/Friendship; The Handicapped; Health/Human Development

**3.59 Millicent the Magnificent.** Alice Bach. New York: Harper & Row, 1978. 45 p. $5.95.

Millicent, a circus acrobat bear, teaches Oliver her acrobatics. Oliver's twin, Ronald, becomes quite jealous. The illustrations are delightful.

*Careers:* Female = 1 Male = 4 Neutral = 0
*Subject Categories:* Animals; Health/Human Development

**3.60ˣ  Happy Endings Are All Alike.** Sandra Scoppettone. New York: Harper & Row, 1978. 201 p. $6.95.

In this tense and honest novel, Sandra Scoppettone explores the array of prejudices and fears about rape, women and lesbianism. This book deals with moral values and the difficulty today's teenagers must face in learning to know and express themselves. Subject matter makes this book more appropriate for mature secondary readers.

*Careers:* Female = 6 Male = 6 Neutral = 0
*Subject Categories:* Families/Friendship; Health/Human Development

**3.61 Jane Addams.** Matthey G. Grant. Minneapolis, MN: Creative Education, 1974. 29 p.

Although she came from a well-to-do family herself, Jane Addams could not forget the faces of the poor factory workers in Illinois. With a friend, she established Hull House in Chicago and began to offer day care services and classes to the neighbors. This sketch is a sound introduction to Jane Addams' life and work.

*Careers:* Female = 2 Male = 2 Neutral = 1
*Subject Categories:* Autobiography/Biography; History

**3.62 Maria Teresa.** Mary Atkinson. Chapel Hill, NC: Lollipop Power, 1979. 39 p. Paper.

Maria Teresa, who has come to a new school, feels sad and alone. When she brings Spanish-speaking puppets to "show and tell" one day, she begins to overcome cultural barriers and make friends.

*Careers:* Female = 1 Male = 1 Neutral = 0
*Subject Categories:* American Ethnic Minority; Families/ Friendship; Cultural Heritage; Picture Book

**3.63 What Will I Be?** Kathleen Krull Cowles. Racine, WI: Western Publishing, 1979. 23 p.

Picture book of children talking about what they would like to do and what they would like to be. Careers portrayed are nonstereotypic, and illustrations show ethnic minorities and disabled children. Excellent introduction to the concept of nontraditional careers for primary children.

*Careers:* Female = 9 Male = 9 Neutral = 0
*Subject Categories:* Careers; Picture Book

**3.64 My Mother and I Are Growing Strong.** Inez Maury. Stanford, CA: New Seed Press, 1978. 28 p.

Delightful story of Emilitia's and her mother's activities while her father is imprisoned for a year. They continue to work in Father's gardening jobs, learn to fix mechanical things and ward off intruders. The text is presented in English and Spanish, and illustrations are charming.

*Careers:* Female = 1 Male = 3 Neutral = 2
*Subject Categories:* American Ethnic Minority; Families/ Friendship; Picture Book

**3.65ˣ Some Lose Their Way.** Frederick J. Lipp. New York: Atheneum, 1980. 118 p. $7.95.

Vanessa and David are outsiders: Vanessa, because she is much younger and smarter (and more timid) than her classmates; David, because he and his father move around so much. Initially enemies, the two young people become friends as they study the effects of industrial pollution on bird migration and natural habitats. Separately and together, David and Vanessa begin to conquer their feelings of loneliness and lack of confidence. Subject matter and formatting make this book more appropriate for junior high readers.

*Careers:* Female = 3 Male = 10 Neutral = 2
*Subject Categories:* Animals; Famileis/Friendship; Health/Human Development

**3.66 The Girl Who Loved Wild Horses.** Paul Goble. Scarsdale, NY: Bradbury Press, 1978. 26 p. $10.95.

A Native American girl lovingly tends her people's horses and has a special understanding of their needs. One day a thunderstorm scatters the herd. She is carried with them to an unfamiliar landscape that is presided over by a spotted stallion, leader of the wild horses. A year later she is reclaimed by hunters from her village. She falls ill and tells the "doctors" that only her return to the wild horses will make her well. Her parents, who love her, agree. She becomes one of the Horse People, running proud and free. Beautifully illustrated book.

*Careers:* Female = 1 Male = 3 Neutral = 1
*Subject Categories:* American Ethnic Minority; Cultural Heritage; Picture Book

**3.67ˣ Oh, Boy! Babies!** Alison Cragin Herzig and Jane Lawrence Mali. Boston: Little, Brown, 1980. 106 p. $9.95.

An irresistible book chronicling the progress of eight fifth and sixth grade boys enrolled in an elective class on infant care. The "hands on" curriculum covers dressing, feeding, diapering, bathing and other responsibilities. Profuse photographs, marvelous dialogue and quotations and information about child care and development make this a winner that is alternately hilarious and touching. Because of subject matter, this book may also be appropriate for intermediate readers.

*Careers:* Female = 2 Male = 1 Neutral = 2
*Subject Categories:* Health/Human Development; Information Book

**3.68ˣ Sweet Whispers, Brother Rush.** Virginia Hamilton. New York: Philomel Books, 1982. 215 p. $10.95.

A powerful and compelling story centering on 14-year-old Teresa—a bright, sensitive black girl. Teresa or "Tree" is filled with love much of the time and responsible for herself and her disabled older brother. During one climatic week, her life is changed by the mysterious appearances of Brother Rush—the handsome stranger who draws her into her family's past and reveals disturbing, even frightening secrets. The story rests on rich characterizations and convincing fantasy as Tree ultimately achieves greater understanding of herself and an enlarged vision of the strong-hearted, mature woman her mother has become. An award-winning novel that will reward the willing reader. Subject matter and format make this book more appropriate for intermediate readers.

*Careers:* Female = 11 Male = 12 Neutral = 8
*Subject Categories:* American Ethnic Minority; Cultural Heritage; Families/Friendship; Health/Human Development

**3.69 Wonder Women of Sports.** Betty Millspap Jones. New York: Random House, 1981. 70 p. $4.99.

Easy-to-read biographies of 12 notable women athletes: Diana Nyad, Billie Jean King, Annie Peck, Nadia Comaneci, Mickey Wright, Wilma Rudolph, Joan Joyce, Kitty O'Neil, Roberta Bingay, Babe Didrickson, Sonja Henie, Althea Gibson. A bit simplistic but serves as an introduction to the subject for primary-grade readers.

*Careers:* Female = 9 Male = 5 Neutral = 6
*Subject Categories:* American Ethnic Minority; Autobiography/ Biography; The Handicapped; Sports

**3.70 Three Days on a River in a Red Canoe.** Vera B. Williams. New York: Greenwillow Books, 1981. 30 p. $9.95.

A young girl describes her adventurous river trip with Mom, Aunt Rosie and cousin Sam. Delightful illustrations depict their preparation and journey and include a surprising amount of specific camping information as this resourceful foursome navigate, fish and explore downstream. Exemplifies sharing of experience and responsibility in nonstereotypical fashion.

*Careers:* Female = 1 Male = 0 Neutral = 0
*Subject Categories:* Families/Friendship; Information Book; Picture Book

**3.71ˣ Tiger Eyes.** Judy Blume. Scarsdale, NY: Bradbury Press, 1981. 206 p. $9.95.

Being 15 going on 16 isn't easy. It's doubly difficult for Davey Wexler, whose family must adjust to the shocking, meaningless murder of Adam Wexler during a store robbery. With her mother and seven-year-old brother, Davey lives for a school year with well-meaning relatives in Los Alamos, New Mexico (known for its part in the development of the A-Bomb). The ironic contrast between national security concerns in the "Bomb City" and the overprotectiveness of her aunt and uncle provides the backdrop for Davey's struggles with her own fears as she recaptures her capacity to think for herself, accepts challenges and meets life with love and laughter again. Her mother's recovery is conveyed convincingly also. Blume effec-

tively challenges stereotypes about Mexican Americans but succumbs in one minor instance to the use of biased language. Subject matter and format make this book more appropriate for older readers.

*Careers:* Female = 9 Male = 9 Neutral = 4
*Subject Categories:* Families/Friendship; Health/Human Development

**3.72 Hiroshima No Pika.** Toshi Maruki. New York: Lothrop, Lee & Shepard, 1982. 45 p. $12.50.

A painful but moving story of survival as related by a seven-year-old Japanese girl named Mii, who tells of what happened to her family on August 6, 1945 in Hiroshima. This award-winning book features beautiful, sensitive illustrations; nonetheless, the scenes of death and destruction are disturbing. Consequently, the book would be best used in a family or classroom setting that encourages questions and discussion.

*Careers:* Female = 2 Male = 3 Neutral = 4
*Subject Categories:* American Ethnic Minority; Families/Friendship; Foreign Countries; History; Picture Book

# Reading Grade Level 4–Harris-Jacobson Formula

**4.1ˣ  Jo, Flo and Yolanda.** Carol de Poix. Chapel Hill, NC: Lollipop Power, 1973. 32 p. $1.75.

Even though they're triplets and share many things in common, Jo, Flo and Yolanda are also unique, and each has her own special interests and dreams. Print size and pictures make this book more appropriate for primary-grade readers.

*Careers:* Female = 3 Male = 1 Neutral = 0
*Subject Categories:* American Ethnic Minority; Families/Friendship; Picture Book

**4.2ˣ  My Doctor.** Harlow Rockwell. New York: Macmillan, 1973. 20 p. $4.95.

A small boy visits his doctor's office and tells about the instruments she uses. Pictures and print size are more appropriate for primary-grade readers.

*Careers:* Female = 2 Male = 0 Neutral = 0
*Subject Categories:* Careers; Health/Human Development; Picture Book; Science

**4.3 The Story of Helen Keller.** Lorena A. Hickok. New York: Grosset & Dunlap, 1958. 181 p. $3.95.

The inspiring life story of Helen Keller, who overcame the disabilities of being blind and deaf through the loving and dedicated teaching of Anne Sullivan.

*Careers:* Female = 14 Male = 37 Neutral = 14
*Subject Categories:* Biography; Families/Friendship; The Handicapped; Health/Human Development

**4.4ˣ  A Little Lion.** Christine Westerberg. Englewood Cliffs, NJ: Prentice-Hall, 1975. 26 p. $4.95.

A group of children who are playing "explorer" make the youngest girl be the "baby lion," but instead she becomes "king of the jungle." Pictures and large print make this book more appropriate for primary-grade readers.

*Careers:* Female = 1 Male = 0 Neutral = 0
*Subject Categories:* Families/Friendship; Picture Book

**4.5 Flat on My Face.** Julia First. New York: Avon/Camelot Books, 1975. 95 p. $1.25. Paper. (Originally published by Prentice-Hall, 1974.)

Although 11-and-1/2-year-old Laura is one of the most sought after players on the boy's Little League baseball practice team, she wants to be "popular" like the other girls in her class. However, through her activities with a young cerebral palsy victim, she learns to become confident in herself and realizes there is room in her life for many different kinds of people.

Book deals with inequitable treatment of girls in organized sports activities and how parents treat boys and girls differently.

*Careers:* Female = 6 Male = 11 Neutral = 7
*Subject Categories:* Families/Friendship; The Handicapped; Health/Human Development; Sports

**4.6 Maria Luisa.** Winifred Madison. Philadelphia, PA: J.B. Lippincott, 1971. 187 p. $4.43.

Maria Luisa, a young Mexican American girl from a small town in Arizona, moves to San Francisco to live with relatives and experiences prejudice for the first time. Story provides a realistic portrait of problems many ethnic minorities face in the public school system as well as a positive portrayal of ethnic minorities and girl/boy friendships. Book also shows the successful results of a special program for students who speak English as a second language.

*Careers:* Female = 11 Male = 15 Neutral = 12
*Subject Categories:* American Ethnic Minority; Families/Friendship; Health/Human Development

**4.7 Are You There God? It's Me, Margaret.** Judy Blume. New York: Dell, 1970. 149 p. $1.50. Paper. (Originally published by The Bradbury Press, 1970.)

A candid and humorous portrayal of a 12-year-old girl's concerns—family relationships, religion, physical maturation, social expectations.

*Careers:* Female = 11 Male = 11 Neutral = 16
*Subject Categories:* Families/Friendship; Health/Human Development; Religion/Mythology

**4.8 The Practical Princess and Other Liberating Fairy Tales.** Jay Williams. New York: Parent's Magazine Press, 1978. 99 p. $5.95.

This book is a collection of six delightful fairy tales, filled with princesses, dragons, witches, princes and enchanters—however, the princesses slay the dragons and rescue the princes! The stories, which include "The Practical Princess," "Stupid Marco," "The Silver Whistle," "Forgetful Fred," "Petronella," and "Philbert the Fearful," reverse the traditional fairy tale roles and provide amusing entertainment throughout.

*Careers:* Female = 7 Male = 13 Neutral = 7
*Subject Categories:* Fantasy, Folk & Fairy Tales

**4.9 Penelope and the Mussels.** Shirley Boccaccio. San Francisco, CA: Joyful World Press, 1971. 22 p. $2.95. Paper.

Penelope, along with her baby brother Peter, a raccoon and a salamander, pilot a plane to the beach to collect mussels for dinner. Book is written in rhyme and delightfully illustrated with collage of photographs and pen and ink drawings.

*Careers:* Female = 1 Male = 2 Neutral = 0
*Subject Categories:* Animals; Families/Friendship; Fantasy, Folk & Fairy Tales; Mystery/Adventure; Picture Book; Poetry/Rhyme

**4.10 Liza Lou and the Yeller Belly Swamp.** Mercer Mayer. New York: Parent's Magazine Press, 1976. 40 p. $5.41.

This amusing story tells how Liza Lou, a young black girl, uses her wit to outfox the devils, gobblygooks, witches and swamp-haunts of Yeller Belly Swamp.

*Careers:* Female = 4 Male = 1 Neutral = 0
*Subject Categories:* American Ethnic Minority; Fantasy, Folk & Fairy Tales; Mystery/Adventure; Picture Book

**4.11 I Climb Mountains.** Barbara Taylor. Toronto, ON: The Women's Press, 1975. 24 p. $3.00. Paper.

Peter finds out his two friends, Lucy and Annie, are just as adventuresome and imaginative as he is.

*Careers:* None shown
*Subject Categories:* Families/Friendship; Picture Book

**4.12ˣ ABC Workbook.** Jean Mangi. Old Westbury, NY: The Feminist Press, 1975. 30 p. $2.25. Paper.

With illustrations showing women and girls in a variety of nontraditional careers and activities, this combined coloring/activity book provides nonsexist examples to help children learn their ABCs. ("My name is Ann. I am an absolutely great astronaut.") Subject matter is more appropriate for the beginning reader.

*Careers:* Female = 16 Male = 1 Neutral = 0
*Subject Categories:* Picture Book

**4.13 The Preacher's Kid.** Rose Blue. New York: Franklin Watts, 1975. 52 p. $5.90.

Linda and her family face rejection because they don't join their community in boycotting the busing of black children to her school. Linda must decide which is more important to her—her values or attending her friend's birthday party.

*Careers:* Female = 4 Male = 4 Neutral = 4
*Subject Categories:* American Ethnic Minority; Cont. Issues/Curr. Events; Families/Friendship; Health/Human Development; Religion/Mythology

**4.14 Moy Moy.** Leo Politi. New York: Charles Scribner's Sons, 1960. 30 p. $6.95.

Story of the celebration of Chinese New Year through the eyes of a young Chinese American girl, Moy Moy.

*Careers:* Female = 2 Male = 2 Neutral = 2
*Subject Categories:* American Ethnic Minority; Families/Friendship

**4.15 Jennifer, Hecate, Macbeth, William McKinley and Me, Elizabeth.** E.L. Konigsburg. New York: Atheneum, 1967. 117 p. $1.95. Paper.

Two lonely girls secretly explore witchcraft together. When they stop pretending to be witches, they become good friends.

*Careers:* Female = 10 Male = 5 Neutral = 10
*Subject Categories:* American Ethnic Minority; Families/Friendship; Mystery/Adventure

**4.16 Iggie's House.** Judy Blume. New York: Dell, 1970. 117 p. $1.25. Paper. (Originally published by The Bradbury Press, 1970.)

Winnie, an active 11-year-old girl who plays ball with the boys, sets out to be a "good neighbor" to the Garbers, a black family who has just moved into the house of her best friend Iggie, whose family has moved away. Life becomes complicated when one of the neighbors tells the Garbers to get out of the neighborhood, and Winnie comes to learn the difference between being a "good neighbor" and being a friend. Sensitive portrayal of conflicts occurring due to prejudice and racism.

*Careers:* Female = 2 Male = 10 Neutral = 2
*Subject Categories:* American Ethnic Minority; Families/Friendship; Health/Human Development

**4.17 She Wanted to Read: The Story of Mary McLeod Bethune.** Ella Kaiser Carruth. Nashville, TN: Abingdon, 1966. 80 p. $2.95.

This book is a biography of Mary McLeod Bethune, a black woman who grew up on a cotton plantation and became a world-famous educator and civic leader.

*Careers:* Female = 18 Male = 20 Neutral = 5
*Subject Categories:* American Ethnic Minority; Biography; History

**4.18ˣ Rafiki.** Nola Langner. New York: Viking Press, 1977. 30 p. $7.95.

Although the king of the African jungle proclaims that only girls do housework and only animals build houses, young Rafiki's arrival changes the order of things. Humorous messages for animals and independent people of all ages, although the pictures and large print make this book more appropriate for primary-grade readers.

*Careers:* Female = 1 Male = 1 Neutral = 0
*Subject Categories:* Animals; Fantasy, Folk & Fairy Tales; Foreign Countries; Picture Book

**4.19 Before the Supreme Court: The Story of Belva Ann Lockwood.** Terry Dunnahoo. Boston: Houghton Mifflin, 1974. 186 p. $4.95.

This biography of a remarkable woman of the nineteenth century depicts the attitudes and discrimination women lived with 100 years ago. Despite obstacles that took years to surmount, Belva Ann Lockwood became a lawyer, was the first woman to practice law before the Supreme Court and ran for the presidency of the United States. Her support of the equal rights movement was a life-long endeavor; she died three years before the 19th Amendment was ratified.

*Careers:* Female = 12 Male = 31 Neutral = 20
*Subject Categories:* Biography; History

**4.20ˣ Tommy and Sarah Dress Up.** Gunilla Wolde. Boston: Houghton Mifflin, 1972. 20 p. $1.25.

In this colorful picture book, a boy and girl play "dress up." Subject matter, pictures and print make this book more appropriate for primary-grade readers.

*Careers:* Female = 0 Male = 0 Neutral = 2
*Subject Categories:* Families/Friendship; Picture Book

**4.21 What Can She Be? A Veterinarian.** Gloria and Esther Goldreich. New York: Lothrop, Lee & Shepard, 1972. 47 p. $4.32.

Simple text and interesting photographs describe Dr. Penny's work as a veterinarian.

*Careers:* Female = 1 Male = 1 Neutral = 2
*Subject Categories:* Animals; Careers; Picture Book; Science

**4.22 Two Tickets to Freedom: The True Story of Ellen and William Craft, Fugitive Slaves.** Florence B. Freedman. New York: Simon & Schuster, 1971. 96 p. $5.95.

A dramatic recounting of the true story of Ellen and William Craft, who escaped from slavery, lived prosperously in England and returned home to the South after the Civil War to open a farm school for their people.

*Careers:* Female = 7 Male = 43 Neutral = 19
*Subject Categories:* American Ethnic Minority; Biography; History; Mystery/Adventure

**4.23 Nothing Is Impossible: The Story of Beatrix Potter.** Dorothy Aldis. New York: Atheneum, 1969. 154 p. $6.95.

This biography of Beatrix Potter tells the story of her lonely and overprotected childhood; her love of animals, children, gardens and life; and the stubborn determination that led her to become a writer and illustrator of children's books despite disapproval from her family.

*Careers:* Female = 13 Male = 19 Neutral = 0
*Subject Categories:* Animals; Biography; Families/Friendship; Foreign Countries; Health/Human Development

**4.24 Rosie and Michael.** Judith Viorst. New York: Atheneum, 1974. 37 p. $6.95.

This delightful picture book is about Rosie and Michael and all the things they do for each other. Their friendship is on an equal basis and is portrayed nonstereotypically.

*Careers:* Female = 1 Male = 5 Neutral = 0
*Subject Categories:* Families/Friendship; Picture Book

**4.25ˣ Cowslip.** Betsy Haynes. Nashville, TN: Thomas Nelson, 1973. 139 p. $5.95.

This is an extremely moving story about 13-year-old Cowslip, a black slave who lives in the South before the Civil War and is sold on the auction block and put in charge of the master's children. The reader sees her move from the belief that blacks are slaves because of God's will to the conviction that all human beings should be free; that she will be as wild and free as the flower for which she's named.

*Careers:* Female = 10 Male = 13 Neutral = 8
*Subject Categories:* American Ethnic Minority; Health/Human Development; History

**4.26ˣ The Cuckoo Tree.** Joan Aiken. Garden City, NY: Doubleday, 1971. 314 p. $4.95.

Smugglers, intrigue and heroism combine in a story about Dido Twite, who saves King James from the insidious Hanoverian plot. Because of the use of dialect and the subject matter, book may be more appropriate for older readers.

*Careers:* Female = 7 Male = 37 Neutral = 1
*Subject Categories:* Foreign Countries; History; Mystery/Adventure

**4.27 Kristy's Courage.** Babbis Friis. New York: Harcourt, Brace & World, 1965. 159 p. $5.95.

Kristy, who has been hit by a car, must learn to live with a scar and nearly unintelligible speech. She learns how to accept herself and deal with her classmates' reactions. There is some sex role and ethnic stereotyping.

*Careers:* Female = 5 Male = 12 Neutral = 7
*Subject Categories:* Families/Friendship; The Handicapped; Health/Human Development

**4.28 What Can She Be? A Lawyer.** Gloria and Esther Goldreich. New York: Lothrop, Lee & Shepard, 1973. 40 p. $4.95.

With simply written text and numerous photographs, this book provides a documentary picture of a lawyer's life. The story shows Ellen Green at work on cases understandable to a young child and thus opens up the profession of law to girls and boys.

*Careers:* Female = 5 Male = 7 Neutral = 5
*Subject Categories:* Careers; Picture Book

**4.29 The Borrowers.** Mary Norton. New York: Harcourt, Brace, Jovanovich, 1952. 180 p. $1.50. Paper.

This is a story of the Borrowers—"Little People" who live within the houses of big people and borrow things.

*Careers:* Female = 3 Male = 6 Neutral = 2
*Subject Categories:* Families/Friendship; Fantasy, Folk & Fairy Tales; Mystery/Adventure

**4.30ˣ Fannie Lou Hamer.** June Jordan. New York: Thomas Y. Crowell, 1972. 40 p. $1.45. Paper.

Biography of Fannie Lou Hamer, a black woman who became a leader in the registration of black voters in the South. This is an excellent portrait of a strong, courageous woman who was beaten and threatened for her convictions, yet continued to encourage blacks to register for the vote. Large type and pictures make this book appropriate for primary-grade readers.

*Careers:* Female = 3 Male = 13 Neutral = 1
*Subject Categories:* American Ethnic Minority; Biography; Cont. Issues/Curr. Events; Picture Book

**4.31 The Empty Schoolhouse.** Natalie Savage Carlson. New York: Harper & Row, 1965. 119 p. $6.49.

This story examines the conflicts and problems arising from school integration through the eyes of 14-year-old Emma, a young black girl growing up in the South, and her 10-year-old sister Lullah.

*Careers:* Female = 6 Male = 12 Neutral = 2
*Subject Categories:* American Ethnic Minority; Cont. Issues/ Curr. Events; Families/Friendship

**4.32 Sojourner Truth: Fearless Crusader.** Helen Stone Peterson. Champaign, IL: Garrard, 1972. 94 p. $4.28.

Story of the life and work of Sojourner Truth, from slavery to freedom, and her struggle to abolish slavery, defend women's rights and help her people after the Emancipation Proclamation.

*Careers:* Female = 15 Male = 19 Neutral = 11
*Subject Categories:* American Ethnic Minority; Biography; History

**4.33ˣ The Story of Ferdinand.** Munro Leaf. New York: Penguin Books, 1977. 68 p. $1.95. Paper. (Originally published by Viking Press, 1936.)

This is a classic story written in 1936 about a nonstereotypic bull. Ferdinand is gentle, quiet, peace-loving and fond of flowers. Although he doesn't like to fight, charge or roar, he is a great big, strong bull. Large print and pictures make this book more appropriate for primary-grade readers.

*Careers:* Female = 1 Male = 3 Neutral = 0
*Subject Categories:* Animals; Fantasy, Folk & Fairy Tales; Foreign Countries; Picture Book

**4.34 Along Sandy Trails.** Ann Nolan Clark. New York: Viking Press, 1969. 30 p. $5.95.

A Papago girl learns about the desert from her grandmother. Book is beautifully illustrated with color photographs of animals, birds, cacti and plants found in the desert.

*Careers:* Female = 2 Male = 1 Neutral = 0
*Subject Categories:* American Ethnic Minority; Families/ Friendship; Picture Book; Science

**4.35 My Mother the Mail Carrier (Mi Mama La Cartera).** Inez Maury. Old Westbury, NY: The Feminist Press, 1976. 28 p. $3.50. Paper.

Five-year-old Lupita talks about her mother, who enjoys being both a mother and a mail carrier. This book is delightfully illustrated and written in English and Spanish.

*Careers:* Female = 3 Male = 0 Neutral = 0
*Subject Categories:* American Ethnic Minority; Families/ Friendship; Picture Book

**4.36 Journey to America.** Sonia Levitin. New York: Atheneum, 1970. 150 p. $.95. Paper.

Lisa, her mother and her two sisters escape from the Nazis and flee to Switzerland as refugees. Although life is difficult for them at first, many people help them until they can join their father in America.

*Careers:* Female = 15 Male = 24 Neutral = 16
*Subject Categories:* Families/Friendship; Foreign Countries; History; Mystery/Adventure

**4.37 Chris Evert, Tennis Pro.** Linda Jacobs. St. Paul, MN: EMC Corporation, 1974. 40 p. $4.95.

A brief biography of tennis pro Chris Evert, whose coolness on the court and tennis mastery have made her a champion.

*Careers:* Female = 1 Male = 2 Neutral = 5
*Subject Categories:* Biography; Sports

**4.38 Mumbet: The Story of Elizabeth Freeman.** Harold W. Felton. New York: Dodd, Mead, 1970. 63 p. $4.50.

Biography of Elizabeth Freeman, who in 1781 became the first slave to win her freedom in the courts of the state of Massachusetts.

*Careers:* Female = 5 Male = 13 Neutral = 3
*Subject Categories:* American Ethnic Minority; Biography; History

**4.39 Mahalia: Gospel Singer.** Kay McDearmon. New York: Dodd, Mead, 1976. 45 p. $4.50.

Biography of Mahalia Jackson, a famous American gospel singer, who overcame poverty and racial prejudice.

*Careers:* Female = 11 Male = 9 Neutral = 10
*Subject Categories:* American Ethnic Minority; Biography; Health/Human Development

**4.40 A Year in the Life of Rosie Bernard.** Barbara Brenner. New York: Harper & Row, 1971. 179 p. $4.79.

Ten-year-old Rosie goes to live with a relative in Brooklyn in the 1930s. During the year she decides to become a doctor, explores her religious background and learns to accept her father's remarriage.

*Careers:* Female = 8 Male = 14 Neutral = 5
*Subject Categories:* Families/Friendship; Health/Human Development; Religion/Mythology

**4.41 Two Piano Tuners.** M.B. Goffstein. New York: Farrar, Straus & Giroux, 1970. 65 p. $5.95.

Story about a young girl who wants to be a piano tuner like her famous grandfather. It explores the importance of choosing a career based on interest instead of expectation or prestige.

*Careers:* Female = 4 Male = 4 Neutral = 0
*Subject Categories:* Families/Friendship; Fine Arts; Health/ Human Development

**4.42 Kids Are Natural Cooks.** Parent's Nursery School. Boston: Houghton Mifflin, 1972. 129 p. $4.95. Paper.

A book of child-tested, natural food recipes for girls and boys to try at home and school, with delightful illustrations and guidelines for teachers and parents.

*Careers:* Female = 2 Male = 1 Neutral = 1
*Subject Categories:* Information Book

**4.43 The Changeling.** Zilpha Keatley Snyder. New York: Atheneum, 1970. 220 p. $.95. Paper.

Though Martha's family disapproves of her friendship with Ivy Carson, it is Ivy who helps Martha develop a sense of her own individuality. Ivy tells Martha she is a changeling—a child of supernatural people. This is Ivy's way of expressing her uniqueness and explaining her special talents.

*Careers:* Female = 12 Male = 9 Neutral = 7
*Subject Categories:* Families/Friendship; Health/Human Development; Fantasy, Folk & Fairy Tales

**4.44 Where the Lilies Bloom.** Vera and Bill Cleaver. New York: New American Library, 1974. 175 p. $1.50. Paper. (Originally published by J.B. Lippincott, 1969.)

A 14-year-old girl living in Appalachia faces adversity with courage and ingenuity and keeps her family together after the death of their father.

*Careers:* Female = 6 Male = 12 Neutral = 5

*Subject Categories:* Families/Friendship; Health/Human Development

**4.45 Notes on the Hauter Experiment: A Journey through the Inner World of Evelyn B. Chestnut.** Bernice Grohskopf. New York: Atheneum, 1975. 135 p. $6.95.

In this science fiction story, Evelyn B. Chestnut finds herself locked away in a world of perfect order from which she cannot escape.

*Careers:* Female = 3 Male = 3 Neutral = 6
*Subject Categories:* Mystery/Adventure; Science Fiction

**4.46 The Ostrich Chase.** Moses L. Howard. New York: Holt, Rinehart & Winston, 1974. 116 p. $5.95.

Although the customs and traditions of the Bushmen culture do not allow girls to hunt and shoot, young Khuana's greatest ambition is to kill an ostrich. She finally realizes her goal after an exciting and dangerous trek across the Kalahari desert with her grandmother. This is a very warm and readable story.

*Careers:* Female = 1 Male = 2 Neutral = 0
*Subject Categories:* Families/Friendship; Foreign Countries; Mystery/Adventure

**4.47 Firegirl.** Gibson Rich. Old Westbury, NY: The Feminist Press, 1972. 46 p. $3.25. Paper.

Brenda, an eight-year-old girl who is fascinated by fire trucks and longs to fight fires, proves to her family and the fire chief that she can fight fires too. Ethnic minorities are well represented in the text and illustrations.

*Careers:* Female = 4 Male = 4 Neutral = 1
*Subject Categories:* Mystery/Adventure; Picture Book

**4.48 Zeely.** Virginia Hamilton. New York: Macmillan, 1967. 122 p. $6.95.

A young, imaginative black girl in the rural South discovers the importance of being herself and holding her head high.

*Careers:* Female = 4 Male = 4 Neutral = 2
*Subject Categories:* American Ethnic Minority; Families/Friendship; Health/Human Development

**4.49 Womenfolk and Fairy Tales.** Rosemary Minard. Boston: Houghton Mifflin, 1975. 163 p. $6.95.

A collection of traditional fairy tales deliberately chosen because they depict girls and women as active, intelligent, competent and brave individuals. Although many of these tales end in marriage, it isn't the main focus of the stories.

*Careers:* Female = 11 Male = 14 Neutral = 2
*Subject Categories:* Fantasy, Folk & Fairy Tales; Mystery/Adventure

**4.50ˣ Memoirs of an Ex-Prom Queen.** Alix Kates Shulman. New York: Bantam Books, 1979. 294 p. $2.25. Paper. (Originally published by Alfred A. Knopf, 1972.)

This novel is about a girl who grows up to be pretty and sexually attractive and is chosen to be "Prom Queen" in high school. The author traces her exploits and the emotional and social significance attached to them. The book is humorous, witty and often painfully realistic. It is likely that almost every woman will identify at some point with the main character as she explores her values and dreams while making mistakes along the way. Her reliance on other people's evaluation of her

physical attributes ("sexy," "beautiful") proves to be the root of many of her problems. The portrayal of explicit sex makes this book more appropriate for mature secondary students.

*Careers:* Female = 10 Male = 18 Neutral = 2
*Subject Categories:* Health/Human Development; Women's Studies

**4.51ˣ The Girls of Huntington House.** Blossom Elfman. New York: Bantam Books, 1978. 213 p. $1.95. Paper. (Originally published by Houghton Mifflin, 1972.)

A warm, touching, sometimes comic, sometimes desperate story of an English teacher who spends a year teaching at a home for unwed mothers. Through her eyes the reader sees the sadness, comedy and reality of junior and senior high school-aged women coping with their pregnancies. Subject matter and formatting make this book more appropriate for junior or senior high readers.

*Careers:* Female = 14 Male = 15 Neutral = 15
*Subject Categories:* Families/Friendship; Health/Human Development

**4.52 Stand Up Lucy.** Elizabeth Hall. Boston: Houghton Mifflin, 1971. 188 p.

Fairly traditional story of a spirited young girl who becomes a part of the suffragist movement despite her father's objections.

*Careers:* Female = 10 Male = 21 Neutral = 9
*Subject Categories:* Families/Friendship; History

**4.53ˣ Our Cup Is Broken.** Florence Crannell Means. Boston: Houghton Mifflin, 1969. 229 p.

A story for mature teenagers about a young Hopi woman caught between two cultures. Adopted by a white family after the death of her parents, Sarah returns to her Hopi village after a broken romance and a nine-year stay with her adoptive family in Kansas. Although she rejects the white culture, she no longer feels accepted by her Hopi people. She is raped by a Hopi man, bears his child and eventually marries another because of the difficulty of living alone in the village. The story is dramatic and somewhat bitter, yet provides insight and a deeper understanding of the Hopi culture and the often deplorable consequences of cultural separation.

*Careers:* Female = 14 Male = 20 Neutral = 12
*Subject Categories:* American Ethnic Minority; Behavioral Science; Cultural Heritage; Health/Human Development

**4.54 How Many Miles to Sundown?** Patricia Beatty. New York: William Morrow, 1974. 22 p.

Story of a spunky 13-year-old girl, Beeler Quiney, and her journey through Texas, New Mexico and the Arizona Territory in the 1880s. Traveling with her is her ornery brother Leo and Nate Graber, who is searching for his missing father. On their journey they meet a variety of colorful characters and encounter bandits and a circus.

*Careers:* Female = 9 Male = 18 Neutral = 17
*Subject Categories:* Families/Friendship; History; Mystery/Adventure

**4.55ˣ I'll Get There. It Better Be Worth the Trip.** John Donovan. New York: Dell, 1979. 158 p. $1.25. Paper. (Originally published by Harper & Row, 1969.)

After his grandmother dies, 14-year-old Davy Ross, along with his dachshund Fred, goes to New York to live with his divorced, alcoholic mother. There he becomes friends with Douglas Altschuller, who shares with Davy the loneliness of a broken home. Drawn to each other in their need for love and companionship, their relationship culminates in an unforeseen moment of open sexuality. A nonstereotypic portrayal of a young man's conflicting emotions as he goes through the pain of adolescence. Subject matter may make this book more appropriate for junior high school readers.

*Careers:* Female = 7 Male = 22 Neutral = 11
*Subject Categories:* Families/Friendship; Health/Human Development

**4.56ˣ  Lisa, Bright and Dark.** John Neufeld. New York: New American Library, 1970. 143 p. $1.50. Paper. (Originally published by S.G. Phillips, 1969.)

Story of 16-year-old Lisa, who is progressively slipping into a world of madness. Because her parents are indifferent, Lisa's three friends join forces to try to help her through "group therapy" sessions. Although the idea of teenagers practicing amateur psychology should not be encouraged and the characters are somewhat stereotypic, this book provides readers with greater understanding of mental illness and how it affects others. Subject matter may be more appropriate for older readers.

*Careers:* Female = 6 Male = 12 Neutral = 5
*Subject Categories:* Behavioral Science; Families/Friendship; The Handicapped; Health/Human Development

**4.57 Dinky Hocker Shoots Smack!** M.E. Kerr. New York: Dell, 1972. 190 p. $1.50. Paper. (Originally published by Harper & Row, 1972.)

Story of the problems and friendship of four teenagers in Brooklyn: Tucker, who wants to be a librarian and has never had a meaningful relationship in his life; Dinky, who is fat and getting fatter; Natalia, who has to go to a special school for emotionally disturbed children; and P. John, who is a 15-year-old "fascist." The story is amusing, often insightful and touching in its portrayal of the problems of teenagers. However, parents do not come off too well in this book. For the most part, the children's problems are portrayed as being the result of their parents' inattention and preoccupation with liberal, "do-gooding" causes.

*Careers:* Female = 8 Male = 22 Neutral = 16
*Subject Categories:* Families/Friendship; The Handicapped; Health/Human Development

**4.58ˣ  The Sexes: Male/Female Roles and Relationships.** Betsy Ryan. New York: Scholastic Book Service, 1975. 186 p. Paper.

A delightful book with more than 100 poems, photographs, songs, cartoons, articles and ads, which explore love, dating, marriage and male and female sex roles today. This book is appropriate for free reading and would also provide an excellent resource for stimulating discussion about female and male roles and relationships in health, social studies or women's studies courses at the junior high or secondary level.

*Careers:* Female = 21 Male = 17 Neutral = 5
*Subject Categories:* Behavioral Science; Health/Human Development; Women's Studies

**4.59 Maria Looney and the Remarkable Robot.** Jerome Beatty, Jr. New York: Avon, 1979. 144 p. $1.50. Paper.

While young moonster Maria Looney is on a gadabout survival test on the South Pole of the moon, she meets Captain John Smith, a crashed earthman, and Tommy Tonn, a robot. Thus begins an adventure in which Maria finds herself rescuing Tommy from the ruthless and greedy Robinson K. Russo and his hooligans after Tommy is robotnapped. Although the careers are stereotyped, Maria is active and adventurous.

*Careers:* Female = 8 Male = 7 Neutral = 10
*Subject Categories:* Mystery/Adventure; Science Fiction

**4.60 The Autobiography of Miss Jane Pittman.** Ernest J. Gaines. New York: Bantam Books, 1972. 246 p. $1.75. Paper. (Originally published by Dial Press, 1971.)

Although this novel about the recollections of a former slave is not a "real" autobiography, the character of Miss Jane Pittman is as real as any you will ever read. The story follows Jane Pittman for 100 years—from her days as a slave, to her participation in one of the first acts of black militancy in the 1960s. Readers will find 100 years of black history brought to life in these pages, but more than that, the character of Jane Pittman—her determination and spirit—is unforgettable. Older readers will also enjoy this book.

*Careers:* Female = 10 Male = 26 Neutral = 4
*Subject Categories:* American Ethnic Minority; Cont. Issues/Curr. Events; Cultural Heritage; History

**4.61ˣ  ABC Play with Me.** Donna Kelly. Racine, WI: Western Publishing, 1978. 23 p.

This delightful book portrays children enjoying play activities on a nonstereotyped basis. Races, sexes, ethnic groups and disabled are represented. ABC format makes this book more appropriate for first graders.

*Careers:* None shown
*Subject Categories:* American Ethnic Minority; Families/Friendship; Health/Human Development

**4.62 Andrea Jaeger Tennis Champion.** Julianna A. Fogel and Mary S. Watkins. New York: J.B. Lippincott, 1980. 41 p. $8.95.

Fourteen-year-old Andrea Jaeger is a determined tennis professional with outstanding drive and discipline. She played twice in Wimbledon and in 1980 advanced to the quarterfinals of the tournament. Written from a first person perspective and generously illustrated with photographs, this description of the dedication and hard work of a young professional athlete is recommended for young readers.

*Careers:* Female = 1 Male = 1 Neutral = 0
*Subject Categories:* Autobiography/Biography; Picture Book; Sports

**4.63 Arthur Mitchell.** Tobi Tobias. New York: Thomas Y. Crowell, 1975. 33 p.

Biography of Arthur Mitchell, the first black dancer of the New York City Ballet, who established the world-renowned Dance Theatre of Harlem. Although there is some sexist language, the story and beautiful illustrations will interest young readers.

*Careers:* Female = 4 Male = 13 Neutral = 6
*Subject Categories:* American Ethnic Minority; Autobiography/Biography; Fine Arts

**4.64 Elizabeth Blackwell, Pioneer Doctor.** Matthew G. Grant. Mankato, MN: Creative Education, 1974. 31 p.

Part of a series entitled *Women of America.* Easy to read and colorfully illustrated, the book traces the career of Elizabeth Blackwell, the first woman physician to graduate in the United States. Blackwell is cited for her courage and dedication in the face of prejudice against women physicians which seemed nearly insurmountable in the first half of the nineteenth century.

*Careers:* Female = 4 Male = 2 Neutral = 1
*Subject Categories:* Autobiography/Biography; Health/Human Development; History

**4.65 Billie Jean King: Queen of the Court.** Carol Bauer Church. Minneapolis, MN: Greenhaven Press, 1976. 65 p.

An interesting account of the tennis career of Billie Jean King. The author's presentation of tennis as a "lady like" sport is overshadowed by the enormous strides that Billie Jean King made for all women athletes. She not only was a superbly skillful tennis champion but also cared about bringing the sport to the people.

*Careers:* Female = 2 Male = 6 Neutral = 0
*Subject Categories:* Autobiography/Biography; Sports

**4.66ˣ Hey, Dollface.** Deborah Hautzig. New York: William Morrow, 1978. 151 p. $6.95.

A perceptive, funny, tender novel about the friendship between two adolescent girls. Val and Chloe love each other, and this frightens both of them. They believe themselves to be heterosexuals, and yet both simultaneously desire and are disturbed by physical closeness. "How do you separate loving as a friend and sexual love—or do they cross over sometimes?" Val wonders. The girls learn that part of growing up involves making their own decisions about what is "right" and "wrong" based on honest feelings. This is not a book about "bisexuality" but about two very real young people learning to define friendship. Subject matter makes book more appropriate for junior high readers.

*Careers:* Female = 12 Male = 13 Neutral = 7
*Subject Categories:* Families/Friendship; Health/Human Development

**4.67 What Can She Be? A Newscaster.** Gloria and Esther Goldreich. New York: Lothrop, Lee and Shepard, 1973. 47 p.

Black and white photographs vividly portray the work of Barbara Lamont, a black newscaster who reports the news on both radio and television in New York City. Good introduction to some of the careers associated with broadcast journalism.

*Careers:* Female = 4 Male = 14 Neutral = 5
*Subject Categories:* American Ethnic Minority; Careers

**4.68 By the Highway Home.** Mary Stolz. New York: Harper & Row, 1971. 194 p. $1.95. Paper.

Catty Reed's beloved brother is killed in Vietnam, her father loses his job and the family moves to another state. Meanwhile, she faces a number of concerns common to young teenagers: an aggravating sister, fears and a first love. Mary Stolz manages to make Catty's story touching without being cloying and deals

sensitively with such topics as death, old age, cowardice and the environment.

*Careers:* Female = 3 Male = 22 Neutral = 10
*Subject Categories:* Families/Friendship; Health/Human Development

**4.69ˣ Window Wishing.** Jeanette Caines. New York: Harper & Row, 1980. 20 p. $7.95.

In this nonsexist and nonracist book, Grandma Mag is an unconventional grandma who wears sneakers, fishes and makes kites. When her two grandchildren visit, they go window wishing and have picnics in the cemetery. This is a delightful book with a text enhanced by true-to-life, nonstereotyped illustrations. Large print makes this book more appropriate for primary-grade readers.

*Careers:* Female = 0 Male = 0 Neutral = 1
*Subject Categories:* American Ethnic Minority; Families/Friendship; Picture Book

**4.70ˣ Daddy Was a Number Runner.** Louise Meriwether. New York: Jove, 1970. 188 p. $1.95. Paper.

This powerful book brings Harlem to life through the eyes of a 12-year-old girl. Her joys and sorrows, pain and triumph belong to the reader. Francie is resourceful and tough with a will to overcome the obstacles of her life. Subject matter may make this book more appropriate for junior high readers.

*Careers:* Female = 6 Male = 20 Neutral = 3
*Subject Categories:* American Ethnic Minority; Health/Human Development; Literature by Women

**4.71 Mary McLeod Bethune.** Eloise Greenfield. New York: Thomas Y. Crowell, 1980. 32 p.

A very readable and interesting account of the life and work of Mary McLeod Bethune. Against great odds, she gained an education and later began her own school. Her life was devoted to the betterment of life for black people. This book is a reminder of the legacy of black women today.

*Careers:* Female = 1 Male = 1 Neutral = 1
*Subject Categories:* American Ethnic Minority; Autobiography/Biography; Cultural Heritage; History

**4.72 I Am the Running Girl.** Arnold Adoff. New York: Harper & Row, 1979. 40 p. $6.95.

Beautifully illustrated and poetic account of a girl's desire to run. This book is very well done and would be interesting to girls interested in sports or achievement of any kind.

*Careers:* None shown
*Subject Categories:* Sports

**4.73 An Eskimo Birthday.** Tom D. Robinson. New York: Dodd, Mead, 1975. 39 p. $5.25.

Rather traditional story about a young Eskimo girl, Eeke, who gets a parka she wants for her birthday.

*Careers:* Female = 3 Male = 3 Neutral = 1
*Subject Categories:* American Ethnic Minority; Families/Friendship

**4.74 The Wind Is Not a River.** Arnold A. Griese. New York: Thomas Y. Crowell, 1978. 108 p. $6.95.

Two children, Sasan and her brother Sidak, are the only villagers to escape the Japanese invasion of their Aleutian island during World War II. The story tells of their struggle for survival as they try to leave the island to get help and their decision to look beyond the label of "enemy" to save a human life.

*Careers:* Female = 0 Male = 3 Neutral = 3
*Subject Categories:* American Ethnic Minority; Cultural Heritage; History; Mystery/Adventure

**4.75ˣ Jemmy.** Jon Hassler. New York: Atheneum, 1980. 175 p. $7.95.

A life of poverty seems to lie ahead for 17-year-old Jemmy Stott who lives just outside a reservation in Minnesota. Her mother, a Chippewa, is dead; her father, a white, is an unemployed alcoholic who has demanded that she quit school to take care of him and her younger brother and sister. The book traces a six-month friendship between Jemmy and a famous painter she meets and his wife; a friendship that changes Jemmy's life as she discovers her own identity—as a Native American, a woman and an artist. Subject matter makes story relevant to older readers.

*Careers:* Female = 8 Male = 15 Neutral = 14
*Subject Categories:* American Ethnic Minority; Families/Friendship; Health/Human Development

**4.76ˣ The Beckoner.** Adrienne Jones. New York: Harper & Row, 1980. 243 p. $8.95.

Kate Duret, a young woman in her early twenties, is on the verge of a psychological breakdown. Gradually, Kate makes peace with herself and finds the strength to follow her grandmother's admonition: "Thou'rt to stand up to life, my bonny." Very few stereotypes in this interesting, positive novel. Subject matter is appropriate for junior and senior high readers.

*Careers:* Female = 7 Male = 13 Neutral = 6
*Subject Categories:* Families/Friendship; Health/Human Development

**4.77 What Can She Be? A Police Officer.** Gloria and Esther Goldreich. New York: Lothrop, Lee and Shepard, 1975. 48 p.

Book explores the jobs of two sisters who are police officers: One works with a rescue squad; the other patrols a neighborhood beat.

*Careers:* Female = 6 Male = 7 Neutral = 5
*Subject Categories:* Careers

**4.78 Me Too.** Vera and Bill Cleaver. Philadelphia, PA: J.B. Lippincott, 1973. 158 p.

A 12-year-old girl takes care of her retarded twin during the summer and sets forth to succeed at teaching her after everyone else has failed. The story realistically gives insights into the prejudices faced by the mentally disabled.

*Careers:* Female = 5 Male = 8 Neutral = 17
*Subject Categories:* Families/Friendship; The Handicapped; Health/Human Development

**4.79 The Boy Who Wanted a Family.** Shirley Gordon. New York: Harper & Row, 1980. 90 p. $7.95.

Seven-year-old Michael, who was bounced from foster home to foster home, wants a family. When a single woman wants to adopt him, he meets a "mom" like he never met before. She has many unusual ideas about their having fun together, and they

have many special times in the year before the adoption is final. This book brings a fresh perspective on family relationships.

*Careers:* Female = 2 Male = 4 Neutral = 0
*Subject Categories:* Families/Friendship

**4.80 The Clever Princess.** Ann Tompert. Chapel Hill, NC: Lollipop Power, 1977. 39 p.

In this delightful fairy tale, Princess Lorna cleverly solves the puzzles of the king's counselors and becomes the ruler over the kingdom. The illustrations portray a variety of roles, nationalities and ages.

*Careers:* Female = 1 Male = 5 Neutral = 0
*Subject Categories:* American Ethnic Minority; Fantasy, Folk & Fairy Tales

**4.81 Self Portrait: Margot Zemach.** Margot Zemach. Reading, MA: Addison-Wesley, 1978. 32 p. $7.95.

With somewhat deceptive simplicity, words and pictures combine to portray a creative, competent and singular woman—the award-winning artist, Margot Zemach. A child of the Depression years, raised by parents in the theatre, Zemach later settled into a close partnership with her husband in the writing and illustrating of children's books and the raising of four daughters in this country and abroad. The illustrations depict scenes from her books in the midst of drawings of her life, including her family's endearing household chaos of pets and possessions. A touching, nonsaccharine glimpse of Margot as artist and mother following her husband's death in 1974. A fine counterpoint to books focusing on more "traditional" family life.

*Careers:* Female = 14 Male = 8 Neutral = 0
*Subject Categories:* Autobiography/Biography; Careers; Families/Friendship; Picture Book

**4.82 Pearl in the Egg.** Dorothy Van Woerkom. New York: Thomas Y. Crowell, 1980. 118 p. $8.95.

Young Pearl, disguised as a boy, and her brother Gavin flee a life of serfdom (in the thirteenth century England) and are befriended by a troupe of entertainers. Gavin seeks his own apprenticeship in the town, but Pearl becomes a minstrel like her new friend Matill Makejoye. Yet, in their travels, she is never free from fear of discovery and a return to her feudal lord. Eventually, the dreaded day arrives and Pearl must choose whether to come to the aid of Sir Geoffrey or allow him and his followers to die at the hands of bandits—thereby leaving her freedom assured. An informative, entertaining story inspired by the fact that court records of King Edward I list Pearl's and Matill's names—two women in a traditionally male role.

*Careers:* Female = 8 Male = 36 Neutral = 12
*Subject Categories:* Families/Friendship; Foreign Countries; History; Mystery/Adventure

**4.83 Anywhere Else But Here.** Bruce Clements. New York: Farrar, Straus & Giroux, 1980. 152 p. $9.95.

Thirteen-year-old Molly Smelter has her work cut out for her. After her father's printing business goes bankrupt, she is determined that she and her father will make a fresh start "anywhere else but here" (Schenectady, New York), where she has lived all her life. A few obstacles exist: her well-meaning Aunt Aurora; Fostra Lee Post, a platitude-quoting member of a self-actualization group, who seems to have designs on the two Smelters; and Fostra's passive-aggressive eight-year-old son who has pyromaniac tendencies. But Molly has her allies also and enough gumption and good heart to surpass all setbacks. Although the aunt is drawn somewhat stereotypically, the presentation of a mutually caring father/daughter relationship is particularly good in this often humorous story.

*Careers:* Female = 8 Male = 10 Neutral = 6
*Subject Categories:* Families/Friendship; Health/Human Development

**4.84 Stories for Free Children.** Letty Cottin Pogrebin (ed.). New York: McGraw-Hill, 1982. 142 p. $14.95.

"You're a free child if you are allowed *to be yourself and true to yourself.*" This definition is put into practice in the 38 short stories, poems, fables, fairy tales and nonfiction pieces comprising the anthology. The book is a companion to *Free to Be...You and Me,* and like the earlier publication, children will relish its contents as will parents and teachers. An excellent resource. Subject matter and format also make this book appropriate for older readers.

*Careers:* Female = 29 Male = 43 Neutral = 33
*Subject Categories:* Anthologies; Families/Friendship; Health/Human Development; Women's Studies

# Reading Grade Level 5–Dale-Chall Formula

**5.1<sup>x</sup> Lordy, Aunt Hattie.** Ianthe Thomas. New York: Harper & Row, 1973. 22 p. $4.95.

This beautifully illustrated picture book written in southern dialect is about Jeppa Lee, a young black girl who wakes up one morning to find her usual routine doesn't apply—it's summer time. Use of illustrations and print size make this book more appropriate for primary-grade readers.

*Careers:* None shown
*Subject Categories:* American Ethnic Minority; Families/Friendship; Picture Book

**5.2<sup>x</sup> The Country Bunny and the Little Golden Shoes.** DuBose Heyward. Boston: Houghton Mifflin, 1939. 45 p. $2.45. Paper.

A cottontail bunny proves herself brave, swift and wise, thus earning the little golden shoes given only to very special Easter bunnies. Because of the subject matter and format, this book is more appropriate for primary-grade readers.

*Careers:* None shown
*Subject Categories:* Animals; Fantasy, Folk & Fairy Tales; Picture Book

**5.3 Sacagawea: The Story of an American Indian.** Betty Westrom Skold. Minneapolis, MN: Dillon Press, 1977. 72 p. $5.95.

A sensitive story about Sacagawea, a Shoshoni woman who acted as guide and interpreter to the Lewis and Clark Expedition in 1804-1805. Gives a good glimpse of several Native American cultures' ways of life.

*Careers:* Female = 4 Male = 18 Neutral = 3
*Subject Categories:* American Ethnic Minority; Biography; History

**5.4 Judy's Journey.** Lois Lenski. New York: Dell, 1978. 212 p. $1.25. Paper. (Originally published by J.B. Lippincott, 1947.)

Realistic and sensitive story of 10-year-old Judy and her migrant worker family as they follow the harvests from Florida to New Jersey. Portrays the struggles and poverty encountered by migrant workers, as well as their indomitable spirit and hope for a better life. Sex and ethnic roles are somewhat stereotypic.

*Careers:* Female = 13 Male = 32 Neutral = 11
*Subject Categories:* Families/Friendship

**5.5 Amy and the Cloud Basket.** Ellen Pratt. Chapel Hill, NC: Lollipop Power, 1975. 38 p. $2.00. Paper.

This delightful, rhyming fairy tale explores the concept of sex role stereotyping. Appealing illustrations show old people, young people, ethnic minorities and the disabled.

*Careers:* Female = 4 Male = 4 Neutral = 0
*Subject Categories:* Fantasy, Folk & Fairy Tales; Picture Book; Poetry/Rhyme

**5.6 The Runaway Summer.** Nina Bawden. Baltimore, MD: Penguin Books, 1976. 175 p. $1.50. Paper. (Originally published by J.B. Lippincott, 1969.)

Mary is sent to live with relatives while her parents are getting a divorce. Though resentful, she makes friends with Simon and helps hide an Indian boy, Krishna, from the police because he was brought into England illegally. Although there is some sex role sterotyping, and at first, Mary is not a very appealing character, her growth provides a positive model.

*Careers:* Female = 8 Male = 17 Neutral = 6
*Subject Categories:* Families/Friendship; Foreign Countries; Health/Human Development; Mystery/Adventure

**5.7<sup>x</sup> The Man Who Didn't Wash His Dishes.** Phyllis Krasilovsky. Garden City, NY: Doubleday, 1950. 28 p. $1.95. Paper.

Although he cooks his own supper, cleans the house by himself and makes his own bed, a man who lives alone can't cope with washing the dishes. Large print and illustrations make this picture book more appropriate for primary-grade readers.

*Careers:* Female = 1 Male = 0 Neutral = 0
*Subject Categories:* Picture Book

**5.8<sup>x</sup> Maria Tallchief.** Tobi Tobias. New York: Thomas Y. Crowell, 1970. 32 p. $1.95. Paper.

This biography of Maria Tallchief, an Osage, tells the story of her hard work and success as a prima ballerina, and her decision to give up her career to devote herself to her husband and daughter. Because of the pictures, large print and short sentences, book may be more appropriate for younger readers.

*Careers:* Female = 6 Male = 9 Neutral = 1
*Subject Categories:* American Ethnic Minority; Biography

**5.9 Susan B. Anthony: Pioneer in Women's Rights.** Helen Stone Peterson. Champaign, IL: Garrard, 1971. 94 p. $4.28.

A biography of Susan B. Anthony, a courageous pioneer in the suffragist movement who worked her entire life to obtain the vote for women and blacks.

*Careers:* Female = 19 Male = 25 Neutral = 7
*Subject Categories:* Biography; History

**5.10ˣ The Terrible Thing that Happened at Our House.**
Marge Blaine. New York: Parent's Magazine Press,
1975. 29 p. $5.41.

In this delightful picture book, a little girl narrates an extensive
complaint about all the changes that occur when her mother
goes back to work—the "Terrible Thing." But together the
family works out a solution to the problem of finding time and
energy to spend together. Subject matter, large print and
wonderful illustrations make this book appropriate for all
ages—from primary-grade readers to adults.

*Careers:* Female = 4 Male = 1 Neutral = 1
*Subject Categories:* Families/Friendship; Picture Book

**5.11ˣ The Sunflower Garden.** Janice May Udry. Irving-
ton-on-Hudson, NY: Harvey House, 1969. 37 p. $4.89.

Pipsa, a young Algonkian girl, is never praised as her five
brothers are. But Pipsa earns her father's admiration when she
raises her own sunflower garden, a first for her people, and kills
a rattlesnake to save her baby brother's life. The pictures, print
size and subject matter may be more appropriate for younger
readers.

*Careers:* Female = 1 Male = 1 Neutral = 0
*Subject Categories:* American Ethnic Minority; Families/
Friendship; Picture Book

**5.12ˣ First Snow.** Helen Coutant. New York: Alfred A.
Knopf, 1974. 33 p.

This is a beautifully written and illustrated story about a
Vietnamese girl, newly arrived in America with her family, who
discovers that her grandmother is dying and searches for its
meaning. As she experiences her first snow, watching a
snowflake melt into water which brings life to a tree, she
discovers the Buddhist belief that "life and death are but two
parts of the same thing." Large print and pictures make this
book appropriate for younger readers.

*Careers:* Female = 5 Male = 4 Neutral = 0
*Subject Categories:* American Ethnic Minority; Families/
Friendship; Health/Human Development; Picture Book

**5.13 Annie and the Old One.** Miska Miles. Boston: Little,
Brown, 1971. 44 p. $6.95.

A young Navajo girl learns to accept the approaching death of
grandmother by seeing that all things return to the earth.
Sensitive illustrations enhance this moving story.

*Careers:* Female = 2 Male = 2 Neutral = 0
*Subject Categories:* American Ethnic Minority; Families/
Friendship; Health/Human Development; Picture Book

**5.14ˣ The Magic Hat.** Kim Westsmith. Chapel Hill,
NC: Lollipop Power, 1973. 47 p. $2.00. Paper.

In this charming story, Polly finds a magic hat in the garbage
dump. She uses the hat to get rid of the mysterious busybody's
fence which separates girls and boys and "girl toys" and "boy
toys." Large print and pictures make this book more appropriate for younger readers.

*Careers:* Female = 0 Male = 1 Neutral = 0
*Subject Categories:* Fantasy, Folk & Fairy Tales; Picture Book

**5.15 Phoebe's Revolt.** Natalie Babbitt. New York: Farrar, Straus & Giroux, 1968. 36 p. $5.95.

A rhyming poem about a turn-of-the-century girl who revolts
against frilly clothes.

*Careers:* Female = 4 Male = 4 Neutral = 1
*Subject Categories:* Families/Friendship; Picture Book; Poetry/
Rhyme

**5.16 Women with a Cause.** Bennett Wayne (ed.). Champaign, IL: Garrard, 1975. 165 p. $4.96.

Four short biographies of important women in United States
history: Anne Hutchinson, Lucretia Mott, Susan B. Anthony
and Eleanor Roosevelt.

*Careers:* Female = 20 Male = 42 Neutral = 15
*Subject Categories:* Biography; History

**5.17ˣ Martin's Father.** Margrit Eichler. Chapel Hill,
NC: Lollipop Power, 1971. 31 p. $1.75. Paper.

Story of a day in the life of Martin and his father, who is a
single parent. The father is shown engaging in numerous
"nurturing" activities with his son. Large print and pictures
make this book more appropriate for primary-grade readers.

*Careers:* Female = 0 Male = 1 Neutral = 0
*Subject Categories:* American Ethnic Minority; Families/
Friendship; Picture Book

**5.18 Mary Jane.** Dorothy Sterling. New York: Scholastic
Book Service, 1971. 218 p. $.95. Paper. (Originally
published by Doubleday, 1959.)

A story of integration, told through the eyes of Mary Jane, who
wants to be a biologist and is one of the first black children to
go to a previously all-white junior high in her town.

*Careers:* Female = 14 Male = 19 Neutral = 15
*Subject Categories:* American Ethnic Minority; Cont. Issues/
Curr. Events

**5.19 Moon Eyes.** Josephine Poole. Boston: Little, Brown,
1965. 151 p. $6.95.

This story of the supernatural finds Kate trying to save herself
and her brother from their aunt and a huge dog with moon eyes.

*Careers:* Female = 6 Male = 10 Neutral = 5
*Subject Categories:* Families/Friendship; Foreign Countries;
Mystery/Adventure

**5.20 Runaway to Freedom: A Story of the Underground
Railway.** Barbara Smucker. New York: Harper & Row,
1977. 154 p. $6.49.

Two young girls escape from slavery and travel a hazardous
route toward freedom in Canada via the underground railroad.

*Careers:* Female = 2 Male = 9 Neutral = 2
*Subject Categories:* American Ethnic Minority; Families/
Friendship; History; Mystery/Adventure

**5.21 True Grit.** Charles Portis. New York: New American Library, 1969. 190 p. $1.25. Paper. (Originally
pubished by Simon & Schuster, 1968.)

A self-reliant, young girl sets out to find her father's murderer.
This is an exciting story from the first page to the last.

*Careers:* Female = 3 Male = 48 Neutral = 6

*Subject Categories:* Families/Friendship; History; Mystery/Adventure

**5.22 Ballet Shoes.** Noel Streatfeild. New York: Random House, 1937. 294 p. $5.39.

This is an interesting tale of how three orphaned girls, adopted by a never-present bachelor, prepare themselves for careers on the stage and to become self-supporting. Money is scarce for the household, and each girl takes seriously the development of her own talents to provide the much needed income.

*Careers:* Female = 7 Male = 12 Neutral = 1
*Subject Categories:* Families/Friendship; Fine Arts; Health/Human Development

**5.23 The Lion, the Witch and the Wardrobe.** C.S. Lewis. New York: Macmillan, 1950. 186 p. $1.95. Paper.

Two brothers and two sisters travel to the fairy tale land of Narnia, where they equally participate in acts of heroism as Aslan, the noble lion, frees Narnia from the spell of the White Witch.

*Careers:* Female = 7 Male = 10 Neutral = 10
*Subject Categories:* Fantasy, Folk & Fairy Tales; Mystery/Adventure

**5.24 Come by Here.** Olivia Coolidge. Boston: Houghton Mifflin, 1970. 239 p. $5.95.

Baltimore in 1900 is the setting for this story of Minty Lou Payson, a black girl whose warm secure world is shattered when her parents are killed in an accident. In the aftermath, she is passed from relative to relative, mistreated and ignored by folks grown callous from lives of hardship and who don't understand her ambition to become a nurse. The story provides an important picture of the results of cultural, economic, physical and social division between blacks and whites. Subject matter makes this book appropriate for older readers.

*Careers:* Female = 11 Male = 24 Neutral = 12
*Subject Categories:* American Ethnic Minority; Families/Friendship; Health/Human Development; History

**5.25 Secret Castle.** Anne Colver. New York: Alfred A. Knopf, 1960. 113 p.

A traditional story about two young girls on vacation who search for a secret treasure to help a friend.

*Careers:* Female = 7 Male = 10 Neutral = 6
*Subject Categories:* Families/Friendship; Mystery/Adventure

**5.26 Tatterhood and Other Tales.** Ethel Johnston Phelps (ed.). Old Westbury, NY: The Feminist Press, 1978. 164 p. $10.95.

Twenty-five fairy and folk tales from a variety of cultures and countries, which portray clever and resourceful heroes and contain good role models for both sexes.

*Careers:* Female = 8 Male = 24 Neutral = 1
*Subject Categories:* Fantasy, Folk & Fairy Tales

**5.27 Mrs. Frisby and the Rats of NIMH.** Robert C. O'Brien. New York: Atheneum, 1971. 233 p. $1.95. Paper.

In this delightful story, a widowed mouse, Mrs. Frisby, solves a pressing family problem with the help of some rats that have escaped from an experimental laboratory.

*Careers:* Female = 4 Male = 12 Neutral = 5
*Subject Categories:* Animals; Families/Friendship; Fantasy, Folk & Fairy Tales

**5.28 Naomi.** Berniece Rabe. New York: Thomas Nelson, 1975. 192 p. $6.95.

Naomi Bradley, an 11-year-old girl growing up on a Missouri farm in the 1930s, goes to a fortune teller who tells her she will die before her fourteenth birthday. The resulting story is a realistic portrayal of Naomi's struggle to avoid what others feel is destined to happen to her and to understand that she, too, can set a goal for herself beyond what society expects of her. Because of the subject matter and dialect, this book may be more appropriate for junior high readers.

*Careers:* Female = 10 Male = 14 Neutral = 8
*Subject Categories:* Families/Friendship; Health/Human Development

**5.29 Heidi.** Johanna Spyri. New York: Penguin Books, 1956. 239 p. $.95. Paper. (Originally published in 1880.)

A warm and engaging story of a little girl who discovers the glorious Swiss alps, the bottomless love of an eccentric grandfather, and the perfect cure for a sick friend. The adult roles are stereotypic; however, Heidi herself is a very positive figure.

*Careers:* Female = 3 Male = 7 Neutral = 0
*Subject Categories:* Families/Friendship; Foreign Countries; Mystery/Adventure

**5.30ˣ It's Not What You Expect.** Norma Klein. New York: Avon, 1974. 128 p. $1.50. Paper. (Originally published by Pantheon, 1973.)

After their father leaves home and moves to New York to become a writer, Carla and Oliver, 14-year-old twins, decide to spend the summer keeping their mother company. They also start a French restaurant with the help of their brother and friends, with Oliver as the chef and Carla as the maitre d'hotel. The summer is confusing for the twins, however. Their father is gone, their older brother's girlfriend ends her pregnancy with an abortion, and their parents are "seeing" other people. But each achieves a growing maturity and understanding of the complexities of life. The characters are delightfully nonstereotypic. The subject matter makes this book appropriate for older readers.

*Careers:* Female = 13 Male = 13 Neutral = 3
*Subject Categories:* Families/Friendship; Health/Human Development

**5.31ˣ The Member of the Wedding.** Carson McCullers. New York: Bantam Books, 1975. 153 p. $1.75. Paper. (Originally published by Houghton Mifflin, 1946.)

A realistic and moving novel of the growing pains of a young girl's adolescence. Twelve-year-old Frankie finds herself searching for the "we of me" after her best friend moves away and her close relationship to her father changes. To combat an overwhelming sense of loneliness and to find someone to belong to, Frankie decides to go with her brother and his new bride after their wedding. This book provides a moving portrait of human beings isolated from one another—man from woman, child from adult and black from white.

*Careers:* Female = 12 Male = 26 Neutral = 13

*Subject Categories:* American Ethnic Minority; Families/ Friendship; Health/Human Development; Literature by Women

**5.32ˣ Making Our Way.** William Loren Katz and Jacqueline Hunt Katz. New York: Dial Press, 1978. 170 p. $7.95. (Originally published by Ethrac Publications, Inc., 1975.)

*Making Our Way* is a profoundly moving collection of personal histories of men and women struggling to survive the squalor surrounding them in turn-of-the-century America. Many of the stories describe the dreams and nightmares of American immigrants. Each person who contributed to the colorful tapestry of this collection was, in one sense, a minority member wrestling with oppression. The authenticity of their portraits provides us with intimate insights, historically and personally. Ethnic minorities are well represented. Book is appropriate for junior high and secondary students.

*Careers:* Female = 40 Male = 165 Neutral = 12
*Subject Categories:* American Ethnic Minority; Autobiography; Behavioral Science; Cultural Heritage; History

**5.33ˣ Lady Sings the Blues.** Billie Holiday. New York: Avon, 1976. 192 p. $2.25. Paper.

Billie Holiday vividly describes her struggles as a black woman, a singer, a wife and drug addict. Her style of writing quickly moves the reader through her life—years crowded with tragic disappointment and bitter sorrow, the exultation of a gifted artist sharing her talent with a devoted audience and the sting of racial prejudice. There are a variety of interesting anecdotes about famous singers, musicians and actors who were part of Holiday's life. The book's realism may make it more appropriate for mature readers.

*Careers:* Female = 8 Male = 11 Neutral = 0
*Subject Categories:* American Ethnic Minority; Autobiography; Cultural Heritage; Fine Arts; Health/Human Development

**5.34 The Maude Reed Tale.** Norah Lofts. New York: Dell, 1974. 190 p. $.95. Paper. (Originally published by Thomas Nelson, 1971.)

In this delightful tale, Maude Reed wants to be a wool merchant like her grandfather, while her twin brother Walter wants to be a traveling minstrel. However, in fifteenth century England, girls are supposed to grow up to become ladies, and boys are supposed to become knights. Maude's mother sends her away to learn the art of being a lady, but after 16 months Maude returns to rescue her mother and grandfather from an unscrupulous scoundrel.

*Careers:* Female = 10 Male = 23 Neutral = 19
*Subject Categories:* Foreign Countries; Health/Human Development; History; Mystery/Adventure

**5.35 Bitter Herbs and Honey.** Barbara Cohen. New York: Lothrop, Lee and Shepard, 1976. 159 p.

Story of a young Jewish girl in the early 1900s who is caught between her parents' goal of finding her a husband and her own goal of going away to college. Her parents' fear that by breaking tradition she will forget her Jewish faith is intensified when she begins secretly dating a "goy"—a stranger. The story portrays Jewish holidays and traditions and provides a better understanding of the Jewish cultural heritage.

*Careers:* Female = 20 Male = 20 Neutral = 13

*Subject Categories:* Cultural Heritage; Families/Friendship; Health/Human Development; History; Religion/Mythology

**5.36 The Min-Min.** Mavis Thorpe Clark. New York: Collier Books, 1978. 216 p. $1.95. Paper. (Originally published by Macmillan, 1969.)

*The Min-Min* is the adventure of young Sylvia Edwards, her unhappy life in a railway worker's camp, her attempt to flee from home and her struggle for personal identity. Her story is one of adolescent rejection of parental apathy and joyless future. Sylvia's personal journey is like that of going after the wondrous Min-Min, discovering, at last, that the wonder is within herself. The roles within the book are traditional; however, prominent men are sensitive and nurturing, and Sylvia herself is self-reliant and single-minded.

*Careers:* Female = 7 Male = 32 Neutral = 3
*Subject Categories:* Behavioral Science; Cultural Heritage; Families/Friendship; Foreign Countries; Health/Human Development; Mystery/Adventure

**5.37 Early Rising.** Joan Clarke. Philadelphia, PA: J.B. Lippincott, 1974. 252 p. $7.95.

Story of a young girl growing up with her brother and sisters in an English village at the turn of the century. The story shows her growth from a headstrong, lively young girl who always finds herself in mischief, into a confident, spirited young woman who realizes there is more to life than marriage—even with a handsome young baron.

*Careers:* Female = 20 Male = 22 Neutral = 16
*Subject Categories:* Families/Friendship; Foreign Countries; Health/Human Development; History

**5.38 The Witch of Blackbird Pond.** Elizabeth George Speare. Boston: Houghton Mifflin, 1958. 249 p. $6.95.

A historical romance (emphasis on romance) about a young girl accused of witchcraft in New England in 1687. The characters are very traditional and the "happily ever after" ending has the "heroine" marrying the "hero." However, the book is entertaining and the major character is spirited and independent.

*Careers:* Female = 9 Male = 17 Neutral = 10
*Subject Categories:* Families/Friendship; History; Mystery/ Adventure

**5.39 The Pigman.** Paul Zindel. New York: Harper & Row, 1968. 182 p.

Story of two high school sophomores, Lorraine Jensen and John Coulan, who come from unhappy homes but whose friendship helps make life tolerable. Together they recount the circumstances surrounding their friendship with a lonely old man, as well as their reaction to and part in his death. The story portrays an "equal" friendship between a girl and a boy, is unsentimental and at times painfully realistic. There are some extremely negative descriptions of acquaintances and family members.

*Careers:* Female = 14 Male = 17 Neutral = 15
*Subject Categories:* Families/Friendship; Health/Human Development

**5.40 Woman Chief.** Rose Sobol. New York: Dell, 1976. 108 p. $1.25. Paper. (Originally published by Dial Press, 1976.)

An easy-to-read fictionalized biography of Woman Chief, a hunter and warrior who became the only woman honored as a chief of the Crows. Her daring and bravery as a warrior brought recognition of her leadership as well as wealth and four "wives." Because Woman Chief was a hunter and warrior during the times of intertribal wars, the story concentrates on the military aspect of the culture and provides little detail of the nonviolent side of Crow society. (The brains of enemies' women and children are bashed in, wounded warriors are scalped, and leggings are fringed with human hair.)

*Careers:* Female = 7 Male = 13 Neutral = 5
*Subject Categories:* American Ethnic Minority; Biography; History; Mystery/Adventure

**5.41ˣ The Heart Is a Lonely Hunter.** Carson McCullers. New York: Bantam Books, 1978. 307 p. $1.95. Paper. (Originally published by Houghton Mifflin, 1940.)

This moving, yet unsentimental novel was written by Carson McCullers at the age of 23. It provides a vividly realistic portrait of the isolation and despair of the poor and disenfranchised—black and white—in a small southern town. The story focuses on Singer, who is deaf, and four characters who bring to him their problems and despair: Mick, a 15-year-old girl seeking beauty in an ugly world; Blount, a bitter, drunken radical; Dr. Copeland, a bitterly disillusioned black doctor; and Biff, a lonely, hardboiled cafe owner. The subject matter may be more appropriate for junior high readers.

*Careers:* Female = 25 Male = 55 Neutral = 44
*Subject Categories:* American Ethnic Minority; Families/Friendship; The Handicapped; Health/Human Development; Literature by Women

**5.42 The Cat Ate My Gymsuit.** Paula Danziger. New York: Dell, 1979. 119 p. $1.25. Paper. (Originally published by Delacorte, 1974.)

Story of 13-year-old Marcy, who is shy, overweight and unhappy at home. However, with the arrival of a new English teacher, who teaches her students to communicate with one another as fellow human beings, Marcy begins to make friends and learns to like herself. Although the characters are not very realistic, the story is amusing and entertaining.

*Careers:* Female = 5 Male = 9 Neutral = 4
*Subject Categories:* Families/Friendship; Health/Human Development

**5.43 What Can She Be? A Farmer.** Gloria and Esther Goldreich. New York: Lothrop, Lee and Shepard, 1976. 44 p.

This picture book depicts the farm work of two women in Maine. While the photographs portray them milking cows, bailing hay and feeding cows, the presentation seems somewhat dated. Additional farm stories in other parts of the country or in more modern agricultural settings could have been added for a more balanced look at a career in farming.

*Careers:* Female = 2 Male = 2 Neutral = 0
*Subject Categories:* Careers; Picture Book

**5.44ˣ Tisha.** Robert Specht. New York: Bantam Books, 1976. 342 p. $2.25. Paper.

The story of a young woman's first year as a a teacher in a one room schoolhouse in the Alaskan bush in 1927. With only a high school education, a year of teaching in Oregon and a lot of courage, 19-year-old Anne Hobbs goes to a small gold-mining community in the Forty Mile country of Alaska. Despite her youth and naïveté, Anne has had a good role model for her adventurous nature in her grandmother, a Native American, who reared her. Much of the action of the book involves Anne's refusal to buckle in to the extreme racism rampant among the white community. Anne, or "Tisha" as the native Alaskan children call their teacher, insists that these children not be excluded from the school and eventually takes into her home two native Alaskan children whose mother has died. She also falls in love with a young man whose mother is an Eskimo, which the community finds unacceptable. It is an exciting and powerful story which at the same time conveys some important themes concerning the conflict between native Alaskan and white values and the pioneering spirit of Alaska. Formatting makes this book more appropriate for the junior and senior high reader.

*Careers:* Female = 11 Male = 20 Neutral = 10
*Subject Categories:* American Ethnic Minority; Cultural Heritage; Mystery/Adventure

**5.45 Dragonwings.** Laurence Yep. New York: Harper & Row, 1975. 248 p. $6.50.

Beautiful portrayal of a close father-son relationship in a Chinese family. Moonshadow and his father Windrider survive the San Francisco earthquake of 1906, learn that it is possible to be friends with white "demons" and together pursue a dream that almost takes precedence over family. *Dragonwings* takes a few Chinese out of the large number of immigrants from China around the turn of the century, frees them from stereotypes and makes them come to life.

*Careers:* Female = 9 Male = 37 Neutral = 11
*Subject Categories:* American Ethnic Minority; Cultural Heritage; Families/Friendship; History

**5.46ˣ Haunted Summer.** Hope Dahle Jordan. New York: Pocket Books, 1969. 150 p. $1.50. Paper.

A very readable story about a high school girl who becomes involved in a hit-and-run accident and struggles with the burden of her secret. Ironically, "Rilla" Marston, who plays golf on the "boys' team" and has a job considered unusual for a girl, is mistaken for a boy by the one witness to her involvement in the crime. But Rilla is not presented as a "tomboy," just a very sensitive young person learning a difficult lesson in life. Subject matter may make this book more appropriate for older readers.

*Careers:* Female = 10 Male = 12 Neutral = 14
*Subject Categories:* Families/Friendship; Health/Human Development

**5.47 Clever Gretchen and Other Forgotten Tales.** Alison Lurie. New York: Thomas Y. Crowell, 1980. 110 p. $7.95.

The heroes of these folk tales are bright, active and brave young women. They hunt, answer riddles, outwit the devil and rescue relatives from danger. The author has made a contribution by rescuing these tales from obscurity.

*Careers:* Female = 6 Male = 11 Neutral = 3
*Subject Categories:* Fantasy, Folk, & Fairy Tales

**5.48 Liking Myself.** Pat Palmer. San Luis Obispo, CA: Impact, 1977. 80 p. $3.95. Paper.

A child-size introduction to concepts of feelings, self-esteem and assertiveness, designed for young readers ages five to nine. Although the illustrations tend toward stereotypes in the roles portrayed, they are racially mixed.

*Careers:* Female = 0 Male = 0 Neutral = 2
*Subject Categories:* Families/Friendship; Health/Human Development

**5.49 Some Things You Just Can't Do by Yourself.** New Seed Collective. Stanford, CA: New Seed Press, 1973. 26 p. Paper.

Humorous illustrations depict boys and girls in various activities that can't be carried out alone. The ideas of companionship and sharing among friends are promoted. Appropriate for all ages.

*Careers:* None shown
*Subject Categories:* American Ethnic Minority; Families/Friendship; Picture Book

**5.50ˣ Leaving Home.** Arlene Kramer Richards and Irene Willis. New York: Atheneum, 1980. 163 p. $8.95.

Written for both girls and boys in senior high school and/or college, this book is about becoming an independent person. Using many examples, both female and male, the authors discuss the conflict young peopple feel between the desire to be on their own and the difficulty they experience in separating themselves psychologically from parents. The case histories clarify the motivations behind varying parental attitudes as well as the internal conflicts of the young people. The ingredients for true independence are explained in a commonsense, nonjudgmental manner, and the message is that "leaving home" is a long process rather than a magical or abrupt change.

*Careers:* Female = 22 Male = 24 Neutral = 18
*Subject Categories:* Behavioral Science; Families/Friendship; Health/Human Development

**5.51 This Time of Darkness.** H.M. Hoover. New York: Viking Press, 1980. 161 p. $9.95.

Amy has spent her entire 11 years living underground in "The City," which is a virtual prison for thousands of people. Residents of "The City" are told that no one lives outside; that outside air is unfit to breathe. Axel, Amy's friend, knows better. He came from outside, and he wants to go back. Together they plan a daring escape. This is a totally absorbing adventure story with underlying themes of the importance of preserving humanity and daring to question artificial limitations. No sexist overtones. Should appeal to a wide age range.

*Careers:* Female = 3 Male = 3 Neutral = 4
*Subject Categories:* Families/Friendship; Mystery/Adventure; Science Fiction

**5.52ˣ O Pioneers!** Willa Cather. Boston: Houghton Mifflin, 1913. $3.95.

To read Willa Cather's account of Swedish immigrants settling Hanover, Nebraska is to be there. Cather's imagery helps readers call on all their senses to know the land and the people in the story. She gives readers a clear view of the wheat fields and an inside look at the characters—their feelings and motivations. Readers will feel the tempo, the intensity, the quality of an existence that came from the earth. While the careers for men mentioned in the book greatly exceed those mentioned for women in both number and consequence, the

notion of sex equity is certainly satisfied here. Marie Tovesky is vivacious, Emil Bergson is sensitive and adventurous and Alexandra Bergson, the main character, is a strong woman with much business sense and much finesse—a fine role model. An excellent book for a high school literature course.

*Careers:* Female = 5 Male = 32 Neutral = 2
*Subject Categories:* Families/Friendship; Cultural Heritage; History; Literature by Women

**5.53 The Hideaway Summer.** Beverly Hollett Renner. New York: Harper & Row, 1978. 134 p. $7.95.

An adventure story in which 14-year-old Addie and her younger brother Clay, 10, spend the summer together in a secret cabin. Addie is quite knowledgeable about "woods living" and is portrayed as assertive and resourceful. The relationship of mutual trust that grows between sister and brother is heartening.

*Careers:* Female = 2 Male = 9 Neutral = 0
*Subject Categories:* Families/Friendship; Mystery/Adventure

**5.54 I'm Deborah Sampson: A Soldier in the War of the Revolution.** Patricia Clapp. New York: Lothrop, Lee & Shepard, 1977. 176 p.

Deborah Sampson was a real person who enlisted as a soldier in the Revolutionary War. She successfully disguised herself as a man and served honorably until the end of the war. This is a fictionalized account of her story. A fast-moving adventure, convincingly and humorously told.

*Careers:* Female = 7 Male = 14 Neutral = 2
*Subject Categories:* History; Mystery/Adventure

**5.55 Going to the Sun.** Jean Craighead George. New York: Harper & Row, 1976. 132 p. $1.50. Paper.

A story of conflicts between families and generations; between hunters and an endangered species. It is also a love story about two young people trying to bridge the conflict, and a growing-up story about a boy with the mind set of a hunter who becomes a man when he decides to serve as protector of the animals he studies.

*Careers:* Female = 3 Male = 18 Neutral = 3
*Subject Categories:* Animals; Families/Friendship; Health/Human Development; Science/Technology

**5.56ˣ Don't Put Vinegar in the Copper.** Kat Wong. San Francisco, CA: Children's Book Press, 1978. 24 p. $4.95.

A bilingual story (English/Chinese) about a confusing, amusing error resulting from the language barrier between young Jenny and her mother. The mother demonstrates by chemical experiment what she meant, and the two strike a bargain: if Jenny will listen more carefully and help with her mother's English, her mother will do more home experiments with her. Subject matter and illustrations may make this book appropriate for young readers.

*Careers:* Female = 1 Male = 1 Neutral = 0
*Subject Categories:* American Ethnic Minority; Cultural Heritage; Families/Friendship; Picture Book

**5.57ˣ Alesia.** Eloise Greenfield and Alesia Revis. New York: Philomel Books, 1981. 62 p. $9.95.

Alesia Revis, an 18-year-old black woman, provides an authentic account of her determined recovery from a disabling accident (nine years earlier) via current diary entries and recollections. Without minimizing the difficulties of her effort, Alesia conveys a memorable impression of a capable, fun-loving teenager in the midst of a caring family and good friends. Drawings and photographs enhance this true story. Because of subject matter, this book is more appropriate for older readers.

*Careers:* Female = 12 Male = 5 Neutral = 3
*Subject Categories:* American Ethnic Minority; Autobiography/ Biography; Families/Friendship; The Handicapped; Health/ Human Development

**5.58 Ida Early Comes over the Mountain.** Robert Burch. New York: Viking Press, 1980. 145 p. $9.95.

Set in rural Georgia during the Depression, this novel recounts the satisfying changes in the lives of the four Sutton children and their father when Ida Early appears on their doorstep. Tall, rangy and jovial, Ida is unconventional in appearance and action (6'6" and dressed in coveralls, she can roll a cigarette with one hand, lasso anything that moves and turn chores into play). Ida soon becomes a special part of the family. Although often humorous, the story makes a telling, but not preachy, point about prejudice—directed in this case at a woman whose characteristics and capabilities are judged "unfeminine" and therefore peculiar. Sadly, all other adult females are depicted stereotypically, but Ida shows the way for being and doing what best suits one.

*Careers:* Female = 12 Male = 5 Neutral = 3
*Subject Categories:* Families/Friendship

**5.59 Lupita Manana.** Patricia Beatty. New York: William Morrow, 1981. 192 p. $8.95.

This novel, based on a true story and considerable research, documents the hardships and terrors of being an illegal alien as seen through the eyes of 13-year-old Lupita. She and her 15-year-old brother, Salvador, are forced by the sudden death of their fisher-father to seek work in southern California to assist their mother and four siblings. Exploited by opportunists on both sides of the border and in constant fear of "la migra" (immigration officials), Lupita and others like her struggle against the odds. Lupita endures what she must, strengthened by her love for her family, while Salvador is drawn increasingly to the material rewards of the new culture. A sympathetic treatment of a complex issue.

*Careers:* Female = 9 Male = 22 Neutral = 6
*Subject Categories:* American Ethnic Minority; Cultural Heritage; Families/Friendship; Foreign Countries

**5.60ˣ Ramona Quimby, Age 8.** Beverly Cleary. New York: William Morrow, 1981. 190 p. $7.95.

Ramona is delightful—also determined, resourceful and independent—as she achieves a not always serene transition to third grade in a new school. Warm and funny but not without bias, e.g., the world is white; cooking and child care are female occupations; boys are active and girls are less physical; growing old is undesirable. Ramona is real, however, and readers will empathize with her misery at throwing up in school and rejoice with her jazzy book report that brings down the classroom. Subject matter and format may make this book more appropriate for younger readers.

*Careers:* Female = 6 Male = 7 Neutral = 1
*Subject Categories:* Families/Friendship

**5.61 Wilderness Challenge.** National Geographic Society. Washington, DC: National Geographic Society, 1980. 104 p. $6.95.

A good introduction for young people to the joys and personal satisfaction that comes from hard, physical effort in such wilderness experiences as kayaking, mountain climbing, horse packing, swamp exploring, backpacking, winter camping and white-water river rafting. Male instructors predominate, but numerous color photographs show girls and boys learning the necessary skills and participating equally in the adventurous outings. The text bears out this equality of experience, while providing considerable sound, factual information about the wilderness.

*Careers:* Female = 4 Male = 7 Neutral = 6
*Subject Categories:* Information Book; Mystery/Adventure

**5.62ˣ Pioneer Women: Voices from the Kansas Frontier.** Joanna L. Stratton. New York: Simon & Schuster, 1982. 319 p. $8.95.

"These stories are the record of the woman side of pioneer life in Kansas" drawn from some 800 accounts covering the latter half of the nineteenth century. Although this was a period when a woman's place was considered to be in the home, these memoirs show that necessity often created different circumstances. Survival required physical stamina, fortitude, resourcefulness, ingenuity and great courage. This chronicle is a testimonial to the many pioneer women who demonstrated these qualities in the midst of physical deprivation, extreme isolation, natural disasters and political upheaval. They were sustained by spiritual faith and the conviction that settling the raw land was important, fulfilling work. Although the book does not include the voices of women on the "margin" of society, nor those who gave up and left, it does provide an admirable addition to pioneer history—both informative and compelling reading. Subject matter and format make this book more appropriate for secondary readers.

*Careers:* Female = 39 Male = 76 Neutral = 38
*Subject Categories:* Cultural Heritage; History; Women's Studies

# Reading Grade Level 6–Dale-Chall Formula

**6.1 She Shoots, She Scores**! Heather Kellerhals-Stewart. Toronto, ON: The Women's Press, 1975. 54 p. $.95. Paper.

Hilary, who likes to play hockey, joins a boy's hockey team. Although at first her team members don't know how to react to her, she shoots, she scores!

*Careers:* Female = 6 Male = 4 Neutral = 1
*Subject Categories:* Families/Friendship; Sports

**6.2 Lady Ellen Grae.** Vera and Bill Cleaver. Philadelphia, PA: J.B. Lippincott, 1968. 124 p. $4.95.

Because she doesn't act "like a lady" and her parents are separating, Ellen Grae is sent to her aunt's house in Seattle to learn the "big values." After a while she returns to Florida because her parents realize that it's more important to be together as a family in the same state—even if mother and father live in different cities.

*Careers:* Female = 9 Male = 19 Neutral = 8
*Subject Categories:* Families/Friendship

**6.3 Emma Tupper's Diary.** Peter Dickinson. Boston: Little, Brown, 1971. 212 p. $5.95.

During her summer vacation to the Scottish Highlands, Emma becomes involved with a "homemade" submarine and prehistoric animals in the loch. She shows courage, intelligence and social conscience in the face of a dangerous and exciting adventure with her cousins.

*Careers:* Female = 7 Male = 29 Neutral = 7
*Subject Categories:* Families/Friendship; Foreign Countries; Mystery/Adventure

**6.4 Farewell to Manzanar.** Jeanne Wakatsuki Houston and James D. Houston. New York: Bantam, 1974. 145 p. $1.75. Paper. (Originally published by Houghton Mifflin, 1973.)

A true story of Jeanne Wakatsuki Houston and her family's imprisonment in Manzanar internment camp—along with 10,000 other Japanese Americans—during World War II. It is a sensitive, moving portrait of the effects of the internment on her family, both before and after the war, and on her life. Ms. Houston was 11 when she left the camp, and she looks back on her experiences with a 30-year perspective.

*Careers:* Female = 16 Male = 44 Neutral = 22
*Subject Categories:* American Ethnic Minority; Families/Friendship; History

**6.5 The Witch's Daughter.** Nina Bawden. New York: Pocket Books, 1973. 212 p. $.95. Paper. (Originally published by J.B. Lippincott, 1966.)

Story of three children—Perdita, a lonely orphan with "second sight"; Janey, a fiercely independent blind girl; and her brother Tim—who are drawn into a dangerous and daring adventure on a remote Scottish island as they become involved in a mystery of stolen jewels and jewel thieves. Through the adventure, Perdita comes to realize that her powers are not a sign of witchcraft, but a special talent.

*Careers:* Female = 8 Male = 10 Neutral = 6
*Subject Categories:* Families/Friendship; Foreign Countries; The Handicapped; Health/Human Development; Mystery/Adventure

**6.6 Master Rosalind.** John and Patricia Beatty. New York: William Morrow, 1974. 208 p. $5.95.

Story of a young girl who masquerades as a boy in Elizabethan England. She is kidnapped from her home in the country and becomes part of a den of thieves in London. She fails at being a pickpocket, however, and joins Will Shakespeare's band of actors, contrary to the law forbidding women to play on the stage. Although she enjoys her actor's life, she begins to realize that someone is trying to kill her, and the exciting story climaxes in a confrontation with the aging Queen Elizabeth. Although the use of Elizabethan terms is somewhat confusing at first, the story is exciting and suspenseful.

*Careers:* Female = 15 Male = 40 Neutral =18
*Subject Categories:* Foreign Countries; History; Mystery/Adventure

**6.7 A Lemon and a Star.** E.C. Spykman. New York: Harcourt, Brace & World, 1955. 214 p. $5.95.

Story of the adventures of two sisters and two brothers at the turn of the century. Although there is little plot or action, story shows boys and girls living and playing together as friends and equals.

*Careers:* Female = 7 Male = 27 Neutral =5
*Subject Categories:* Families/Friendship

**6.8 Nilda.** Nicholasa Mohr. New York: Bantam, 1974. 247 p. $1.25. (Originally published by Harper & Row, 1973.)

This story realistically depicts the daily life of a Puerto Rican girl living in Spanish Harlem. The reader can sense that there is hope for Nilda, and her dying mother's advice is at once both timeless and timely.

*Careers:* Female = 15 Male = 25 Neutral = 14
*Subject Categories:* American Ethnic Minority; Families/Friendship; Health/Human Development

**6.9 Nine Lives of Moses.** Marion Fuller Archer. Chicago: Albert Whitman, 1968. 160 p. $4.75.

Traditional story of 12-year-old Charlotte and her journey across the country with her mother and brother in a wagon train to Oregon. With them on their journey is Charlotte's odd-eyed, black cat Moses, who at first is resented and disliked by most of the travelers, but eventually is accepted as part of the wagon train. Although some of the characters are portrayed stereotypically, Charlotte's mother provides a strong, positive role model.

*Careers:* Female = 5 Male = 21 Neutral = 6
*Subject Categories:* Animals, Families/Friendship, History, Mystery/Adventure

**6.10 Women of Courage.** Dorothy Nathan. New York: Random House/Windward, 1964. 175 p. $.75. Paper.

Well-written biographies of five outstanding women: Susan B. Anthony, Jane Addams, Mary McLeod Bethune, Ameilia Earhart and Margaret Mead. Each biography describes the social conditions during each woman's life.

*Careers:* Female = 20 Male =51 Neutral = 42
*Subject Categories:* American Ethnic Minority; Biography; Families/Friendship; History; Mystery/Adventure

**6.11 Queenie Peavy.** Robert Burch. New York: Viking Press, 1966. 159 p. $6.95.

Realistic and sensitive story of a 13-year-old girl whose chip on the shoulder gives way to a more positive interactive style.

*Careers:* Female = 2 Male = 7 Neutral = 2
*Subject Categories:* Families/Friendship; Health/Human Development

**6.12ˣ Did You Ever?** Paula Goldsmid. Chapel Hill, NC: Lollipop Power, 1971. 30 p. $1.75. Paper.

This rhyming picture book asks children to think about what they like to do, to encourage them to think about what they would like to be. Pictures and formatting style make this book more appropriate for primary-grade students.

*Careers:* Female = 4 Male = 3 Neutral = 3
*Subject Categories:* Careers; Picture Book

**6.13 A Proud Taste for Scarlet and Miniver.** E.L. Konigsberg. New York: Atheneum, 1973. 198 p. $1.95.

The story of Eleanor of Aquitaine, as told by three friends and Eleanor herself, after they have all reached Heaven. As Queen of England, Eleanor was a woman of action and a patron of the arts. The reader gets a vivid look at twelfth century England and France.

*Careers:* Female = 8 Male = 30 Neutral = 33
*Subject Categories:* Biography; Foreign Countries; History

**6.14 The Endless Steppe: A Girl In Exile.** Esther Hautzig. New York: Scholastic Book Services, 1968. 238 p. $1.25. Paper. (Originally published by Thomas Y. Crowell, 1968.)

This is a true story of a young Polish Jewish girl and her family, who are exiled to Siberia by the Russians in 1940. The book is extremely moving and convincingly portrays the deprivation and extreme hardship endured—and conquered—by Esther and her family in their five-year exile.

*Careers:* Female = 17 Male = 28 Neutral = 22
*Subject Categories:* Families/Friendship; Foreign Countries; History; Mystery/Adventure

**6.15 Women at Their Work.** Betty Lou English. New York: Dial Press, 1977. 47 p. $6.95.

A collection of 21 short, simply written essays of 21 women (including several ethnic minorities) who talk about their nontraditional careers—ranging from jockey and firefighter to judge and chemist. Essays are accompanied by photographs showing the women at their work.

*Careers:* Female = 44 Male = 9 Neutral = 11
*Subject Categories:* American Ethnic Minority; Careers; Picture Book

**6.16 The Search for Charlie.** Paige Dixon. New York: Atheneum, 1976. 90 p. $4.95.

While Jane Woden is studying for her college exams in Massachusetts, her brother Charlie is kidnapped from her family's Montana ranch. She catches a plane home to help in the search and, with her friend Vic, packs into the mountains in pursuit of the kidnapper and her brother. There Jane confronts violence not only from the kidnapper but from within herself. Excellent portrait of a competent young woman.

*Careers:* Female = 4 Male = 13 Neutral = 6
*Subject Categories:* Families/Friendship; Health/Human Development; Mystery/Adventure

**6.17ˣ Mary's Monster.** Ruth VanNess Blair. New York: Coward, McCann & Geoghegan, 1975. 61 p. $5.95.

A true story of Mary Anning, whose discoveries of the Ichthyosaurus and other dinosaur fossils in the cliffs of Lyme Regis, England, advanced the study of geology and had a great effect on the scientists of the 1800s. Because of the large print, pictures and dialogue, this book appears more appropriate for younger readers.

*Careers:* Female = 6 Male = 16 Neutral = 8
*Subject Categories:* Biography; Families/Friendship; Foreign Countries; History; Mystery/Adventure; Science

**6.18ˣ The Squire's Name.** P.C. Asbjornsen. New York: Atheneum, 1976. 28 p. $6.95.

In this humorous Norwegian folk tale, a daughter spoils the plans between her father and a rich squire for her marriage. Illustrations and a large print make this picture book more appropriate for younger readers.

*Careers:* Female = 2 Male = 5 Neutral = 0
*Subject Categories:* Fantasy, Folk, & Fairy Tales; Picture Book

**6.19 Tall and Proud.** Vian Smith. New York: Pocket Books, 1968. 179 p. $1.25. Paper. (Originally published by Doubleday, 1967.)

A young English girl becomes disabled by polio. She overcomes her disability and the pain of learning how to walk again through a desire to ride her horse, King Sam.

*Careers:* Female = 4 Male = 16 Neutral = 31
*Subject Categories:* Animals; Families/Friendship; Foreign Countries; The Handicapped; Health/Human Development

**6.20 Miss Hickory.** Carolyn Sherwin Bailey. New York: Puffin/Penguin Books, 1978. 122 p. $1.50. (Originally published by Viking, 1946.)

This story depicts the adventures of a country doll made of an apple wood twig, with a hickory nut as a head. It beautifully describes how animals live through the winter and how Miss Hickory survives that New Hampshire season. This is an excellent read-aloud book for third and fourth graders.

*Careers:* Female = 1 Male = 5 Neutral = 0
*Subject Categories:* Animals; Fantasy, Folk, & Fairy Tales; Science

**6.21 Adventures of B.J. The Amateur Detective.** Toni Sortor. Nashville: Abingdon Press, 1975. 94 p. $3.50.

Eleven-year-old B.J. becomes involved in a shoplifting case her mother (a detective) is working on. It is an entertaining story, and B.J. is a positive character; however, the story contains some subtle sterotyupic behaviors and attitudes.

*Careers:* Female = 6 Male = 7 Netural = 3
*Subject Categories:* Families/Friendship; Mystery/Adventure

**6.22ˣ This Time, Tempe Wick?** Patricia Lee Gauch. New York: Coward, McCann & Geoghegan, 1974. 43 p. $5.95.

This folk tale, which historians say may be true, is about a big, strong, clever girl who outwits two British soldiers from stealing her horse during the Revolutionary War in America. Print size and use of pictures makes this book appropriate for younger readers.

*Careers:* Female = 2 Male = 9 Neutral = 0
*Subject Categories:* Fantasy, Folk, & Fairy Tales; History; Mystery/Adventure; Picture Book

**6.23 Harriet Tubman: Conductor on the Underground Railroad.** Ann Petry. New Yokr: Pocket Books, 1971. 221 p. $1.25. Paper. (Originally published by Thomas Y. Crowell, 1955.)

Harriet Tubman escapes from slavery to freedom through the Underground Railroad—a series of secret hiding places along the route to the North. But she returns again and again to help hundreds of other slaves escape to freedom and becomes known as the "Moses" of her people.

*Careers:* Female = 15 Male = 32 Netural = 19
*Subject Categories:* American Ethnic Minority; Biography; History; Mystery/Adventure

**6.24 Women of the West.** Dorothy Levenson. New York: Franklin Watts, 1973. 85 p. $4.47.

This is a well-written and interesting examination of the role played by women on the American frontier. Portrays women—black, white and Native American—in a variety of careers, from cowgirl to teacher to saloonkeeper to governor.

*Careers:* Female = 47 Male = 35 Neutral = 10
*Subject Categories:* History; Women's Studies

**6.25 Emmeline and Her Daughters: The Pankhurst Suffragettes.** Iris Noble. New York: Julian Messner, 1971. 184 p. $5.29.

This is a fascinating history of the women's suffragist movement in England, which was led by Emmeline Pankhurst and her daughters Christabel, Sylvia and Adela. The political struggles and personal sacrifices portrayed provide a story of courage and inspiration with relevance for today.

*Careers:* Female = 35 Male = 37 Neutral = 28
*Subject Categories:* Biography; Families/Friendship; Foreign Countries; History; Women's Studies

**6.26 The Liberation of Clementine Tipton.** Jane Flory. Boston: Houghton Mifflin, 1974. 214 p. $5.95.

Ten-year-old Clementine Tipton gains some new ideas and learns she has a variety of options for her life during the excitement and activities surrounding Philadelphia's centennial celebration in 1876 and the growing women's movement.

*Careers:* Female = 18 Male = 31 Neutral = 21
*Subject Categories:* Families/Friendship; Health/Human Development; History

**6.27 Julie of the Wolves.** Jean Craighead George. New York: Harper & Row, 1972. 170 p.

A 13-year-old Eskimo girl, Miyax (her English name is Julie), becomes lost in the Alaskan wilderness after running away from an intolerable family situation. This is an outstanding story of her survival—her bravery, creativity and resourcefulness. Depicts the Eskimo way of life as well as white influences on the culture.

*Careers:* Female = 8 Male = 9 Neutral = 15
*Subject Categories:* American Ethnic Minority; Animals; Health/Human Development; Mystery/Adventure

**6.28ˣ Phillis Wheatley: America's First Black Poetess.** Miriam Morris Fuller. Champaign, IL: Garrard, 1971. 92 p. $4.28.

Biography of Phillis Wheatley who, despite slavery and poverty, became America's first black poet in the eighteenth century. Large print and pictures make this book appropriate for younger readers.

*Careers:* Female = 11 Male = 19 Neutral = 5
*Subject Categories:* American Ethnic Minority; Biography; History; Poetry

**6.29 A Wrinkle in Time.** Madeline L'Engle. New York: Farrar, Straus & Giroux, 1962. 211 p. $6.95.

An excellent story describing the adventures of Meg, brother Charles and friend Calvin as they experience a tesseract, or wrinkle in time, in their search for Meg's missing father.

*Careers:* Female = 4 Male = 3 Neutral = 2
*Subject Categories:* Mystery/Adventure; Science Fiction

**6.30 Leo the Lioness.** Constance C. Greene. New York: Viking Press, 1970. 118 p. $6.95.

This is a good story about what it means to be 13 years old, as Tibb faces the harsh truth of reality when she questions standards of behavior.

*Careers:* Female = 5 Male = 4 Neutral = 3
*Subject Categories:* Families/Friendship; Health/Human Development

**6.31 The Taste of Spruce Gum.** Jacqueline Jackson. Boston: Little, Brown, 1966. 212 p. $6.95.

The life of Libby Fletcher is difficult when she moves to a lumber camp in Vermont and must adjust to a new stepfather after her father dies. Story is set in the early 1900s.

*Careers:* Female = 10 Male = 17 Neutral = 11
*Subject Categories:* Families/Friendship; Health/Human Development; History

**6.32 Dust of the Earth.** Vera and Bill Cleaver. New York: New American Library, 1977. 153 p. $1.25. Paper. (Originally published by J.B. Lippincott, 1975.)

When 14-year-old Fern and her family move to a farm in South Dakota, they face a variety of challenges and hardships. Fern is a strong-willed, capable young girl.

*Careers:* Female = 6 Male = 26 Neutral = 12
*Subject Categories:* Families/Friendship

**6.33 The Egypt Game.** Zilpha Keatley Snyder. New York: Atheneum, 1967. 215 p. $1.95. Paper.

Six children become involved in an exciting game that turns an abandoned storage yard into Egypt. They become so involved in the game that they forget their parents' warnings about a disturbed person who has murdered a child in the neighborhood. This story shows boys and girls of different ethnic groups playing together as equals.

*Careers:* Female = 11 Male = 15 Neutral = 8
*Subject Categories:* American Ethnic Minority; Families/Friendship; Health/Human Development; Mystery/Adventure

**6.34 Charlotte Forten: Free Black Teacher.** Esther M. Douty. Champaign, IL: Garrard, 1971. 142 p. $2.59.

Biography of Charlotte Forten, a young, free black woman who devoted her life to teaching and helping her people, before and after the Civil War.

*Careers:* Female = 17 Male = 35 Neutral = 22
*Subject Categories:* American Ethnic Minority; Biography; History

**6.35 The Tamarack Tree.** Betty Underwood. Boston: Houghton Mifflin, 1971. 230 p. $5.95.

This story depicts the role of women in the mid-1800s—the roles of wife, childbearer and husband's property. It shows a young orphaned girl learning of these constraints and working to obtain an education that will permit her some control over and independence in her own life.

*Careers:* Female = 2 Male = 10 Neutral = 3
*Subject Categories:* Families/Friendship; Health/Human Development; History

**6.36 The House without a Christmas Tree.** Gail Rock. New York: Alfred A. Knopf, 1974. 87 p. $4.95.

With the help of her grandmother, 10-year-old Addie gets a Christmas tree for her home, even though her father objects. This is a sensitive story about a young girl growing up during the 1940s.

*Careers:* Female = 3 Male = 3 Neutral = 0
*Subject Categories:* Families/Friendship; Health/Human Development

**6.37 Classmates by Request.** Hila Colman. New York: William Morrow, 1964. 187 p. $3.95.

Ten teenagers ask to be transferred to an all-black school to help integrate it. The problems arising from this situation are shown through the eyes of Carla and Ellen as they struggle to learn to live with each other's differences. The story is captivating and very realistic; may be more appropriate at the secondary level.

*Careers:* Female = 6 Male = 17 Neutral = 5
*Subject Categories:* American Ethnic Minority; Cont. Issues/Curr. Events; Families/Friendship; Health/Human Development

**6.38 A Feast of Light.** Gunilla Norris. New York: Alfred A. Knopf, 1967. 126 p.

A nine-year-old Swedish girl comes to America to live and finds everything new and strange. She learns she has to reach out in order to make new friends and to feel at home in her new country.

*Careers:* Female = 4 Male = 3 Neutral = 1
*Subject Categories:* Families/Friendship; Health/Human Development

**6.39 The Headless Cupid.** Zilpha Keatley Snyder. New York: Atheneum, 1971. 203 p. $1.95. Paper.

Black magic and witchcraft are used by Amanda to help her work out her feelings of hostility toward her mother, her new stepfather and his children.

*Careers:* Female = 8 Male = 14 Neutral = 7
*Subject Categories:* Families/Friendship; Health/Human Development; Mystery/Adventure

**6.40 Clara Barton: Founder of the American Red Cross.** Helen Dore Boylston. New York: Random House, 1955. 177 p. $4.39.

This biography of Clara Barton is a simply written account of her childhood, her heroic service to soldiers on the battlefields of the Civil War and her successful efforts to start a national Red Cross organization in the United States. Barton's compelling desire to be of service to others enabled her to accomplish what others of her time thought no woman capable of doing. Because of the large print size, this book is appropriate for younger readers.

*Careers:* Female = 15 Male = 28 Neutral = 23
*Subject Categories:* Biography; Health/Human Development; History

**6.41 Susette La Flesche: Voice of the Omaha Indians.** Margaret Crary. New York: Hawthorne Books, 1973. 171 p. $5.95.

Biography of Susette La Flesche, "Bright Eyes," who in the late 1800s campaigned for citizenship for her people, the Omahas.

*Careers:* Female = 15 Male = 29 Neutral = 15
*Subject Categories:* American Ethnic Minority; Biography; Families/Friendship; History

**6.42 America's First Woman Astronomer: Maria Mitchell.** Rachel Baker and Joanna Baker Merlen. New York: Julian Messner, 1969. 186 p. $3.34.

Mitchell, a modest, quiet woman, gains fame when she is the first to discover a previously unrecorded comet. The emphasis on her two lost loves tends at times to overshadow the contributions she made as an astronomer and professor of astronomy at Vassar.

*Careers:* Female = 11 Male = 25 Neutral = 2
*Subject Categories:* Biography; History; Science

**6.43 Claudia, Where Are You?** Hila Colman. New York: William Morrow, 1969. 191 p.

Sixteen-year-old Claudia, frustrated and feeling out-of-place with her parents' upper-middle class suburbia lifestyle, runs away to New York City to try to make it on her own. Although the story is rather traditional, romanticized and not always realistic, Claudia is independent and takes risks, providing an interesting hero.

*Careers:* Female = 13 Male = 21 Neutral = 12
*Subject Categories:* Families/Friendship; Health/Human Development

**6.44ˣ  The Street.** Ann Petry. New York: Pyramid Publications, 1961. 270 p. $1.25. Paper. (Originally published by Houghton Mifflin, 1946.)

A tender, angry and depressingly realistic story of a young black woman trapped in the ghetto nightmare of Harlem. Through stark and vivid images, the reader sees Lutie Johnson work, study, scrimp and battle for a better life for herself and her son, only to be repeatedly beaten down by the vice and violence of "the street." This is a moving and well-written book which treats sex and brutality with candor; more appropriate for mature readers.

*Careers:* Female = 24 Male = 53 Neutral = 24
*Subject Categories:* American Ethnic Minority; Behavioral Science; Families/Friendship; Health/Human Development

**6.45ˣ  Leap before You Look.** Mary Stolz. New York: Harper & Row, 1972. 259 p.

An account of 14-year-old Jimmie Gavin's struggle to cope with her parents' divorce and the resulting shattering of her family. While many female characters appear stereotyped as frigid housewives, swooning adolescents, traditional grandmothers or beguiling seductresses, Jimmie, although surrounded by these limited personalities, admirably grows beyond her role models as she begins to develop her own unique, adult self. Young people experiencing the impact of divorce will find solace in Jimmie's maturation from rage and rejection to acceptance and understanding.

*Careers:* Female = 21 Male = 31 Neutral = 34
*Subject Categories:* Behavioral Science; Families/Friendship; Health/Human Development

**6.46 First Woman Ambulance Surgeon: Emily Barringer.** Iris Noble. New York: Julian Messner, 1962. 192 p. $3.34.

A fictionalized biography of Emily Dunning Barringer, the first American woman doctor who was allowed to intern in a hospital, a position that entitled her to practice medicine on equal terms with men. This very readable story provides a look at the prejudice and harassment experienced by women in the medical profession in the late 1800s, as well as the courage, tenacity and sacrifice of one woman to open the doors of medicine for herself and others of her sex. Dr. Barringer is presented as being slender, attractive and very feminine; as having the perfect, understanding husband; and of being a

devoted wife and mother as well as being a hardworking physician—a superwoman.

*Careers:* Female = 26 Male = 38 Neutral = 26
*Subject Categories:* Biography; Careers; Health/Human Development; History

**6.47 Israel's Golda Meir: Pioneer to Prime Minister.** Iris Noble. New York: Julian Messner, 1974. 189 p. $5.29.

A very readable biography of Golda Meir, who traveled from a poverty-stricken girlhood in Milwaukee to leadership of the state of Israel. The book provides a fascinating portrait of the development of a powerful world leader, as well as the founding and growth of a new nation. Some use of sexist language throughout the book.

*Careers:* Female = 20 Male = 35 Neutral = 40
*Subject Categories:* Biography; Foreign Countries; History

**6.48 A Tree Grows in Brooklyn.** Betty Smith. New York: Perennial Library, 1968. 430 p. $1.95. Paper. (Originally published by Harper & Row, 1943.)

With sensitivity and imagery, Betty Smith tells of Francie Nolan's growing up in poverty during the early 1900s in Brooklyn. The captivating theme is Francie's steadfastness—her vitality that prevails in spite of harsh living conditions. The author skillfully portrays the personalities of Francie, her brother, mother and father and develops the relationships between these characters in an unforgettable way. Older readers should also enjoy this book.

*Careers:* Female = 28 Male = 41 Neutral = 11
*Subject Categories:* Families/Friendship; Health/Human Development; Literature by Women

**6.49 Nectar in a Sieve.** Kamala Markandaya. New York: New American Library, 1954. 189 p. $1.75. Paper. (Originally published by John Day, 1954.)

This novel is the poignant narrative of the life of a peasant woman, Rukmani, in her changing homeland of India. During her harsh life as the wife of a poor tenant farmer, she has to face devastating monsoons, droughts and diseases as well as the deterioration and death of many members of her family. *Nectar in a Sieve* is a powerful statement of survival and an authentic historical account.

*Careers:* Female = 14 Male = 34 Neutral = 3
*Subject Categories:* Behavioral Science; Cultural Heritage; Families/Friendship; Foreign Countries; Health/Human Development; Literature by Women; Women's Studies

**6.50ˣ  Daughter of Earth.** Agnes Smedley. Old Westbury, NY: The Feminist Press, 1976. 412 p. $4.50. Paper.

An autobiographical novel about a woman born to an impoverished midwest farm family in the 1890s. The reader sees her struggle to overcome the scars of her childhood and her vow to never love or have children, which she believes are the downfall of all women. Although living in poverty in order to maintain self-sufficiency, she also manages to become educated, to help other members of her family, and to work for political and social causes. The author paints a vivid and often painful picture of a lonely woman struggling through the many hardships of being an independent woman in a changing world. This book examines many nontraditional roles, careers and families with an emphasis on the feminist viewpoint. The subject matter is particularly appropriate for high school students.

*Careers:* Female = 21 Male = 43 Neutral = 2
*Subject Categories:* Health/Human Development; Women's Studies

**6.51 Transport 7-41-R.** T. Degens. New York: Viking Press, 1974. 171 p. $5.95.

Story of a 13-year-old girl's hardships and strength as she travels on a group transport out of the Russian sector into the British sector of defeated Nazi Germany in 1946. Traveling under false papers and without her parents, she is free and completely independent, counting only on her own resourcefulness. But when an elderly man's wife dies in the night, she finds herself drawn into helping the man wheel the corpse through crowded refugee camps and across police borders so that he can fulfill a promise and bury his wife in Cologne.

*Careers:* Female = 3 Male = 21 Neutral = 21
*Subject Categories:* Families/Friendship; Foreign Countries; History; Mystery/Adventure

**6.52 Ariel: Poems by Sylvia Plath.** Sylvia Plath. New York: Harper & Row, 1965. 85 p. $2.25. Paper.

A collection of Sylvia Plath's final poems before her suicide. The power of her poetry is a result of her honest portrayal of other people, other things and herself. Her poems contain many demeaning terms used to describe women and minorities, as well as much explicitness of language. However, *Ariel* is valuable as a brilliant articulation of madness and self-destruction.

*Careers:* Female = 8 Male = 10 Neutral = 3
*Subject Categories:* Behavioral Science; Health/Human Development; Literature by Women; Poetry/Rhyme; Women's Studies

**6.53 After the Wedding.** Hila Colman. New York: William Morrow, 1975. 189 p.

In the year after their marriage, Katie and Peter find themselves growing apart. Eighteen-year-old Katie wants to continue living in the country and be free to work on her pottery; Peter wants to move to New York, join the tennis club and advance his career as assistant producer on a soap opera. As the story moves to its inevitable climax, the reader is caught up in the anguish of their struggle to ease the tensions that are driving them apart. This novel probes questions that many young women face today. What should be the role of a wife? What are the responsibilities of husbands and wives to each other? What are their responsibilities to fulfill their individual desires and expectations? What are their responsibilities to fulfill their individual desires and expectations/

*Careers:* Female = 18 Male = 25 Neutral = 5
*Subject Categories:* Families/Friendship; Health/Human Development

**6.54ˣ Are You in the House Alone?** Richard Peck. New York: Viking Press, 1976. 156 p. $6.95.

A frank and realistic story about a high school girl who is raped, and who discovers she's been a victim of a crime that punishes the innocent and lets the criminal go free. The book offers a chilling view of the reality of how rape cases are treated by the police and in the courts, and the difficulty family and friends have in dealing with the issue. Although the careers

presented are very stereotypic, the book provides a needed look at a vicious crime and its aftermath and asks the reader to confront some difficult questions. Subject matter may make this book more appropriate for older readers.

*Careers:* Female = 12 Male = 21 Neutral = 12
*Subject Categories:* Behavioral Science; Families/Friendship; Health/Human Development

**6.55ˣ The Bell Jar.** Sylvia Plath. New York: Bantam Books, 1972. 216 p. $2.50. Paper. (Originally published by Harper & Row, 1971.)

A thinly disguised autobiography covering six months in the life of 20-year-old Sylvia Plath, who provides a self portrait of a very fragile young woman. Through vivid images, the reader sees Plath's descent into madness, her mental breakdown, and her attempted suicide. Subject matter may make this book more appropriate for older readers.

*Careers:* Female = 24 Male = 29 Neutral = 13
*Subject Categories:* Autobiography/Biography; Behavioral Science; Families/Friendship; Health/Human Development; Literature by Women

**6.56 Hey, White Girl!** Susan Gregory. New York: W.W. Norton, 1970. 221 p. $8.95.

Based on a daily diary kept by the author, this book is about a suburban white girl's senior year in an all-black high school on Chicago's West Side, the year before the 1968 riots. It tells of her experiences, her friendships and her growing understanding and appreciation of the culture and courage of blacks in the ghetto. In her preface, the author warns the reader that the intense experience of being totally immersed in the black world produces what the reader may view as patronizing or exaggerated expressions of the beauty of blackness, particularly when reacting to pointed contrasts between white and black. Yet the book is not at all sentimental and ends with a quote from Malcolm X who said that sincere whites should work with their own kind in conjunction with blacks working with the black community to bring about change. The author makes repeated references to the black *man* and the white *man* when talking about women and men.

*Careers:* Female = 12 Male = 28 Neutral = 14
*Subject Categories:* American Ethnic Minority; Cont. Issues/Curr. Events; Cultural Heritage; Families/Friendship; Health/Human Development

**6.57 Fifth Chinese Daughter.** Jade Snow Wong. New York: Harper & Row, 1945. 246 p. $8.27.

This is a simply told, fascinating tale of Jade Snow Wong, the fifth older sister of the Wong family, and her life growing up in San Francisco's Chinatown during the Depression. Born into a household where propriety and decorum reigned, where only Chinese was spoken, and where respect and obedience to elders and family were unquestioned, Jade Snow finds herself caught between the rigid teachings of her family and the search for personal identity and achievement. The book vividly portrays the rich cultural heritage of Chinese Americans and presents a warm portrait of a young woman's relationship to her family as she matures into adulthood. Older readers will also enjoy this book.

*Careers:* Female = 23 Male = 36 Neutral = 39
*Subject Categories:* American Ethnic Minority; Autobiography/Biography; Cultural Heritage; Families/Friendship; Health/Human Development

**6.58 Tell Me a Riddle.** Tillie Olsen. New York: Dell, 1979. 125 p. $1.25. Paper.

In four timeless short stories, Tillie Olsen explores the struggles and pain of contemporary existence, with verbal richness and beauty that no reader will forget. Included are "I Stand Here Ironing"; "Hey Sailor, What Ship?"; "O Yes"; and "Tell Me a Riddle." This collection would be an excellent resource for a high school literature class.

*Careers:* Female = 5 Male = 17 Neutral = 5
*Subject Categories:* Families/Friendship; Health/Human Development; Essays/Short Stories; Literature by Women; Women's Studies

**6.59 Feminine Plural: Stories by Women about Growing Up.** Stephanie Spinner. New York: Macmillan, 1972. 240 p. $5.95.

This excellent collection of 10 short stories by women includes: Carson McCuller's "Wunderkind"; Doris Lessing's "Notes for a Case History"; Colette's "Green Sealing Wax"; Shirley Ann Grau's "Miss Yellow Eyes"; Katherine Ann Porter's "Virgin Violetta"; R. Prawer Jhabvala's "My First Marriage"; Edna O'Brien's "Irish Revel"; Kay Boyles' "Your Body is a Jewel Box"; Tillie Olsen's "O Yes"; and Flannery O'Connor's "A Temple of the Holy Ghost." The stories are about growing up and new beginnings which in some cases mean the end of romantic illusion and learning the rules of adult behavior. An excellent anthology for use in a high school literature class or for free reading.

*Careers:* Female = 26 Male =45 Neutral = 29
*Subject Categories:* Health/Human Development; Anthologies; Essays/Short Stories; Literature by Women; Women's Studies

**6.60 Fat Jack.** Barbara Cohen. New York: Atheneum, 1980. 182 p. $8.95.

Story of two high school seniors, Judy Goldstein, who is bright and active in school affairs but considers herself plain and not overwhelmingly popular, and Jack Muldoon, a very fat transfer student who is the butt of some of the students' jokes. Judy and Jack become friends and together become involved in the senior play, Shakespeare's *Henry IV Part One*, during which they learn to understand the meaning of friendship and betrayal.

*Careers:* Female = 12 Male = 20 Neutral = 10
*Subject Categories:* Families/Friendship; Health/Human Development

**6.61 Childtimes: A Three Generation Memoir.** Eloise Greenfield and Lessie Jones Little. New York: Thomas Y. Crowell, 1970. 176 p. $7.95.

Three black women—grandmother, mother, daughter—share memories of their childhoods growing up black in America between the 1890s and 1940s. Their memories are filled with family who lived and loved and struggled to stay together and grow in rural North Carolina and Washington, D.C.

*Careers:* Female =10 Male = 39 Neutral = 8
*Subject Categories:* American Ethnic Minority; Cultural Heritage; Families/Friendship; Women's Studies

**6.62 Don't Play Dead before You Have to.** Maia Wojciechowska. New York: Harper & Row, 1970. 115 p.

When Byron, age 14, first meets Charlie, age 5, he tells him he's only there to sit for him; he doesn't intend to be his pal.

However, a deep friendship develops in which both boys learn from each other and grow as persons. The story is told from Byron's perspective—a "tell it like it is" view of the adult world as seen by a teenager who doesn't want to be a "sheep going by some book, memorizing a whole lot of insane rules, made up by God knows who, that don't make any sense." Charlie, who is less tough than Byron, attempts suicide when he becomes depressed about his isolation and his parents' divorce. Byron's insights are at times both hilarious and heartbreaking.

*Careers:* Female = 7 Male = 35 Neutral = 16
*Subject Categories:* Families/Friendship; Health/Human Development

**6.63 Lady for the Defense: A Biography of Belva Lockwood.** Mary Virginia Fox. New York: Harcourt, Brace, Jovanovich, 1975. 158 p. $6.50.

Born in 1830, Belva Lockwood was the first woman lawyer, the first woman lawyer allowed to practice before the Supreme Court and the first female candidate for president of the United States. She fought for the rights of all minorities, sponsoring the first black man allowed to practice law before the Supreme Court and winning for the Cherokee several million dollars owed them by the U.S. Government. She was also a leader in the campaign for world peace. The book is an absorbing and easy-to-read account of an unforgettable woman.

*Careers:* Female = 27 Male = 39 Neutral =10
*Subject Categories:* Autobiography/Biography; History; Women's Studies

**6.64 Dorothy Day: Friend of the Poor.** Carol Bauer Church. Minneapolis, MN: Greenhaven Press, 1976. 85 p.

A biography of Dorothy Day, a socialist newspaper reporter who became founder of *The Catholic Worker* newspaper, a labor organizer and the instigator of a large number of social service programs for the working poor and unemployed. Poor herself from childhood, Dorothy had always been struck by the misery of those with even less. Determined to work for causes that would improve the conditions of those in poverty, she became involved with the "radicals" of the 1920s and 1930s: socialists and communists who seemed to share her ideals. After her conversion to Catholicism, she decided to work for the poor within a religious framework.

*Careers:* Female = 7 Male = 16 Neutral = 7
*Subject Categories:* Autobiography/Biography; History; Religion/Mythology

**6.65 Once at the Weary Why.** Mildred Lawrence. New York: Harcourt, Brace & World, 1969. 189 p. $3.75.

The story of Cammy Chase, a high school girl who becomes derailed from her personal value system. Feeling confused after her parents' divorce and remarriage, she becomes involved with the "in" crowd at school. Normally a good student with many enthusiasms and close friendships, Cammy's pursuit of sophistication affects her grades, relationships with family and friends and interest in life in general. The parental roles are somewhat stereotyped—Cammy's mother works only out of financial necessity; her new husband prefers her to stay at home. However, a young male protagonist is shown as a sensitive, caring individual without any loss of masculinity.

*Careers:* Female = 8 Male = 14 Neutral = 12

*Subject Categories:* Families/Friendship; Health/Human Development

**6.66ˣ  Plays by and about Women.** Victoria Sullivan and James Hatch (eds.). New York: Random House, 1974. 421 p. $3.95. Paper.

This collection of plays includes Alice Gerstenberg's *Overtones*; Lillian Hellman's *The Children's Hour*; Clare Booth's *The Women*; Doris Lessing's *Play with a Tiger*; Megan Terry's *Calm Down Mother*; Natalia Ginzburg's *The Advertisement*; Maureen Duffy's *Rites*; and Alice Childress' *Wine in the Wilderness*. All of the plays are written from a female, but not necessarily feminist, point of view and deal with a wide range of themes. Some of the plays are experimental in form. Due to subject matter, language, violence, and/or sophisticated form, all except *Overtones* are recommended for mature readers.

*Careers:* Female = 45 Male = 56 Neutral = 11
*Subject Categories:* American Ethnic Minority; Cont. Issues/Curr. Events; Drama; Women's Studies

**6.67 What Can She Be? A Legislator.** Gloria and Esther Goldreich. New York: Lothrop, Lee and Shepard, 1978. 46 p. $4.95.

Simple text and photographs follow Carol Bellamy as her career moves from being a New York State senator to the first woman ever elected as president of the New York City Council. No ethnic minorities are represented in the various careers depicted.

*Careers:* Female = 11 Male = 8 Neutral = 7
*Subject Categories:* Careers

**6.68 Summer of My German Soldier.** Bette Greene. New York: Dial Press, 1973. 230 p. $7.95.

During her twelfth summer, Patty Bergen learns the meaning of love from a German prisoner of war who has been brought to a prison camp near the small Arkansas town where Patty lives. The prisoner, Frederick Anton Riker, escapes from the camp, and Patty hides him from the authorities in some rooms above her garage. He becomes her friend during the short time he stays there and makes her feel she is a person of value. He even risks his life one evening by coming out of hiding to help Patty when her father is senselessly beating her. Although Patty has to pay for her friendship with Anton—she is sent to a girls' reformatory for her "crime"—the reader is left with the feeling that Patty will always remain a person of value.

*Careers:* Female = 13 Male = 46 Neutral = 23
*Subject Categories:* Families/Friendship; Health/Human Development

**6.69 Science Experiments You Can Eat.** Vicki Cobb. New York: J.B. Lippincott, 1972. 127 p. $4.95. Paper.

Contains 39 edible experiments that can be performed in the home kitchen and will make learning about science fun. Ways to investigate the properties of solutions, suspensions, colloids and emulsions; the cooking action of microbes and enzymes; and phenomena concerning carbohydrates, fats and proteins are presented in an understandable and entertaining manner. The author takes for granted that both boys and girls can be cooks and experimenters and that the adult cook in the house is not necessarily the mother. These are excellent enrichment activities as well as a source of classroom and "science fair" demonstrations.

*Careers:* Female = 0 Male = 2 Neutral = 6
*Subject Categories:* Science/Technology

**6.70 I Always Wanted to Be Somebody.** Althea Gibson. New York: Harper & Row, 1958. 176 p. $8.79.

Autobiography of a tennis champion. Althea Gibson grew up in black Harlem, and at first her desire to "be somebody" consisted of skipping school, getting in fights and not coming home some nights. Becoming involved in tennis almost by accident, Gibson very slowly focused on the sport as a better way to find an identity. She is frank about the racial prejudice she has experienced but refuses to make tennis a vehicle for militancy. Certain now of her identity, she says, "I'm a tennis player, not a Negro tennis player."

*Careers:* Female = 27 Male = 50 Neutral = 20
*Subject Categories:* American Ethnic Minority; Autobiography/Biography; Sports

**6.71ˣ  Mrs. Dalloway.** Virginia Woolf. New York: Harcourt, Brace, Jovanovich, 1925. 296 p. $2.95. Paper.

This classic novel explores the hidden springs of thought and action in one day of a woman's life and is recommended for highly motivated mature readers due to its complex style and focus on thought rather than plot. The careful reader will note that the most anguished people in the book—whether male or female—have been placed by society, sex or circumstances into the role of observer; only the "doer" escapes. Mrs. Dalloway takes one of the few "doing" paths open to women in her day—that of perpetual hostess. The major theme of the novel touches women and men equally: the inability of the characters to communicate beyond mere platitudes with other human beings.

*Careers:* Female = 24 Male = 47 Neutral = 21
*Subject Categories:* Literature by Women

**6.72 Girl Sports.** Karen Folger Jacobs. New York: Bantam Books, 1978. 180 p. $1.50. Paper.

Fifteen girls ages 9 to 17, representing a variety of ethnic minority groups, tell what it's like to train, compete, win or lose in sports ranging from soccer to wrestling. Many of the girls compete in sports that until recently were considered reserved for "boys only." Now girls are skateboarding, shooting pool and driving motorcycles. An inspiring book about young women who are successful competitors with rightfully earned self-respect.

*Careers:* Female = 32 Male = 33 Neutral = 15
*Subject Categories:* American Ethnic Minority; Health/Human Development; Sports

**6.73 The Mouse, The Monster and Me.** Pat Palmer. San Luis Obispo, CA: Impact, 1977. 78 p. $3.95. Paper.

Excellent nonsexist promotion of assertive behavior by using mice and dragons as representing undesirably passive or aggressive behavior. Highly recommended.

*Careers:* Female = 0 Male = 0 Neutral = 8
*Subject Categories:* Health/Human Development

**6.74ˣ  By and about Women: An Anthology of Short Fiction.** Beth Kline Schneiderman (ed.). New York: Harcourt, Brace, Jovanovich, 1973. 325 p.

A collection of short stories by well-known American and British women writers. The stories represent a variety of experiences encountered by women, with an emphasis on the necessity of coping with life. It should be noted that none of the stories focus on women in even slightly nontraditional careers; "coping" often means learning to live with defeat. A few of the stories contain explicit sexual references, and the subject matter may make this anthology more appropriate for senior high readers. However, the selective teacher will find examples of fine literature which will serve as valuable catalysts for thought and provocative class discussion.

*Careers:* Female = 32 Male = 49 Neutral = 40
*Subject Categories:* Anthologies; Essays/Short Stories; Literature by Women; Women's Studies

**6.75 Selma, Lord, Selma.** Sheyann Webb and Rachel West Nelson. University, AL: University of Alabama Press, 1980. 147 p. $9.95.

Sheyann Webb and Rachel West Nelson were eight and nine years old in 1965, a landmark year in the history of the Civil Rights Movement. They vividly recall their experiences as aware and sensitive members of that movement in Selma, Alabama.

*Careers:* Female = 7 Male = 23 Neutral = 13
*Subject Categories:* American Ethnic Minority; Cont. Issues/Curr. Events

**6.76 Chief Sarah.** Dorothy Nafus Morrison. New York: Atheneum, 1980. 170 p. $9.95.

Biography of Sarah Winnemuca, a Paiute woman who fought for Native American rights as a lecturer, writer and school administrator. An informative and interesting glimpse into the changing world of Native Americans from the mid to the late nineteenth century.

*Careers:* Female = 19 Male = 38 Neutral = 30
*Subject Categories:* American Ethnic Minority; Autobiography/Biography; Cultural Heritage; History; Women's Studies

**6.77 America's First Woman Chemist: Ellen Richards.** Esther M. Douty. New York: Julian Messner, 1961. 191 p. $3.34.

Biography of Ellen Richards, one of the first graduates of Vassar College, the first woman student at MIT, the first woman instructor at MIT and the first professional woman chemist in America. The story brings the field of chemistry alive for many who might ordinarily overlook it as a career option.

*Careers:* Female = 24 Male = 30 Neutral = 4
*Subject Categories:* Autobiography/Biography; Careers; History; Science/Technology

**6.78 Barefoot in the Grass: The Story of Grandma Moses.** William H. Armstrong. Garden City, NY: Doubleday, 1970. 96 p. $4.95.

*Barefoot in the Grass* is a delightful tale of Anne Mary Robertson's lifetime, particularly her wonderful childhood. Later to become Grandma Moses, a world renowned artist, Anne Mary Robertson maintained a marvelous sense of humor and a crystal clear memory throughout her long and eventful life.

*Careers:* Female = 9 Male = 35 Neutral = 8
*Subject Categories:* Autobiography/Biography; Fine Arts

**6.79 Ludell.** Brenda Wilkinson. New York: Harper & Row, 1975. 170 p.

The first in a series of books about Ludell, a black girl growing up in a small Georgia town. Although poverty and segregation are obvious factors in Ludell's life, this is an upbeat, positive story about a girl just entering puberty, told from Ludell's point of view.

*Careers:* Female = 11 Male = 15 Neutral = 3
*Subject Categories:* American Ethnic Minority; Families/Friendship; Health/Human Development

**6.80 Bouquets for Brimbal.** J.P. Reading. New York: Harper & Row, 1980. 186 p. $8.95.

Macey Beacon, 18, attempts to sort out feelings of love for her best friend, Annie, and for her boyfriend, Don. Learning that Annie is gay forces Macey to re-examine her stereotypical views about homosexuals; Macey is confused about love, sex and commitment in relationships. Although Macey struggles with her confusion and insecurities, the reader feels that she is growing and will reach new understandings with her "web" of feelings.

*Careers:* Female = 4 Male = 2 Neutral = 0
*Subject Categories:* Families/Friendship; Health/Human Development

**6.81 I Know Why the Caged Bird Sings.** Maya Angelou. New York: Bantam Books, 1971. 246 p. $2.25. Paper.

Extremes of circumstances and feelings make Maya Angelou's childhood in a rural community in the 1930s a remarkable narrative. More remarkable still is Angelou's skill, imagination and generosity in sharing these circumstances and feelings with the reader. A moving and important autobiographical narrative for our times.

*Careers:* Female = 20 Male = 47 Neutral = 16
*Subject Categories:* American Ethnic Minority; Autobiography/Biography; Families/Friendship; Literature by Women

**6.82 I Carve Stone.** Joan Fine. New York: Thomas Y. Crowell, 1979. 53 p. $7.95.

This book shows how various tools are used to transform a block of stone to a shining marble piece of sculpture. Well illustrated with black and white photographs.

*Careers:* Female = 1 Male = 0 Neutral = 0
*Subject Categories:* Careers; Fine Arts

**6.83ˣ My Little Book of Cats.** N. Gretchen Greiner. Racine, WI: Whitman, 1976. 22 p.

A picture book about cats, their likes and dislikes, habits and personalities. Illustrations portray ethnic minorities and the disabled. Individual cats are referred to as "he" and "she." More appropriate for primary grade children because of formatting.

*Careers:* Female = 1 Male = 1 Neutral = 0
*Subject Categories:* Animals; Picture Book

**6.84 Margaret Sanger: Pioneer of Birth Control.** Laurence Lader and Milton Meltzer. New York: Dell, 1974. 190 p. $.95. Paper.

This biography of Margaret Sanger encompasses her whole life, from her birth in 1879 in New York to her death in Arizona in 1966. Described are the seeds that started her deep involvement in the birth control movement as well as the many overwhelming obstacles she faced to achieve her goals. Realistically shown are the personal sacrifices she made to further the movement and her lack of any private or family life for many years. Methods of birth control and how conception takes place are discussed in the book in a very positive and easily understandable way. The book itself is not sexist, but does portray accurately the sexism to be found in this country at the turn of the century through today.

*Careers:* Female = 12 Male = 28 Neutral = 38
*Subject Categories:* Autobiography/Biography; Cont. Issues/ Curr. Events; Health/Human Development; History; Women's Studies

**6.85 Listen to Your Kitten Purr.** Lilo Hess. New York: Charles Scribner's Sons, 1980. 30 p. $8.95.

This book describes the plight of abandoned animals through Mindy who, after the near drowning of her five kittens, is spayed by her new owners. Photographs show how safely and professionally the spaying is done.

*Careers:* Female = 0 Male = 2 Neutral = 0
*Subject Categories:* Animals; Science/Technology

**6.86ˣ Ruby.** Rosa Guy. New York: Viking Press, 1976. 217 p. $8.95.

Ruby is an 18-year-old black girl from the West Indies who lives in Harlem with her overbearing father and bookworm sister. In her loneliness and isolation she reaches out to find love with another student, Daphne, who challenges her both emotionally and intellectually. A well-written and sensitive portrait of two young women in love. Daphne, the more mature and independent of the two, recognizes when their relationship must end and breaks it off. Ruby has a difficult time accepting Daphne's rejection and her feelings of abandonment. Mature subject matter makes this book more appropriate for senior high readers.

*Careers:* Female = 10 Male = 9 Neutral = 6
*Subject Categories:* American Ethnic Minority; Families/ Friendship; Health/Human Development

**6.87 A Christmas Memory.** Truman Capote. New York: Random House, 1956. 45 p.

An autobiography of the years when, as a youngster, Truman Capote lived with a family of distant and elderly cousins in a small town in rural Alabama. This touching, warm story is primarily about his fond remembrances of one of the cousins, an elderly woman, and the way they celebrated Christmas in spite of their poverty.

*Careers:* Female = 5 Male = 11 Neutral = 3
*Subject Categories:* Autobiography/Biography; Families/ Friendship

**6.88 Sam.** Barbara Corcoran. Bloomfield, CT: Atheneum, 1967. 219 p. $.95. Paper.

Sam is a 15-year-old girl living on a small island with her family. No one else lives on the island, and Sam was schooled at home by her father until her junior year in high school. Sam's father and brother believe that people are "no good" and shun involvement outside the immediate family, but Sam learns that she has to make her own decisions about life.

*Careers:* Female = 4 Male = 18 Neutral = 9

*Subject Categories:* Animals; Families/Friendship; Health/Human Development

**6.89ˣ Women of Crisis: Lives of Struggle and Hope.** Robert Coles and Jane Hallowell Coles. New York: Dell, 1978. 291 p. $.95. Paper.

Five poor, working class American women—two whites, one black, one Eskimo, and one Chinese—describe in their own words their hopes, dreams, fears, conflicts and struggles. Despite the fact that none of these women sees herself as a feminist or as politically aware or educated, each shares a common sense of what it is like to grow up as a woman in America. The authors provide additional information and observations producing a book in which complex issues of race, class and sex vividly come to life. Subject matter makes this book more appropriate for secondary students.

*Careers:* Female = 33 Male = 31 Neutral = 20
*Subject Categories:* American Ethnic Minority; Behavioral Science; Cultural Heritage; Women's Studies

**6.90 Of Love and Death and Other Journeys.** Isabelle Holland. New York: J.B. Lippincott, 1975. 159 p.

In this often humorous, often serious and insightful novel, the author writes with understanding about a young girl's experiences of the joy and grief of life. The central character, Meg Grant, age 16, has a turning point which changes her life dramatically. The fact that none of the characters is stereotyped makes this a delightful, fresh book.

*Careers:* Female = 5 Male = 12 Neutral = 6
*Subject Categories:* Families/Friendship; Health/Human Development

**6.91 A Long Way from Verona.** Jane Gardam. New York: Collier, 1971. 277 p. $1.25. Paper.

A somewhat traditional yet entertaining story about 13-year-old Jessica Vye, a girl growing up in England during World War II. Although most of the peripheral characters are stereotypic, Jessica, who is certain she will become a writer, is fiercely independent and self-sufficient. Use of English dialects occasionally may be confusing to the reader.

*Careers:* Female = 12 Male = 23 Neutral = 16
*Subject Categories:* Families/Friendship; Foreign Countries

**6.92 The Golda Meir Story.** Margaret Davidson. New York: Charles Scribner's Sons, 1976. 211 p. $6.95.

This biography of Golda Meir opens with her life at the age of four, depicts her family's immigration and life in America and concludes with her emigration to Israel and her involvement in that country's growth. The story provides the reader with insights into the persecutions the Jewish people have faced for centuries and the Arab resentment of Israel's formation. Racist attitudes toward Jews are realistically depicted in the book but are not emphasized.

*Careers:* Female = 13 Male = 30 Neutral = 22
*Subject Categories:* Autobiography/Biography; Foreign Countries; Religion/Mythology

**6.93 Black Cow Summer.** Richard Graber. New York: Harper & Row, 1980. 212 p. $9.95.

Set in a small Minnesota town during the 1930s, this story presents love, friendship, family relationships, economic adversity, danger and death from the perspective of a teenage boy becoming an adult. During the summer, Ray Deck falls in love with Mary Ellen, a new girl in town from Missouri. His relationship with Mary Ellen causes conflict with his mother, who disapproves of "hillbillies," and with Mary Ellen's step-brothers, who seem determined to break up the romance. At summer's end Mary Ellen leaves town after her stepfather dies. This forces Ray to attempt to come to terms with his feelings and future.

*Careers:* Female = 4 Male = 20 Neutral = 4
*Subject Categories:* Families/Friendship; Health/Human Development

**6.94ˣ  Daddy Is A Monster . . . Sometimes.** John Steptoe. New York: J.B. Lippincott, 1980. 29 p. $8.95.

Vividly illustrated picture book about a young father and his two children. Bweela and her brother Javaka affectionately share their feelings about how their daddy has a way of turning into a scary monster when they are "being kind of messy," or making some noise or pushing him too far. Formatting makes this book more appropriate for primary-grade children.

*Careers:* Female = 0 Male = 3 Neutral = 0
*Subject Categories:* American Ethnic Minority; Families/Friendship; Picture Book

**6.95ˣ  "I Am Cherry Alive," The Little Girl Sang.** Delmore Schwartz. New York: Harper & Row, 1958. 32 p. $7.95.

Beautiful illustrations add charm to a young girl's hymn to life in this delightful picture book for primary-grade children.

*Careers:* None shown
*Subject Categories:* Health/Human Development; Picture Book

**6.96 Contributions of Women: Labor.** Marcia McKenna Biddle. Minneapolis, MN: Dillon Press, 1979. 126 p. $8.95.

Chapter-length biographies of five women prominently involved in the U.S. labor movement: Mother Jones, Mary Heaton Vorse, Frances Perkins, Addie Wyatt and Dolores Huerta (capsule biographies of 10 other women labor leaders are included). These life stories are impressive and instill pride in women's contributions and achievements in this field, as well as documenting cruel and discriminatory practices against workers in general and women and minorities in particular. An excellent book.

*Careers:* Female = 41 Male = 46 Neutral = 30
*Subject Categories:* American Ethnic Minority; Autobiography/Biography; Cont. Issues/Curr. Events; History; Women's Studies

**6.97 Susannah and the Blue House Mystery.** Patricia Elmore. New York: E.P. Dutton, 1980. 164 p. $9.95.

Blond Lucy plays Dr. Watson to her black and brainy friend Susannah's Sherlock Holmes as they sift through clues in the old blue house leading to a missing will and hidden treasure (valuable antiques). Highly readable, with well-drawn major characters. The book presents a variety of family arrangements and subtly pokes holes in some common racial and sex role stereotypes. This story is a considerable improvement on Nancy Drew, while retaining much of the appeal of that genre.

*Careers:* Female = 10 Male = 3 Neutral = 7
*Subject Categories:* American Ethnic Minority; Families/Friendship; Mystery/Adventure

**6.98 Only Love.** Susan Sallis. New York: Harper & Row, 1980. 250 p. $9.95.

Fanny Adams is a 16-year-old paraplegic who has a short time to live. Her sense of mischief, adventure and humor enliven the hospital where she has come to stay and bring delight to her fellow residents, young and old. Her biggest challenge is Lucas Hawkins, who has lost both legs as a result of a recent motorbike accident. With Fanny's help, he comes out of his room and enters her heart as she does his. A nonsentimental story about love in all its aspects.

*Careers:* Female = 7 Male = 12 Neutral = 8
*Subject Categories:* Families/Friendship; The Handicapped; Health/Human Development

**6.99 The Journey of the Shadow Bairns.** Margaret J. Anderson. New York: Alfred A. Knopf, 1980. 177 p.

Young Margaret and four-year-old Robbie are orphaned by the sudden death of their parents shortly before the family was to migrate from Scotland to Canada in 1903. Rather than be separated, Margaret and Robbie slip away from Glasgow for the long journey by ship and rail, hoping to find an aunt and uncle in Manitoba. Knowing they dare not attract attention to themselves, Margaret tells Robbie that they will play at being shadow children—a survival tactic that plays a large part in their successful overcoming of difficulties. Author has drawn on historical pioneer records. Margaret's determination and optimism appear characteristic of the period and place.

*Careers:* Female = 9 Male = 17 Neutral = 13
*Subject Categories:* Families/Friendship; Foreign Countries; History

**6.100 The Maid of the North: Feminist Folktales from around the World.** Ethel Johnston Phelps. New York: Holt, Rinehart & Winston, 1981. 176 p. $10.95.

Twenty-one tales (drawn primarily from Northern Europe) all featuring spirited, courageous women. There isn't a single, hand-wringing, blond and beautiful female in the whole lot—and the heroes' determination in facing the problems at hand is remarkable. Some tales are poignant; many are light-hearted. All provide a fine antidote to the more typical portrayals of women in standard folktale collections.

*Careers:* Female = 10 Male = 22 Neutral = 7
*Subject Categories:* American Ethnic Minority; Fantasy, Folk & Fairy Tales

**6.101 The Skull in the Snow and Other Folktales.** Toni McCarty. New York: Delacorte Press, 1981. 87 p. $7.45.

A collection of 14 tales honoring the female folk hero. These simple retellings are gathered from all over the world and feature women who rely on their common sense, courage and ingenuity (plus the usual magical interventions common to all folk tales). With but two exceptions, each hero operates within the domestic role specific to her culture, but these women are neither timid nor passive. Fine illustrations complement the text.

*Careers:* Female = 7 Male = 15 Neutral = 6
*Subject Categories:* American Ethnic Minority; Cultural Heritage; Foreign Countries; Fantasy, Folk & Fairy Tales

**6.102ˣ  Cowgirls: Women of the American West.** Teresa Jordan. Garden City, NY: Anchor Press, 1982. 301 p. $19.95.

Cowboy legends permeate our culture, but stories about grown-up cowgirls are much rarer. This book sets the record straight by providing the first extended look at the cowboy's full-fledged female counterpart—the cowgirl who works outside on the range or in the rodeo on a regular basis. Oral histories of 30 women of varying ages and circumstances, interspersed with photographs and capsule quotations from a variety of sources, provide a collective portrait of women who endure hard labor and adversity, develop or retain their independence and discover a special joy in their work. Unlike the so-called Prairie Madonnas, cowgirls demonstrated their courage and spunk outside the traditional domestic sphere. A number show little sympathy for "Women's Lib stuff," but in so doing they reflect the usual western rancher's distaste for national movements and pride in an ability to go it alone. An informative, entertaining, sympathetic and enriching collection of minibiographies. Subject matter and format make this book more appropriate for secondary readers.

*Careers:* Female = 52 Male = 42 Neutral = 21
*Subject Categories:* Autobiography/Biography; Women's Studies

# Reading Grade Level 7–Dale-Chall Formula

**7.1 The Forge and the Forest.** Betty Underwood. Boston: Houghton Mifflin, 1975. 255 p. $6.95.

This vivid historical novel speaks clearly to the issues of the present. An orphaned French girl's life in the United States becomes a turmoil of conflicting emotions toward the iron-willed pastor who is her guardian, the growing abolitionist movement and the role of women in her society.

*Careers:* Female = 13 Male = 44 Neutral = 30
*Subject Categories:* Families/Friendship; Health/Human Development; History

**7.2 The Lark and the Laurel.** Barbara Willard. New York: Harcourt, Brace & World, 1970. 207 p. $5.95.

Cecily Jolland, who has lived a doll-like, passive existence, is left with her aunt when her father is forced to flee England upon the ascension of Henry Tudor to the throne in 1485. Although at first Cecily is resistant to her aunt and the simple country life, she soon gains confidence in herself as an independent young woman as she works, does chores and learns she is not her father's property to do with as he wills.

*Careers:* Female = 11 Male = 30 Neutral = 8
*Subject Categories:* Families/Friendship; Foreign Countries; History; Mystery/Adventure

**7.3 The Black Stallion and the Girl.** Walter Farley. New York: Random House, 1971. 196 p. $1.75. Paper.

Alec alienates the trainer at his race horse farm when he hires a girl to work with the colts. Story deals with the problems encountered when a female enters a nontraditional career.

*Careers:* Female = 6 Male = 20 Neutral = 18
*Subject Categories:* Animals; Cont. Issues/Curr. Events; Families/Friendships

**7.4 Magic at Wychwood.** Sally Watson. New York: Alfred A. Knopf, 1970. 128 p.

In this captivating tale, Princess Elaine, who doesn't faint or flirt as princesses are supposed to, sets out to prove to her tutor that magic exists as well as science. Among the characters are sorcerers, witches, a thing that goes bump in the night, roaming sheets, a mechanical horse and a chair that comes to life.

*Careers:* Female = 11 Male = 19 Neutral = 6
*Subject Categories:* Fantasy, Folk & Fairy Tales

**7.5 Maria Sanford: Pioneer Professor.** Lucie Hartley. Minneapolis, MN: Dillon Press, 1977. 95 p. $5.95.

Biography of Maria Sanford (1836–1920), whose teaching career spanned 54 years and who became the first woman college professor in the United States.

*Careers:* Female = 15 Male = 23 Neutral = 20
*Subject Categories:* Biography; History

**7.6 Zanballer.** R.R. Knudson. New York: Dell, 1974. 143 p. $1.25. Paper. (Originally published by Delacorte Press, 1972.)

In this amusing story, eighth grader Suzanne "Zan" Hagen leads her football team of former dance students to victory in the Dogwood Mini-Bowl despite the principal's objections and boys' harassment. She's helped by her friend and classmate, "science whiz" Arthur Rinehart, who acts as the team's coach.

*Careers:* Female = 8 Male = 15 Neutral = 12
*Subject Categories:* Families/Friendship; Sports

**7.7ˣ Doctor Mary's Animals.** Beverley Allinson. Toronto, ON: D.C. Heath, Canada Ltd., 1975. 30 p. Paper.

This book is the story of a veterinarian and her work. Interesting photographs show her in the animal hospital and on house calls with a young friend. Large print and pictures make this book more appropriate for upper primary- or lower intermediate-grade readers.

*Careers:* Female = 1 Male = 1 Neutral = 1
*Subject Categories:* Animals; Careers; Picture Book; Science

**7.8ˣ Fresh Fish and Chips.** Jan Andrews. Toronto, ON: Canadian Women's Educational Press, 1973. 24 p. $2.00. Paper.

When the children decide they want fresh fish for dinner, mother goes out and catches not only fish, but also octopus, whale, squid, crab and lobster. Large print and illustrations make this amusing picture book more appropriate for primary-grade readers.

*Careers:* Female = 1 Male = 1 Neutral = 0
*Subject Categories:* Animals; Families/Friendship; Fantasy, Folk & Fairy Tales; Picture Book; Poetry/Rhyme

**7.9ˣ Three Stalks of Corn.** Leo Politi. New York: Charles Scribner's Sons, 1976. 28 p. $6.95.

This beautifully illustrated story is about a young Mexican American girl who lives with her grandmother in a California barrio. The text is sprinkled with Spanish, and Mexican legends, food, customs and other cultural traditions are portrayed. The illustrations and print size make this book more appropriate for primary- or early intermediate-grade readers; good read-aloud story.

*Careers:* Female = 4 Male = 4 Neutral = 1
*Subject Categories:* American Ethnic Minority; Families/Friendship; Picture Book

**7.10 Oh Lizzie! The Life of Elizabeth Cady Stanton.** Doris Faber. New York: Pocket Books, 1974. 172 p. $.75. Paper. (Originally published by Lothrop, Lee & Shepard, 1972.)

A well-written account of Elizabeth Cady Stanton's life. In depicting her commitment to and involvement in the women's rights movement, especially obtaining the right to vote, the book reveals much about the historical position of women in the United States.

*Careers:* Female = 15 Male = 26 Neutral = 18
*Subject Categories:* Biography; History

**7.11 Daughter of the Mountains.** Louise Rankin. New York: Pocket Books, 1968. 212 p. $1.25. Paper. (Originally published by Viking Press, 1948.)

This is a touching story of a 12-year-old Tibetan girl's love for her dog. When the dog is stolen by a wool-trader, she travels alone and on foot from the mountains to the coast of India to retrieve her beloved pet.

*Careers:* Female = 6 Male = 23 Neutral = 16
*Subject Categories:* Animals; Foreign Countries; Mystery/Adventure

**7.12 They Wouldn't Quit.** Ravina Gelfand and Letha Patterson. Minneapolis, MN: Lerner, 1962. 54 p. $3.95.

Short biographies of 10 men and four women who overcame their physical disabilities to achieve their goals.

*Careers:* Female = 13 Male = 35 Neutral = 18
*Subject Categories:* Biography; The Handicapped

**7.13 National Velvet.** Enid Bagnold. New York: Pocket Books, 1935. 214 p. $1.50. Paper.

Fourteen-year-old Velvet Brown wins the Grand National, the greatest steeplechase in the world. This is the story of how she wins her horse in a lottery and through deception (since women couldn't ride in the Grand National) enters the steeplechase and wins. She's disqualified, but not unhappy, because she only wanted her horse to be able to show his greatness.

*Careers:* Female = 9 Male = 31 Neutral = 21
*Subject Categories:* Animals; Families/Friendship; Foreign Countries

**7.14 Sing to the Dawn.** Mingfong Ho. New York: Lothrop, Lee & Shepard, 1975. 158 p. $6.50.

An excellent story of a young Thai girl's determination to continue her education in the city, despite competition from her brother and opposition from her father.

*Careers:* Female = 3 Male = 10 Neutral = 9
*Subject Categories:* Families/Friendship; Foreign Countries

**7.15 Rebecca of Sunnybrook Farm.** Kate Douglas Wiggin. New York: Airmont, 1967. 255 p. $.75. Paper.

This classic story portrays a fresh, delightful 10-year-old girl whose charm, optimistic spirit and resourcefulness assist her in

contending with two demanding aunts. Roles within the book are quite traditional; however, Rebecca herself is very positive as is the overall tone of the book.

*Careers:* Female = 6 Male = 6 Neutral = 1
*Subject Categories:* Families/Friendship; Health/Human Development

**7.16 The Secret Garden.** Frances Hodgson Burnett. New York: Dell, 1978. 298 p. $1.50. Paper. (Originally published by J.B. Lippincott, 1938.)

The story of a spoiled and strong-willed girl, who through her friendships with two other children grows in her ability to look beyond herself. The three children, two boys and a girl, are presented in a positive manner where distinctions are not made on the basis of sex. The adults, however, are presented in very traditional roles.

*Careers:* Female = 5 Male = 8 Neutral = 1
*Subject Categories:* Families/Friendship; Health/Human Development

**7.17 The Senator from Maine: Margaret Chase Smith.** Alice Fleming. New York: Dell, 1976. 131 p. $1.25. Paper. (Originally published by Thomas Y. Crowell, 1969.)

A biography of Margaret Chase Smith who served in both houses of Congress and who was one of the first women in the country to be a candidate for president of the United States. Although this book provides a positive example of a successful woman in politics, it presents her in terms of some very traditional stereotypes.

*Careers:* Female = 19 Male = 30 Neutral = 3
*Subject Categories:* Biography; Cont. Issues/Curr. Events

**7.18 Time at the Top.** Edward Ormondroyd. Berkeley, CA: Parnassus Press, 1963. 176 p. $5.95.

As she is riding the elevator up to her apartment, a young girl suddenly finds herself carried from 1968 back into the past to the year 1881. This engrossing story is filled with mystery and suspense and also provides a good picture of American life in the 1880s.

*Careers:* Female = 6 Male = 26 Neutral = 5
*Subject Categories:* Fantasy, Folk & Fairy Tales; History; Mystery/Adventure

**7.19 Shirley Chisholm.** Susan Brownmiller. New York: Pocket Books, 1972. 121 p. $.75. Paper. (Originally published by Doubleday, 1970.)

This is an excellent biography of Shirley Chisholm, the first black woman elected to the U.S. Congress. Good portrait of a strong, independent woman—the influences on her life, the issues she must face and her nonstereotypic marriage.

*Careers:* Female = 22 Male = 25 Neutral = 23
*Subject Categories:* American Ethnic Minority; Biography; Families/Friendship

**7.20 To the Barricades: The Anarchist Life of Emma Goldman.** Alix Shulman. New York: Thomas Y. Crowell, 1971. 235 p. $6.95.

A fiercely feminist biography of Emma Goldman, who was once called "the most dangerous woman in America" because of her anarchist beliefs. Her hatred of oppression caused her to support with revolutionary zeal causes still of concern today— women's rights, birth control, peace and the fight against censorship.

*Careers:* Female = 10 Male = 22 Neutral = 14
*Subject Categories:* Biography; History; Mystery/Adventure

**7.21 Maggie Rose: Her Birthday Christmas.** Ruth Sawyer. New York: Harper & Row, 1952. 151 p. $4.79.

Maggie Rose Bunker, an imaginative and hard working eight-year-old, lives in a shack with her ma and pa and six brothers and sisters on the wrong side of the Point, a resort spot near Bangor, Maine. The Bunkers are warm, laughing and singing folk but do little work and rely mainly on the generosity of their neighbors. Maggie Rose, however, goes to work picking berries so that she can invite *all* the neighbors for a Christmas birthday party. When the money that she worked so hard to save is stolen, her family is motivated to go to work so that she can have the party on which she counted.

*Careers:* Female = 4 Male = 14 Neutral = 6
*Subject Categories:* Families/Friendship

**7.22ˣ  The Princess and the Admiral.** Charlotte Pomerantz. Reading, MA: Addison-Wesley, 1974. 46 p. $5.50.

This is a delightful tale based on Kubla Khan's invasion of Vietnam. It tells how Princess Mat-Mat devises a clever plan so that her people—fisherfolk and farmers—defeat the Admiral and his invading forces. Type size and illustrations make this book more appropriate for younger readers.

*Careers:* Female = 4 Male = 8 Neutral = 3
*Subject Categories:* Fantasy, Folk & Fairy Tales; Foreign Countries; Mystery/Adventure

**7.23  Contributions of Women: Education.** Mary W. Burgess. Minneapolis, MN: Dillon Press, 1975. 142 p. $6.95.

This book provides biographical sketches of six American women who were pioneers in the field of education—Emma Hart Willard, Mary Lyon, Martha Berry, Patty Smith Hill, Florence Sabin and Mary McLeod Bethune. Each sketch traces the early interests, hardships and eventual successes in furthering American education.

*Careers:* Female = 11 Male = 15 Neutral = 5
*Subject Categories:* American Ethnic Minority; Biography; History

**7.24  An Album of Women in American History.** Claire R. and Leonard W. Ingraham. New York: Franklin Watts, 1972. 88 p. $4.33.

This book is a survey of notable women in American history, from the colonial times to the present. The reader is introduced to the accomplishments of hundreds of women, including blacks, Native Americans and whites, through brief biographies and numerous pictures.

*Careers:* Female = 62 Male = 3 Neutral = 1
*Subject Categories:* American Ethnic Minority; History

**7.25  I'm Nobody! Who Are You? The Story of Emily Dickinson.** Edna Barth. New York: The Seabury Press, 1971. 128 p. $6.95.

A biography of Emily Dickinson who chose to live in solitude and rarely left her home in Amherst but whose sensitive poetry broke nineteenth century literary norms. This book, which includes over 35 of her poems, also speculates on her secret love disappointment which may have caused her to become a recluse.

*Careers:* Female = 9 Male = 16 Neutral = 9
*Subject Categories:* Biography; Families/Friendship; Fine Arts; Poetry/Rhyme

**7.26  Contributions of Women: Sports.** Joan Ryan. Minneapolis, MN: Dillon Press, 1975. 135 p. $6.95.

Short biographies of six women who not only were champion athletes—setting world records and winning gold medals—but also contributed greatly to the acceptance of women in sports. Those featured are Babe Didrikson Zaharias (outstanding golfer and track star); Kathy Kusner (Olympic equestrian and big-league jockey); Wilma Rudolph (Olympic runner); Billie Jean King (tennis champion); Peggy Fleming (figure skating champion); and Melissa Belote (Olympic swimmer).

*Careers:* Female = 23 Male = 24 Neutral = 17
*Subject Categories:* American Ethnic Minority; Biography; Families/Friendship; Health/Human Development; Sports

**7.27  Famous Modern American Women Athletes.** Helen Hull Jacobs. New York: Dodd, Mead, 1975. 132 p. $4.95.

Short biographies of eight outstanding American women athletes who were Olympic stars, record setters and professional athletes, including Judy Cook Soutar, Janet Lynn, Micki King, Kathy Whitworth, Cindy Nelson, Shirley Babashoff, Billie Jean King and Francie Larrieu.

*Careers:* Female = 14 Male = 15 Neutral = 5
*Subject Categories:* Biography; Sports

**7.28  Downright Dencey.** Caroline Dale Snedeker. Garden City, NY: Doubleday, 1927. 314 p. $3.95.

The absorbing story of a Quaker girl whose sense of justice and need for forgiveness from the boy she injures puts her in almost continual conflict with her family. The two main characters, Dencey and Sam Jetsam, are very well developed and sympathetically portrayed.

*Careers:* Female = 4 Male = 8 Neutral = 2
*Subject Categories:* Families/Friendship; Mystery/Adventure

**7.29  Life with Working Parents.** Esther Hautzig. New York: Macmillan, 1976. 124 p. $6.95.

A cheerful, informative guide written particularly for boys and girls who live in households with a single parent, two working parents or where no one person assumes 100 percent responsibility for housekeeping. Young persons reading this book will be delighted and encouraged to realize all the things they can do to make a household run smoothly: caring for younger children, plants and pets; cooking; organizing; cleaning; and doing simple repairs. These all help develop a sense of responsibility and pride in looking out for oneself. The author avoids sex role stereotypes in both parent careers and family responsibilities. Practical suggestions for meals, crafts and family entertainment make this very enjoyable reading.

*Careers:* Female = 2 Male = 3 Neutral = 15
*Subject Categories:* Families/Friendship; Information Book

**7.30  Fighting Shirley Chisholm.** James Haskins. New York: Dial Press, 1975. 211 p. $7.95.

This is an easy-to-read biography of Shirley Chisholm, a "fighter" known for not giving up in the face of adversity and one of the most influential black politicians in recent years. The author follows Chisholm's life from Brooklyn ward politics to a close election in which she becomes the first black woman elected to serve in the House of Representatives. This book places special emphasis on Chisholm's close family tie with her father and her parents' almost obsessive goal to educate their children.

*Careers:* Female = 14 Male = 14 Neutral = 2
*Subject Categories:* American Ethnic Minority; Biography

**7.31 Daughter of Discontent.** Hila Colman. New York: William Morrow, 1971. 191 p.

After being raised by her mother, 17-year-old Katherine spends the summer in New York with her father, becoming reacquainted after a seven-year absence. While working on his election campaign, a variety of events causes her to examine the "roles" played by men and women around her, explore her growing sexuality and determine the kind of woman she wants to be and how she's going to get there.

*Careers:* Female = 17 Male = 27 Neutral = 28
*Subject Categories:* Families/Friendship; Health/Human Development

**7.32 Somebody's Angel Child: The Story of Bessie Smith.** Carman Moore. New York: Dell, 1969. 126 p. $.95. Paper. (Originally published by Thomas Y. Crowell, 1969.)

This biography of Bessie Smith provides an easy-to-read portrait of the woman. It shows how "Mr. Blues" shadowed her life and how she expressed in her music the misery of being poor and black in the early 1900s.

*Careers:* Female = 3 Male = 22 Neutral = 26
*Subject Categories:* American Ethnic Minority; Biography; Cultural Heritage; Fine Arts

**7.33 The Wife of Martin Guerre.** Janet Lewis. Chicago: The Swallow Press, 1975. 109 p. $2.95. Paper. (Originally published by The Colt Press, 1941.)

An intriguing tale set in sixteenth century France in which young Bertraude comes to believe that the Martin Guerre who returns from the wars after an eight-year absence is not the same man she married at the age of 11. The ironic yet tragic ending to the novel will move the reader to Bertraude's plight, accused by her family of being insane and by herself of committing a mortal sin under the eyes of God and her religion.

*Careers:* Female = 6 Male = 12 Neutral = 13
*Subject Categories:* Foreign Countries; History; Women's Studies

**7.34 Jubilee.** Margaret Walker. New York: Bantam Books, 1967. 416 p. $1.95. Paper. (Originally published by Houghton Mifflin, 1966.)

A powerfully moving novel of the Old South and the Civil War, told through the eyes of Vyry Brown, daughter of a black slave and her white "master." Based on the life of Margaret Walker's great grandmother, this novel is dramatic, rich in detail and presents a portrait of a compassionate, strong and independent woman whose courage and integrity enable her spirit to triumph over the degrading bondage of her times.

*Careers:* Female = 12 Male = 48 Neutral = 25
*Subject Categories:* American Ethnic Minority; Cultural Heritage; Families/Friendship; Health/Human Development; History

**7.35 The Silent Storm.** Marion Marsh Brown and Ruth Crone. Nashville, TN: Abingdon, 1963. 250 p.

A very readable and entertaining biography of Annie Sullivan Macy, the teacher who brought the deaf and blind Helen Keller out of darkness. The book traces Annie's life from her destitute childhood, through the years she acted as Helen's teacher, companion and interpreter while Helen worked on her degree from Radcliffe.

*Careers:* Female = 14 Male = 24 Neutral = 11
*Subject Categories:* Biography; The Handicapped; Health/Human Development; History

**7.36 My Antonia.** Willa Cather. Boston: Houghton Mifflin, 1918. 372 p. $4.95.

This literary classic is a moving portrait of an American pioneer woman. While many of the female careers mentioned in the book are rather menial ones, women are not shown to be second-rate by Willa Cather. The central figure, Antonia, is depicted as a child, as a woman of great physical and moral strength and as a person of tremendous warmth and humanness. The book should be read for the experience of losing one's self in Cather's magnificent images.

*Careers:* Female = 11 Male = 54 Neutral = 1
*Subject Categories:* Families/Friendship; History; Literature by Women

**7.37 Free to Choose: Decision-Making for Young Men.** Joyce Slayton Mitchell. New York: Dell, 1977. 261 p. $1.75. Paper. (Originally published by Delacorte, 1976.)

An anthology of brief essays offering young men (and women) a wealth of information and advice on matters of personal, social, educational and career development. The selections provide a discussion of the variety of choices men and women must make, including sexual, relationship, liberation, turning-on, spiritual, athletic and educational choices. This book would be particularly appropriate for use in health, career guidance and social studies classes, as well as for free reading. Although the book is aimed primarily toward college-bound students, some information is also provided on military and occupational trades.

*Careers:* Female = 8 Male = 37 Neutral = 59
*Subject Categories:* Careers; Health/Human Development

**7.38 Other Choices for Becoming a Woman.** Joyce Slayton Mitchell. New York: Dell, 1975. 267 p. $1.25. Paper. (Originally published by KNOW, Inc., 1974.)

This anthology of brief essays provides a wealth of information designed to help young women (and men) realize their potential in today's world and to encourage them to explore the wide range of careers and lifestyles from which they can choose. The information provided is organized around sexual, relationship, beauty, turning-on, spiritual and educational choices and is geared for college-bound young women. Its companion book, *Free to Choose: Decision-Making for Young Men,* offers additional information on military and nonprofessional career choices.

*Careers:* Female = 23 Male = 8 Neutral = 57

*Subject Categories:* Careers; Health/Human Development; Women's Studies

**7.39 Women's Rights.** Janet Stevenson. New York: Franklin Watts, 1972. 90 p. Paper.

An introductory history of the battle to obtain votes for women in America. Short biographies of suffragists, fictionalized chapters and brief excerpts from primary source materials help make this a very readable, supplementary text for junior high students.

*Careers:* Female = 23 Male = 25 Neutral = 14
*Subject Categories:* History; Women's Studies

**7.40 Women in Television.** Anita Klever. Philadelphia, PA: Westminster Press, 1975. 142 p. $5.95.

Thirty-seven women—each with a different job—talk about their careers in television, off camera and on. In brief, first-person interviews, each woman talks about what she does, how she got to her position, and the "rocky road of making it." Because this book offers a look at personal job histories, it is less dry than many "career" books for girls. It provides a fascinating look at a fast-paced, competitive and often glamorous industry with a wide variety of career possibilities for young women.

*Careers:* Female = 30 Male = 35 Neutral = 51
*Subject Categories:* Careers; Fine Arts; Women's Studies

**7.41 Billie Jean.** Billie Jean King with Kim Chapin. New York: Harper & Row, 1974. 208 p. $6.95.

This autobiography gives a very human account of the numerous struggles of a female athlete. Billie Jean King describes her career as a tennis player, her marriage, her family and other significant people and events in her life. She reveals a very feminist attitude when she discusses traditional inequality of the sexes in sports and her fight for women's equality in tennis. She describes her traditional family background, her expectations for marriage and includes a chapter on women's liberation and its effects. This book provides an interesting account of the life of an ambitious, athletic and sensitive woman.

*Careers:* Female = 7 Male = 12 Neutral = 1
*Subject Categories:* Autobiography; Sports

**7.42ˣ The Bluest Eye.** Toni Morrison. New York: Pocket Books, 1972. 160 p. $1.95. Paper. (Originally published by Holt, Rinehart & Winston, 1970.)

This beautifully written and poignant depiction of life in the black rural South in the late 1930s is narrated by one of the main characters, a young girl named Claudia. From Claudia's childish yet penetrating perspective, the reader learns about the lives of the poor Breedlove family members and particularly the events leading up to the tragic end for young Pecola Breedlove. Pecola, who feels that by being black she cannot be attractive or worthy, finds the only way she can escape the pain is in another world of her own making. The rather vivid description of the father raping his daughter may demand a more mature audience than the average seventh-grade level reader.

*Careers:* Female = 7 Male = 16 Neutral = 4
*Subject Categories:* American Ethnic Minority; Cultural Heritage; Families/Friendship; History; Literature by Women

**7.43 Thank You All Very Much.** Margaret Drabble. New York: New American Library, 1969. 144 p. $1.50. Paper.

(Originally published by William Morrow, 1965 under the title *The Millstone*.)

Rosamund, an English graduate student who lives in her absent parents' posh London flat, is pleased with her independent, "well-organized" life. Her academic research and two undemanding boyfriends require no intimacy and little commitment from her. However, when Rosamund loses her virginity and becomes pregnant after an evening spent with a casual friend, she must deal with emotions and feelings her ordered life had not allowed her. The ensuing story of Rosamund's pregnancy, the birth of her daughter and the subsequent overpowering feelings of love for and involvement with another human being—her daughter—is unsentimental, funny and moving. An excellent story for mature young readers.

*Careers:* Female = 21 Male = 25 Neutral = 18
*Subject Categories:* Foreign Countries; Health/Human Development; Literature by Women

**7.44 Listen for the Fig Tree.** Sharon Bell Mathis. New York: Avon, 1975. 143 p. $1.25. Paper. (Originally published by Viking Press, 1974.)

A dramatically realistic story about a young black girl growing up in New York. Sixteen-year-old Muffin has been blind since the age of 10 and wants to be a lawyer. She cooks, sews, is self-sufficient and looks after her mother, who seeks refuge in alcoholism from the grief and pain of her husband's murder. Through the support of black friends, neighbors and her first Kwanza, an African harvest celebration, Muffin finds the courage and strength she needs to grow and survive. The book emphasizes the importance of black pride and unity and is extremely positive in portraying realistic, nonstereotypic characters. An excellent book!

*Careers:* Female = 3 Male = 9 Neutral = 18
*Subject Categories:* American Ethnic Minority; Cultural Heritage; Families/Friendship; The Handicapped; Health/Human Development

**7.45 What Can She Be? An Architect.** Gloria and Esther Goldreich. New York: Lothrop, Lee & Shepard, 1974. 48 p.

This introduction to a career in architecture uses black and white photographs and simple text to describe architect Susan Broday's projects and daily work. Although ethnic minorities are fairly well represented in the photographs, no women are shown in any of the career roles associated with the field of architecture, such as construction workers and contractors.

*Careers:* Female = 2 Male = 7 Neutral = 5
*Subject Categories:* Careers

**7.46 The World of Mary Cassatt.** Robin McKown. New York: Thomas Y. Crowell, 1972. 253 p.

This biography provides an interesting look at the world of Mary Cassatt, an Impressionist painter and printmaker whose daring use of color and strong line set her apart from most of her American contemporaries and placed her on terms of equality with the most advanced French artists of her day. In telling Mary Cassatt's story, the author has also provided vivid portraits of colleagues and friends—Degas, Manet, Cezanne, Renoir, Pissarro, Monet and Morisat. The biography, generously illustrated with black and white photographs of the works of Cassatt and her fellow artists, brings to life a proud, independent and talented woman.

*Careers:* Female = 20 Male = 63 Neutral = 39
*Subject Categories:* Autobiography/Biography; Fine Arts

**7.47 Crazy Salad: Some Things about Women.** Nora Ephron. New York: Alfred A. Knopf, 1975. 201 p. $7.95.

Twenty-five articles written by Nora Ephron for several different magazines. Some articles are political in nature and all are somewhat satirical. Topics include women's liberation, politics, the women of Israel, consciousness-raising groups and several individual women, including Dorothy Parker. Ephron takes a piercing look at these topics but also produces articles that are fun to read. Secondary students should enjoy this book also.

*Careers:* Female = 42 Male = 24 Neutral = 3
*Subject Categories:* Cont. Issues/Curr. Events; Essays/Short Stories; Women's Studies

**7.48 The Loon Feather.** Iola Fuller. New York: Harcourt, Brace & World, 1940. 419 p.

A beautifully written story told through the eyes of an Ojibway girl that sensitively portrays the relationships between Native American people and white settlers—traders, voyageurs and fur trappers—in the North Country during the early 1800s. Oneta's life becomes inexorably bound to the white world after her father, Tecumseh, dies and her mother marries Pierre, a fur company employee and a Frenchman with an aristocratic background. When Oneta is 12, her mother dies unexpectedly, and she chooses to remain with her stepfather rather than return to her mother's people. Much to her surprise, Oneta is sent to be educated in a convent in Quebec. When she returns home after 12 years, outwardly she is a refined and educated young woman, but inwardly she has retained many of her Ojibway beliefs. These beliefs and the courage imparted to her from her childhood help save the lives of her white family during an uprising caused by her stepfather's cruel and insulting treatment of a Native American trapper.

*Careers:* Female = 10 Male = 42 Neutral = 15
*Subject Categories:* American Ethnic Minority; Cultural Heritage; History

**7.49 Women Working: An Anthology of Stories and Poems.** Nancy Hoffman and Florence Howe (eds.). Old Westbury, NY: The Feminist Press, 1979. 264 p. Paper.

An excellent collection of 34 short stories and poems about women working: in the office, in the factory and at home, as artists, political activists, servants and professionals. More than half the selections focus on women doing unpaid work, which commonly goes unrecognized as "work." Many unknown women writers are represented, as well as better known authors such as Willa Cather and Sholem Asch. Interesting biographical information on the authors and poets and a thoughtful introduction to each section.

*Careers:* Female = 83 Male = 54 Neutral = 18
*Subject Categories:* Anthologies; Essays/Short Stories; Literature by Women; Poetry/Rhyme; Women's Studies

**7.50 Black Artists of the New Generation.** Elton C. Fax. New York: Dodd, Mead, 1977. 361 p. $9.95.

In this follow-up to *Seventeen Black Artists*, Elton Fax (a black artist) profiles nine women and 11 men, black artists of a new generation. The artists come from virtually every section of the country with widely divergent backgrounds and different modes of artistic expression. In every case, however, they share the experience of being black in America and a determination to follow a dream. Readers of all races will be inspired by their stories.

*Careers:* Female = 66 Male = 107 Neutral = 27
*Subject Categories:* American Ethnic Minority; Autobiography/Biography; Careers; Cultural Heritage; Fine Arts

**7.51 Dreams in Harrison Railroad Park.** Nellie Wong. Berkeley, CA: Kelsey Street Press, 1977. 45 p. $3.75. Paper.

Through her poems, Nellie Wong shares the poignant dreams of her mother and other recent Chinese immigrants who long for life as they remember it back in China. She also writes of the frustration and self-contempt felt by many caught between two worlds—struggling to be Americans and renouncing their Chinese ancestry on the one hand, but recognizing the impossibility and undesirability of giving up their cultural heritage on the other. One feels the reverence Nellie has for her parents and ancestors as well as the anger at the reality of being a minority woman in the United States.

*Careers:* Female = 2 Male = 5 Neutral = 5
*Subject Categories:* American Ethnic Minority; Cultural Heritage; Poetry/Rhyme

**7.52 Women and Fiction: Short Stories by and about Women.** Susan Cahill (ed.). New York: New American Library, 1975. 379 p. $2.95. Paper.

*Women and Fiction* provides the reader with a very rich portrait of the lives of women from all walks of life. This selection of short stories by some of our most creative modern writers will especially appeal to readers from high school age on up. The ironies, tragedies, joys and day-to-day experiences of women from all socioeconomic strata of society are portrayed. The introduction and brief biographical sketch of each of the 26 authors also add to the reader's understanding of the struggle which many of these writers experienced to become career fiction writers.

*Careers:* Female = 50 Male = 46 Neutral = 27
*Subject Categories:* American Ethnic Minority; Health/Human Development; Essays/Short Stories; Literature by Women; Women's Studies

**7.53 Jacob Have I Loved.** Katherine Paterson. New York: Thomas Y. Crowell, 1980. 215 p. $8.95.

Growing up on a tiny Chesapeake Bay island during World War II, 13-year-old Louise fights inner battles of her own. She feels that her twin sister is the loved and pampered one, and she hates her for it. Rebelling against a strict religious upbringing, she feels hated even by God. Because of the war, she is temporarily allowed to have an occupation normally closed to women. When the war ends, however, her plans to become a doctor are discouraged because she is a woman. Slowly, Louise begins to find her own identity and a valued place in the world of work and love.

*Careers:* Female = 12 Male = 24 Neutral = 4
*Subject Categories:* Families/Friendship; Health/Human Development

**7.54 Ludell's New York Time.** Brenda Wilkinson. New York: Harper & Row, 1980. 184 p. $8.95.

The third in a series of books about Ludell, a black girl from the South. After her grandmother's death, Ludell is forced to live with her mother in New York City. There, she has to deal with homesickness, separation from her fiance, a clash between her "country" values and city sophistication and a different kind of racial prejudice.

*Careers:* Female = 19 Male = 17 Neutral = 11
*Subject Categories:* American Ethnic Minority; Families/ Friendship; Health/Human Development

**7.55 I Love Myself When I Am Laughing.** Alice Walker (ed.). Old Westbury, NY: The Feminist Press, 1979. 313 p. $6.95. Paper.

Subtitled *A Zora Neale Hurston Reader*, this volume represents autobiography, folklore, reportage, essays, articles and fiction from the pen of the late black writer. Zora Neale Hurston was a brilliant writer; yet she died penniless in a Florida welfare home having had to fight for recognition as a legitimate "voice" throughout her career. Her stories reflect a deep sense of racial pride, the inequality between men and women and the basic strength of women. Someone described Zora Neale Hurston as "a person who is not humbled by second place." The description also fits the women Hurston writes about. A "must" book for senior high students.

*Careers:* Female = 31 Male = 57 Neutral = 22
*Subject Categories:* American Ethnic Minority; Autobiography/ Biography; Cultural Heritage; Essays/Short Stories; Literature by Women

**7.56 Maria Montessori: Knight of the Child.** Bruno Leone. St. Paul, MN: Greenhaven Press, 1978. 58 p.

An interesting and informative biography about one of the most remarkable innovators in the field of education—Maria Montessori. In addition to introducing a new method of teaching children, she became their champion and challenged society to recognize the dignity and social rights of children. Dr. Montessori became Italy's first woman doctor, was honored twice as a candidate for the Nobel Peace Prize and by the end of her illustrious life was renowned and respected throughout the world for her efforts.

*Careers:* Female = 14 Male = 13 Neutral = 5
*Subject Categories:* Autobiography/Biography; Health/Human Development

**7.57 Women Who Shaped History.** Henrietta Buckmaster. New York: Macmillan, 1966. 181 p. $1.95. Paper.

The nineteenth century reflected a turbulent social order in America; turmoil and bloodshed resulted from the conflict over the monolithic slavery order in the South and the industrial development of the North. Powerful protests against the inequalities of the time resulted from the clashing of these dual systems. Women had few legal rights; racial injustice was rampant; and the need for medical and penal reform was emerging. Among the dedicated people who fought for reform were six remarkable women who helped shape the history of America—Dorthea Dix, Prudence Crandall, Elizabeth Cady Stanton, Elizabeth Blackwell, Harriet Tubman and Mary Baker Eddy. These women refused to accept the inequities of their society and therefore established a marked effect upon their own era and the course of American history.

*Careers:* Female = 36 Male = 56 Neutral = 36
*Subject Categories:* American Ethnic Minority; Autobiography/ Biography; History; Women's Studies

**7.58 Rose Kennedy: No Time for Tears.** Carol Bauer Church. Minneapolis, MN: Greenhaven Press, 1976. 79 p.

This life story of Rose Kennedy is presented in a precise and refreshing manner. Rose Kennedy's life has been many-faceted and her determination to maintain her strength, faith and family's spirit in the face of adversity, tragedy and struggle is inspiring and challenging to the reader.

*Careers:* Female = 6 Male = 21 Neutral = 6
*Subject Categories:* Autobiography/Biography; Families/ Friendship; Religion/Mythology

**7.59 Roll of Thunder, Hear My Cry.** Mildred D. Taylor. New York: Dial, 1976. 276 p. $8.95.

Set in Mississippi at the height of the Depression, this Newbery Medal book is the story of a young black girl, Cassie Logan, and her family. Cassie has been raised to be independent and unafraid by parents who are proud of the land they own and are determined not to lose it, their humanity or their self-respect during turbulent times.

*Careers:* Female = 3 Male = 14 Neutral = 8
*Subject Categories:* American Ethnic Minority; Families/ Friendship

**7.60ˣ Nothing but a Dog.** Bobbi Katz. Old Westbury, NY: The Feminist Press, 1972. 30 p. Paper.

Sex neutral presentation of the theme that no *thing* can replace a dog. Whimsical illustrations add to the appeal of this book to young readers. Although the child-dog relationship is somewhat idealized, this picture book is highly recommended as nonsexist material for primary-grade students.

*Careers:* None shown
*Subject Categories:* Animals; Picture Book

**7.61 Motherlove: Stories by Women about Motherhood.** Stephanie Spinner (ed.). New York: Dell, 1978. 249 p. $2.25. Paper.

This excellent collection of short stories by women about motherhood includes Colette's "Bastienne's Child"; Gail Godwin's "Dream Children"; Katherine Mansfield's "At Lehmann's"; Penelope Gilliat's "Come Back If It Doesn't Get Better"; Alice Walker's "Everyday Use"; Jean Stafford's "Cops and Robbers"; Nadine Gorimer's "A Chip of Glass Ruby"; Joanne Greenburg's "Hunting Season"; Rosellen Brown's "Good Housekeeping"; Maxine Kingston's "Shaman"; Mary Lavin's "Happiness"; Joyce Carol Oates' "The Children"; Edna O'Brien's "Cords"; Merrill Joan Gerber's "Forty Watts"; Tillie Olsen's "I Stand Here Ironing"; and Grace Paley's "Faith in a Tree." The stories are about the deepest feelings of motherhood and are touching, funny, revealing and at times brutally honest. Oates' "The Children" contains a particularly violent description of child abuse.

*Careers:* Female = 24 Male = 38 Neutral = 14
*Subject Categories:* Families/Friendship; Health/Human Development; Anthologies; Essays/Short Stories; Literature by Women; Women's Studies

**7.62 Cameras and Courage: Margaret Bourke-White.** Iris Noble. New York: Julian Messner, 1973. 189 p.

"Face your fears—and *do* something," Margaret Bourke-White was taught as a child. "Maggie" became a fearless doer; world-renowned for her sensitive photographic interpretations of war, revolution and poverty. At the peak of her career she battled Parkinson's disease with the same courage she had summoned as bombs fell around her; she was responsible for bringing that illness "out of the closet." Well-written biography of a remarkable woman.

*Careers:* Female = 21 Male = 60 Neutral = 38
*Subject Categories:* Autobiography/Biography; Careers; Fine Arts; The Handicapped

**7.63 Jenny Kimura.** Betty Cavanna. New York: William Morrow, 1964. 217 p.

Jenny Kimura Smith has lived the first 16 years of her life in Japan with her Japanese mother and American father. At the beginning of a summer visit with her American grandmother in the United States, Jenny feels caught between two worlds; she is considered "strange" by both the majority of Japanese at home and by the Americans she meets. All Jenny can do is follow her father's advice to "be herself." In having the courage to do so, she learns the real meaning of having "the best of both worlds." In a sensitive, nonjudgmental manner, the book examines traditional female/male roles and attitudes in both cultures, as well as differences in perception between age groups.

*Careers:* Female = 13 Male = 25 Neutral = 20
*Subject Categories:* American Ethnic Minority; Cultural Heritage; Families/Friendship; Foreign Countries; Health/Human Development

**7.64 What Can She Be? A Geologist.** Gloria and Esther Goldreich. New York: Lothrop, Lee & Shepard, 1976. 47 p.

This book is an introduction to a geologist's work. The main character teaches geology and helps choose sites for bridges and highways. Black and white photographs show her at work and help to explain the tools she uses.

*Careers:* Female = 3 Male = 3 Neutral = 0
*Subject Categories:* Careers; Science/Technology

**7.65 The Woman Warrior: Memories of a Girlhood among Ghosts.** Maxine Hong Kingston. New York: Random House, 1977. 243 p. $2.95. Paper. (Originally published by Alfred A. Knopf, 1976.)

Engrossing essays about growing up as a Chinese American girl in California. There is a wonderful mixture of tales and dreams conveying cultural mores and beliefs with a poignant picture of life as an American-born Chinese girl trying to reconcile the traditions of the old with the need to survive in the new. Both anger and compassion come through in the telling; the reader can sense the constant dilemma the author felt as a child of two worlds.

*Careers:* Female = 19 Male = 14 Neutral = 18
*Subject Categories:* American Ethnic Minority; Cultural Heritage; Foreign Countries; Essays/Short Stories

**7.66 From Parlor to Prison.** Sherna Gluck (ed.). New York: Random House, 1976. 285 p. $3.95. Paper.

Five American suffragists talk about their lives in this collection of oral histories. All five were involved in the early twentieth century suffrage movement. Neither prominent leaders nor "unsung heroes" of the movement, their stories lend another dimension to the history of the struggle for women's rights.

*Careers:* Female = 69 Male = 74 Neutral = 16

*Subject Categories:* Autobiography/Biography; History; Women's Studies

**7.67 Go Well, Stay Well.** Toeckey Jones. New York: Harper & Row, 1979. 202 p. $7.95.

Becky and Candy are two 15-year-old girls living in South Africa. Becky is black and Candy is a wealthy white girl. Under South Africa's apartheid government, friendship between the two poses many seemingly insurmountable obstacles. An excellent story about politics, prejudice and understanding.

*Careers:* Female = 7 Male = 11 Neutral = 5
*Subject Categories:* Cont. Issues/Curr. Events; Cultural Heritage; Foreign Countries

**7.68 Women in Sports: Swimming.** Diana C. Gleasner. New York: Harvey House, 1975. 63 p.

These five stories about young women who are swimmers reveal the enormous amount of skill, self-discipline, stamina and fortitude involved in their sport. These young women are competitive and determined to excel. This book is highly recommended to highlight the contributions of women athletes.

*Careers:* Female = 2 Male = 5 Neutral = 1
*Subject Categories:* Sports

**7.69ˣ Song of Sedna.** Robert D. SanSouci. Garden City, NY: Doubleday, 1981. 27 p. $8.95.

A retelling of an old legend about the transformation of an Eskimo maiden into the goddess of the sea. Sedna is strongwilled and skillful, and she must call on her courage to meet a series of challenges lying between her and her destiny. Having won the throne, she proves she can retain it by exercising wisdom and mercy as well. Splendid illustrations dramatize the interplay between humans and spirits, both evil and good, and evoke the richness of the Eskimo's culture. Subject matter and illustrations make this book more appropriate for young readers.

*Careers:* Female = 1 Male = 1 Neutral = 1
*Subject Categories:* American Ethnic Minority; Cultural Heritage; Fantasy, Folk & Fairy Tales; Picture Book

**7.70 She Never Looked Back: Margaret Mead in Samoa.** Sam and Beryl Epstein. New York: Coward, McCann & Geoghegan, 1980. 54 p. $5.99.

An informative, well-illustrated account of the nine months of field work by Margaret Mead in 1925 that led to her enormously popular book, *Coming of Age in Samoa.* The book contains interesting information about anthropology and treats the Samoan culture respectfully. It also portrays Mead as a courageous and committed young woman who considered her life's work to be adding to the world's store of knowledge.

*Careers:* Female = 8 Male = 16 Neutral = 12
*Subject Categories:* Autobiography/Biography; Behavioral Science; Cultural Heritage; Foreign Countries; Health/Human Development

**7.71 The Night Journey.** Kathryn Lasky. New York: Frederick Warne, 1981. 150 p. $8.95.

Rachel, a contemporary 13-year-old, finds herself living an almost second, underground life through her great-grandmother Sashie's reminiscences. Sashie's Jewish family escaped from Tsarist Russia when Rachel was just nine years old. A superbly told story of risk, danger, cooperation and resourcefulness juxtaposed with the present. The book highlights the reality of religious persecution, pride in the continuity of one's culture and the many roads to freedom. Notable for demonstrating nurturing fathers and the qualities linking four generations of women. Exciting and enriching reading.

*Careers:* Female = 8 Male = 11 Neutral = 7
*Subject Categories:* Cultural Heritage; Families/Friendship; Foreign Countries; Mystery/Adventure

**7.72 Country of Broken Stone.** Nancy Bond. New York: Atheneum, 1980. 271 p. $10.95.

"In the course of her 14 years, Penelope had developed considerable personal resources," and she needs them all in this crucial summer at Wintergas, an isolated country house in the north of England. Penny is not only sorting out the relationship and responsibilities of an expanded family—an American stepmother and her three children grafted onto her life with her charming, somewhat self-centered father and her rebellious older brother—but she's struggling to achieve friendship with Randall, one of the local farm boys. Through him, she becomes increasingly aware of the violent history and ominous present of the countryside; past and present culminate in a dramatic climax that tests all of Penelope's loyalties. The story provides a good example of how prejudice originates and demonstrates the personal effort required to dissolve barriers between people. In addition to the vivid portrayal of Northumberland, the book conveys an excellent understanding of relationships among diverse, hardly perfect, but always real, human beings.

*Careers:* Female = 10 Male = 17 Neutral = 10
*Subject Categories:* Families/Friendship; Foreign Countries; Health/Human Development; Mystery/Adventure

**7.73 The Trouble with Princesses.** Christie Harris. New York: Atheneum, 1980. 170 p. $9.95.

Seven stories representing folktale princesses of the new world—the Northwest coastal Indians who carried the royal bloodlines of the great families in the clans. The trouble with these princesses (as in their European counterparts) is that sometimes they were too spirited to stand by and do nothing in a bad situation; often their suitors had to accomplish "impossible" tasks to win them; sometimes they fell into dire straits, and it took magic to rescue them; and at times they defied their parents and insisted on choosing their own mates. The book is an excellent contribution to Native American legends. In two of the stories, the princesses passively await rescue by action-oriented males.

*Careers:* Female = 4 Male = 8 Neutral = 4
*Subject Categories:* American Ethnic Minority; Cultural Heritage; Fantasy, Folk & Fairy Tales; Mystery/Adventure

# Reading Grade Level 8–Dale-Chall Formula

**8.1 American Painter in Paris: A Life of Mary Cassatt.**
Ellen Wilson. New York: Farrar, Straus & Giroux, 1971.
197 p. $4.95.

The story of a single-minded artist whose work won her the critical acclaim of her contemporaries in France and is among America's finest painting. Mary Cassatt accomplished this at a time when women were discouraged from pursuing careers.

*Careers:* Female = 17 Male = 31 Neutral = 22
*Subject Categories:* Biography; Fine Arts

**8.2ˣ Miss Bianca.** Margery Sharp. New York: Dell,
1977. 152 p. $1.25. Paper. (Originally published by Little,
Brown, 1962.)

Miss Bianca, a white mouse with lots of common sense who is chairperson of the Mouse Prisoners Aid Society, rescues a little girl from a wicked duchess. Although there is some sex role stereotyping throughout the book—"witchy" females, males can't cook—Miss Bianca is strong and brave and uses her wits. This is an excellent read-aloud story for younger children.

*Careers:* Female = 8 Male = 22 Neutral = 6
*Subject Categories:* Animals; Fantasy, Folk & Fairy Tales;
Mystery/Adventure

**8.3 Famous Spies.** Frank Surge. Minneapolis, MN:
Lerner, 1969. 62 p. $3.95.

This book depicts the lives and exploits of six male and eight female spies beginning with Delilah and ending with Banda, Mata Hari's daughter. Although there is some stereotyping of women—Delilah learns Samson's secrets by "nagging" him and "applying her arts"—some very courageous, inventive and practical female spies are also portrayed.

*Careers:* Female = 17 Male = 34 Neutral = 18
*Subject Categories:* Biography; Foreign Countries; Mystery/
Adventure

**8.4 I, Charlotte Forten, Black and Free.** Polly Longsworth. New York: Thomas Y. Crowell, 1970. 233 p.
$6.95.

During the mid-nineteenth century, blacks, even those born to free and prosperous families, were subjected to prejudice and discrimination. This biography of Charlotte Forten, an outstanding black woman who became a teacher and part of the antislavery movement, provides insight into the situation of blacks of that period, both free and slaves.

*Careers:* Female = 9 Male = 52 Neutral = 29

*Subject Categories:* American Ethnic Minority; Biography;
Health/Human Development; History

**8.5 Patriots in Petticoats.** Patricia Edwards Cline. New
York: Dodd, Mead, 1976. 144 p. $4.95.

Stirring biographies of women and girls during the Revolutionary War and the War of 1812, which show the vital role they played in the fight for America's independence.

*Careers:* Female = 13 Male = 23 Neutral = 8
*Subject Categories:* Biography; History; Mystery/Adventure

**8.6 Women Who Win.** Francene Sabin. New York:
Random House, 1975. 166 p. $3.95.

Biographical sketches of 14 women athletes which portray the women's athletic prowess as well as the psychological and emotional obstacles that confronted them in their athletic careers. This book provides good role models for girls interested in pursuing a career in sports.

*Careers:* Female = 11 Male = 21 Neutral = 0
*Subject Categories:* Biography; Sports

**8.7 American Women in Sports.** Phyllis Hollander. New
York: Grosset & Dunlap, 1972. 112 p.

A series of brief sketches of 52 American women athletes, from the early pioneers who had to overcome society's disapproval of women athletes, to the athletes of today who have entered and excelled in new areas of competition as well as fought for equal professional standing and remuneration.

*Careers:* Female = 29 Male = 36 Neutral = 13
*Subject Categories:* Biography; Sports

**8.8 Why Am I So Miserable If These Are the Best Years
of My Life?** Andrea Boroff Eagan. Philadelphia, PA: J.P.
Lippincott, 1976. 241 p. $7.95.

A positive, helpful guide for young women to learn how to have more control over their lives, to enjoy their school years and to make good choices for the future. The author frankly discusses sex and birth control in a clear, concise and objective way. Physiological, emotional and social aspects of sex are thoroughly discussed in regard to both girls and boys. The book emphasizes throughout the need to develop good decision-making skills that will affect future career plans, interpersonal relationships and one's overall happiness. The author has a good sense of humor and enormous respect for young women's potential for growth.

*Careers:* Female = 14 Male = 7 Neutral = 20

*Subject Categories:* Families/Friendship; Health/Human Development; Women's Studies

**8.9 Young and Female.** Pat Ross (ed.). New York: Vintage Sundial, 1972. 107 p. $2.95. Paper. (Originally published by Random House, 1972.)

An anthology of easy-to-read, first-person accounts of turning points in the lives of eight American women: Shirley MacLaine, Shirley Chisholm, Dorothy Day, Emily Hahn, Margaret Sanger, Althea Gibson, Edna Ferber and Margaret Bourke-White. The selections have been taken from the women's autobiographies, where they describe with spirit, self-confidence and humor how they overcame the limited roles traditionally assigned to girls. Appropriate for free reading or as supplemental classroom text.

*Careers:* Female = 37 Male = 34 Neutral = 17
*Subject Categories:* American Ethnic Minority; Autobiography; Careers; Women's Studies

**8.10 Women of Wonder: Science Fiction Stories by Women about Women.** Pamela Sargent (ed.). New York: Vintage, 1974. 285 p. $1.95. Paper.

An excellent anthology of 12 intriguing and well-written science fiction stories by women, in which women characters play major roles. In addition to biographical sketches and brief introductions to the authors and stories, the editor provides a thoughtful, well-researched discussion on the role of women in the time-honored, male preserve of science fiction. The introduction provides an excellent resource for a class of women and science fiction or other literature units focusing on the science fiction genre. Several stories explore changing sex roles and sexual mores and are perhaps most appropriate for mature readers; one of the stories portrays a particularly brutal rape.

*Careers:* Female = 61 Male = 51 Neutral = 43
*Subject Categories:* Anthologies; Essays/Short Stories; Literature by Women; Science Fiction; Women's Studies

**8.11 The Prime of Miss Jean Brodie.** Muriel Sparks. New York: Dell, 1978. 156 p. $1.25. Paper. (Originally published by J.B. Lippincott, 1961.)

*The Prime of Miss Jean Brodie* probes with skill the halcyon years of a fiercely independent and unorthodox schoolteacher and her relationship with six favorite pupils. How Miss Brodie enjoys, exploits and ultimately becomes a victim of her vaunted "prime" forms the basis of this novel.

*Careers:* Female = 14 Male = 12 Neutral = 3
*Subject Categories:* Foreign Countries; Health/Human Development; Literature by Women

**8.12 Law and the New Woman.** Mary McHugh. New York: Franklin Watts, 1975. 107 p.

This book is part of an exciting new series designed to help young women choose lifestyles and careers best suited to their interests and talents. The author encourages young women to pursue a law career if they have the fundamental qualifications: good LSAT scores, high grade-point average and a sincere interest in investing the time and energy in a legal education. She describes law school and the many kinds of job opportunities open to law graduates. The author further explains that law is a good career to choose if one is interested in women's issues because it touches so many different areas, such as education, politics and business.

*Careers:* Female = 12 Male = 7 Neutral = 13
*Subject Categories:* Careers

**8.13 Kathe Kollwitz: Life in Art.** Mina C. Klein and H. Arthur Klein. New York: Schocken Books, 1976. 182 p. $6.95. Paper. (Originally published by Holt, Rinehart & Winston, 1972.)

This is the life of Kathe Kollwitz (1867–1945) told through her art. The title of the book is apt, as the artist's life and art were so completely intertwined. Kathe Kollwitz worked in a number of media, including drawing, etching, lithographing, sculpting and woodcutting. Her work expressed her personal concern with Germany's social ills of her time. Probably the most intense experience in Kollwitz's life that was reflected in her art was the death of one of her sons in World War I. Her priorities, she claimed, were her children, her companion-husband and her work. The story of the last years of Kollwitz's life and art gives a devastating perspective on the repression of art in Hitler's Germany. The book is a valuable lesson in art, feelings, and history.

*Careers:* Female = 8 Male = 37 Neutral = 8
*Subject Categories:* Biography; Fine Arts; Foreign Countries; History

**8.14 A Very Easy Death.** Simone de Beauvoir. New York: Warner Books, 1977. 123 p. $1.95. Paper. (Originally published by Librairie Gallimard, 1973.)

Within this work the author explores through her mother's dying and death her relationship to her mother, the process of dying and the mystery of human existence. It is a powerfully moving book which examines the day-by-day tragedy of the death of a person who values each final instant.

*Careers:* Female = 6 Male = 5 Neutral = 1
*Subject Categories:* Behavioral Science; Families/Friendship; Health/Human Development; Literature by Women

**8.15 George Sand.** Ruth Jordan. London: Constable, 1976. 367 p.

A biography of Aurore Dupin de Francueil Dudevant who, under the name of George Sand, became one of the best-known literary figures in nineteenth century France. Although the biography is somewhat dry and would provide heavy reading for a high school student, the author provides a well-researched look at the life, works and personal relationships of this complex and controversial woman. The numerous excerpts from the writings of George Sand, as well as from the writings of her peers and contemporaries, are particularly intriguing.

*Careers:* Female = 27 Male = 73 Neutral = 56
*Subject Categories:* Biography; Foreign Countries; History; Literature by Women

**8.16 Enchantress from the Stars.** Sylvia Louise Engdahl. New York: Atheneum, 1970. 275 p. $.95. Paper.

In this fascinating science fiction story, a team of field agents from the anthropological service of a superior civilization joins forces with two Younglings on a dangerous mission. Together they save Andrecia, a medieval earth-like planet, from colonization by the Imperial forces and their fire-eating, dragon-like rock crusher. Although Elana is only a first-phase student at the elite and rigorous Service Academy, she stows away on the mission and ultimately comes to learn she has the bravery and dedication required of all agents by the Oath—even if that should include the sacrifice of her life.

*Careers:* Female = 3 Male = 17 Neutral = 18
*Subject Categories:* Mystery/Adventure; Science Fiction

**8.17 A Room of One's Own.** Virginia Woolf. New York: Harvest/Harcourt, Brace, Jovanovich, 1929. 118 p. $2.45. Paper.

A delightful essay exploring the reasons why women haven't contributed more greatly in quantity and quality to the writing of fiction. In Woolf's view there is a very practical reason for this: a great writer needs a fixed income and a room of one's own, neither of which has been accessible to women.

*Careers:* Female = 20 Male = 26 Neutral = 32
*Subject Categories:* Literature by Women; Women's Studies

**8.18 The Yellow Wallpaper.** Charlotte Perkins Gilman. Old Westbury, NY: The Feminist Press, 1973. 63 p. $1.95. Paper. (Originally published by Small, Maynard, 1899.)

This fascinating short story about a woman's descent into madness offers a penetrating look at the debilitating and devastating roles of submission forced on many nineteenth century women in marriage. The tersely written account provides an atmosphere of increasing tension as the narrator slips deeper into madness to escape the pressures of her times. An excellent afterword discussing the work itself, as well as the life and times of the author, is provided.

*Careers:* Female = 5 Male = 6 Neutral = 2
*Subject Categories:* Behavioral Science; Health/Human Development; Literature by Women; Women's Studies

**8.19ˣ Fanshen the Magic Bear.** Becky Sarah. Stanford, CA: New Seed Press, 1973. 22 p. Paper.

Laura rides her pony, Marigold, around the kingdom collecting rent for the king from all of the people. Because the people are poor and must sacrifice to pay the rent, Laura begins to dislike her job. Fanshen, a legendary she-bear, appears to her and encourages Laura to stop collecting rent for the king. Laura leads a protest, and as a result, the kingdom is divided into parcels for the people. A positive story of an assertive girl who takes initiative to rectify an unjust situation. Print size and illustrations make this book more appropriate for primary or young intermediate readers.

*Careers:* Female = 3 Male = 4 Neutral = 0
*Subject Categories:* Fantasy, Folk & Fairy Tales

**8.20 And All Her Paths Were Peace.** Emil Lengyel. Nashville, TN: Thomas Nelson, 1975. 136 p.

When Bertha von Suttner won the Nobel Peace Prize in 1905, she was the first woman peace laureate and the first woman to receive any Nobel award unshared with a man. Von Suttner was born into an aristocratic family in Austria in 1843 and grew up there, enjoying music, literature and languages. The travels of her middle years exposed her to the wars of Europe and Asia. She developed the viewpoint that nations could live peaceably by working together to settle differences and rejected the notion that gathering weapons would be a deterrent to war. Von Suttner lectured avidly and prolifically and wrote novels on her antiwar theme. Lengyel's account of Bertha von Suttner's life includes the stories of her successes in a 40-year loving

relationship with her husband and in her world-renowned career.

*Careers:* Female = 8 Male = 27 Neutral = 3
*Subject Categories:* Autobiography/Biography; Foreign Countries; History; Women's Studies

**8.21 Deadline.** Kathleen A. Begley. New York: Dell, 1977. 169 p. $1.50. Paper.

Kathleen Begley's story of her experiences as a newspaper reporter is a fascinating behind-the-scenes look at a large daily newspaper. It also is an example of the hard work and determination it takes to become a good reporter. Begley obviously loves her job but does not try to glamorize it for the reader.

*Careers:* Female = 22 Male = 52 Neutral = 28
*Subject Categories:* Careers

**8.22 Doctors for the People.** Elizabeth Levy and Mara Miller. New York: Dell, 1979. 111 p. $1.25. Paper. (Originally published by Alfred A. Knopf, 1977.)

Profiles of two women and three men doctors. All not only care for but care about their patients, and they have placed commitment to patient care above anything else. One of the women is a black surgeon and legislator; the other is a feminist gynecologist. The men include a geneticist, a family practitioner and a general practitioner who works with migrant farm workers. In addition to the individual profiles, the book describes a unique clinic for teenagers which provides a wide range of medical, psychological and vocational services.

*Careers:* Female = 11 Male = 15 Neutral = 21
*Subject Categories:* Careers; Health/Human Development

**8.23 The Cancer Lady: Maud Slye and Her Heredity Studies.** J.J. McCoy. New York: Thomas Nelson, 1977. 184 p. $6.95.

This is a story of cancer research—more than a biography of geneticist Maud Slye. Other than glimpses of her poetry and the fact that she cried over the deaths of laboratory mice, the author tells almost nothing about her personal life and nothing at all about her childhood. The reader does find out a lot about her work: cancer research. Maud Slye's mouse studies proved that heredity was a factor in cancer, a theory that was not accepted by the majority of cancer researchers in her day. Working with little money, assistance or support of any kind, Slye devoted her life to something that is a common diagnostic tool today. Because of its technical style, this book may be most appropriate for serious secondary science students.

*Careers:* Female = 1 Male = 17 Neutral = 11
*Subject Categories:* Autobiography/Biography; Careers; Science/Technology

**8.24 The Gender Trap: A Closer Look at Sex Roles (Book 1: Education and Work).** Carol Adams and Rae Laurikietis. London: Academy Press, 1977. 116 p. $4.50. Paper. (Originally published by Quartet Books, 1976.)

Designed for high school-aged young people, this book deals with basic issues of women and work. It discusses how parents and the educational system mold and perpetuate stereotyped behaviors and career expectations for girls and boys. It provides statistics, quotes, cartoons, interviews and stories focusing on the world of work from a feminist perspective. Although adapted for American audiences, this book was written by two English authors and provides the English outlook.

*Careers:* Female = 57 Male = 40 Neutral = 7
*Subject Categories:* Behavioral Science; Careers; Women's Studies

**8.25 Marie Curie.** Robert Reid. New York: New American Library, 1974. 284 p. $2.25. Paper.

A well-researched biography of the famous chemist, physicist and discoverer of radium. Working in a time when higher education was closed to women in her native Poland and male supremacy in science unquestioned, Marie Curie found her own way. Her marriage was an emotional and scientific partnership, and although she had a devoted and close relationship with her two daughters, she never allowed motherhood to derail her from professional goals. She was twice the winner of the Nobel prize and acknowledged around the world for her contribution to science. Not one of her achievements came easily, but every one was based solely on merit.

*Careers:* Female = 26 Male = 58 Neutral = 34
*Subject Categories:* Autobiography/Biography; History; Science/Technology

**8.26 I Never Promised You A Rose Garden.** Joanne Greenberg. New York: New American Library, 1964. 256 p. $1.75. Paper. (Originally published by Holt, Rinehart & Winston.)

A sensitive, moving story of the three years Deborah, an emotionally disabled 16-year-old, spends in a mental hospital. Her relationships with her family are crucial to the reasons she is there and to her recovery. These relationships are unravelled through discussions between Deborah and her psychiatrist, who is trying to bring Deborah back to reality from the imaginary world in which she has been living for years—an absorbing journey from madness to reality.

*Careers:* Female = 6 Male = 5 Neutral = 7
*Subject Categories:* Behavioral Science; Families/Friendship; Health/Human Development

**8.27 Careers in Conservation.** Ada and Frank Graham. San Francisco, CA: Sierra Club/Charles Scribner's Sons, 1980. 166 p. $9.95.

Thirteen profiles of women and men who work in conservation. Some work outdoors studying birds, plants and animals; some are in government; others work in a laboratory. Students may not be aware that many of these jobs exist, and the book should encourage anyone who may be interested in the wide area of conservation. An appendix of suggestions and references for the reader who would like to find out more about working in this field is attached.

*Careers:* Female = 17 Male = 50 Neutral = 43
*Subject Categories:* Careers; Science/Technology

**8.28 Male & Female under 18.** Nancy Larrick and Eve Merriam (eds.). New York: Avon, 1973. 188 p. $1.50. Paper.

In 1972, over 2,500 young people responded to a flyer asking them the following questions: What does it mean to be a girl in 1972? Or a boy? What do I think of my parents' roles as mothers and fathers? Or the adults around me as men and women? What do I see as the advantages or disadvantages in my sex role in today's world? How can I make the most of myself as a male or female? Many of the poems and short prose statements they wrote in answer to the questions are included in this book. Ranging from ages 8 to 18, these young people come from every geographic area, economic level and ethnic background. This is an excellent book for free reading or as a catalyst for language arts activities.

*Careers:* Female = 9 Male = 18 Neutral = 4
*Subject Categories:* American Ethnic Minority; Cont. Issues/Curr. Events; Health/Human Development; Poetry/Rhyme

**8.29 Bella Abzug.** Doris Faber. New York: Lothrop, Lee & Shepard, 1976. 156 p.

In this lively book, Doris Faber traces the career of Bella Abzug as student leader, young lawyer, antiwar leader and congresswoman. This book goes behind Abzug's sensational publicity to reveal the ideals and actions that brought her to national attention.

*Careers:* Female = 16 Male = 21 Neutral = 8
*Subject Categories:* Autobiography/Biography; Women's Studies

**8.30 Sea and Earth: The Life of Rachel Carson.** Philip Sterling. New York: Dell, 1974. 189 p. $.95. Paper. (Originally published by Thomas Y. Crowell, 1970.)

Biography of Rachel Carson, the author of *Silent Spring*, which dealt with human abuses of the environment. The biography takes us back to Carson's childhood and the beginnings of her passion for nature. We see the reasons behind her strong desire to write and share her feelings with her readers. An inspiring portrait of how a "quiet woman" can produce a huge impact on current thought.

*Careers:* Female = 17 Male = 29 Neutral = 6
*Subject Categories:* Autobiography/Biography; Cont. Issues/Curr. Events; Science/Technology

**8.31 Martha Quest.** Doris Lessing. New York: New American Library, 1970. 248 p. $3.95. Paper. (Originally published by Simon & Schuster, 1952.)

The first in a five-part series entitled *Children of Violence*, this novel concerns a teenage girl, Martha Quest, who is of British descent growing up in the veld of South Africa in the 1930s. Her parents are farmers and seem to live in a world of regret and disappointment about what might have been. Martha feels nothing but disgust and desire to escape from this "small world," so she goes to the city and finds a secretarial job in a law office. Soon she is swept away by the wild and rebellious social group that frequents The Sports Club. Lessing provides a powerful description of a woman who is odds with others but cannot assert herself or her true feelings. Many women can identify with Martha, her rebellion and attempts at liberation. Many women can identify with Martha and her rebelli Regardless of where she is, she is at odds with others but cannot assert herself or her true feelings. Many women ca Regardless of where she is, she finds herself at odds with those around her but cannot assert herself or her true feelings. who is at odds with others but cannot assert herself or her true feelings. Many women csan identify with Martha and her rebellion.who is at odds with others but cannot assert herself or her true feelings. Many women can identify with Martha and her rebellion.

*Careers:* Female = 26 Male = 25 Neutral = 17
*Subject Categories:* Foreign Countries; History; Literature by Women

**8.32 Gaudy Night.** Dorothy L. Sayers. New York: Avon, 1968. 383 p. $2.50. Paper. (Originally published by Harper & Row, 1936.)

When Harriet Jane attended the Oxford reunion known as the "Gaudy," the prim academic setting was haunted by a rash of bizarre pranks: scrawled obscenities, burnt effigies and poison pen letters—including one that said, "Ask your boyfriend with the title if he likes arsenic in his soup." While Harriet initially undertakes to solve the mystery, she recognizes her own limitations and, in the end, calls in her paramour in stereotypic fashion to solve the case. The look at varying values is interesting even though the book ends on a predictable note.

*Careers:* Female = 19 Male = 14 Neutral = 4
*Subject Categories:* Foreign Countries; Literature by Women; Mystery/Adventure

**8.33 A Time for Everything.** Susan Sallis. New York: Harper & Row, 1979. 218 p. $7.95.

A book about growing up in wartime England. Lily Freeman enters adolescence near the beginning of World War II and matures in many ways by the time it has ended. "Was growing up simply a process of discovering that security was insecure and that infallibility was always supremely fallible?" Lily asks. She finds that her question contains only part of the truth. British "hill country" dialect and references appropriate to the time-frame may be somewhat intimidating for the immature reader.

*Careers:* Female = 7 Male = 21 Neutral = 4
*Subject Categories:* Families/Friendship; Foreign Countries; Health/Human Development

**8.34ˣ Free To Be...You and Me.** Marlo Thomas, et al. (eds.). New York: McGraw-Hill, 1974. 143 p. $6.95. Paper.

A delightful, nonsexist collection of songs, stories, poems and pictures designed to expand young children's personal horizons and dispel myths and limiting stereotypes. Children, parents and teachers will find it both entertaining and thought provoking.

*Careers:* Female = 21 Male = 23 Neutral = 7
*Subject Categories:* Careers; Families/Friendship; Health/Human Development; Fantasy, Folk & Fairy Tales; Poetry/Rhyme

**8.35 Wild Animals, Gentle Women.** Margery Facklam. New York: Harcourt, Brace, Jovanovich, 1978. 127 p. $5.95.

The author reflects an avid interest and respect for the animal world by her portrayal of 11 unusually dedicated and extraordinary women scientists. The book introduces us to the San Diego Zoo's first woman zookeeper; to Ruth Harkness, who in 1936 brought the first panda from the Himalayas into the Western world; to renowned primatologists Jane Goodall, Birute Galdikas and Dian Fossey; and to seven other equally devoted women scientists engaged in their individual pursuits.

*Careers:* Female = 26 Male = 31 Neutral = 54
*Subject Categories:* Animals; Autobiography/Biography; Careers; Science/Technology

**8.36 Breakthrough: Women in Religion.** Betsy Covington Smith. New York: Walker, 1978. 139 p. $7.95.

This is a highly readable and informative account of women who were able to become members of the clergy, the most exclusively male vocation. The lives of five women and their career struggles are examined. Portraits of Protestant, Catholic and Jewish women are examined.

*Careers:* Female = 18 Male = 17 Neutral = 14
*Subject Categories:* Religion/Mythology; Women's Studies

**8.37 Life in the Iron Mills.** Rebecca Harding Davis. Old Westbury, NY: The Feminist Press, 1972. 174 p. $3.50. Paper.

The first part of this book is the short story, "Life in the Iron Mills," originally published in the *Atlantic Monthly* in 1861. The last part is a biographical account of Rebecca Harding Davis written by Tillie Olsen. Contemporary readers may not appreciate or understand the story or the contribution it made to American literature without reading the biographical account. Tillie Olsen quotes a great deal from Rebecca Harding Davis's later writings and shows the reader that she never achieved the degree of greatness shown in her first work probably due to her marriage and family interests.

*Careers:* Female = 11 Male = 16 Neutral = 11
*Subject Categories:* Autobiography/Biography; History; Literature by Women

**8.38 Against Rape.** Andra Medea and Kathleen Thompson. New York: Farrar, Straus & Giroux, 1974. 147 p. $2.25. Paper.

A discussion of the varied aspects of rape: why it happens so commonly, how it affects women's daily lives and why rape rates are skyrocketing. The authors have provided a practical guide for women on how to train for self-defense, how to be alert in the home and on the street, what to do should a rape occur and how to deal with guilt feelings. The information contained in this book is excellent and valuable; however, at times, the authors' anger turns into antimale rhetoric. Especially recommended for teenage hitchhikers.

*Careers:* Female = 1 Male = 8 Neutral = 0
*Subject Categories:* Health/Human Development; Women's Studies

**8.39 The Dollmaker.** Harriette Arnow. New York: Avon, 1972. 608 p. $2.25. Paper. (Originally published by Macmillan Company, 1954.)

This powerful and tragic novel is the story of the emotional destruction of a woman, a family and perhaps a nation. Gertie Nevels, a strong, confident, yet inarticulate woman from the hills of Kentucky, is able to live totally off the land and love every ounce of energy she puts back into it. However, when forced to move with her family to Detroit during World War II, she never adjusts, never regains her confidence and dignity, never has an opportunity to develop her talents and use her strength and energy. She watches her family disintegrate and blames herself for the tragedy that befalls them. This novel presents a compelling picture of a nation of people uprooted and forced to turn on each other in hatred. All the horrors of war, depression, poverty, urban alienation and labor unrest are portrayed.

*Careers:* Female = 14 Male = 48 Neutral = 9
*Subject Categories:* Behavioral Science; Cultural Heritage; History; Literature by Women

**8.40 Hannah Senesh: Her Life and Diary.** Hannah Senesh. New York: Schocken Books, 1973. 257 p. Paper. (Originally published by Hakibbutz Hameuchad Publishing House, 1966.)

Hannah Senesh, Israel's national hero, is remembered as a poet and a martyr. Safe in Palestine during World War II, she volunteered for a mission to help rescue Jews in her native Hungary. She was captured by the Nazis, imprisoned and tortured, and was executed at the age of 23. This book contains the diary she kept from the age of 13, letters to family and comments by her mother and two friends.

*Careers:* Female = 15 Male = 29 Neutral =14
*Subject Categories:* Autobiography/Biography; Cultural Heritage; Foreign Countries; History

**8.41 In Her Own Image: Women Working in the Arts.** Elaine Hedges and Ingrid Wendt. Old Westbury, NY: The Feminist Press, 1980. 301 p. Paper.

Excellent anthology of works of Western women in the arts, represented by selections from their poetry, fiction, autobiographies, essays, journals, letters and photographs of sculpture, paintings, graphics, photography, ceramics, needlework, music and dance. In all these forms, the women are making statements about their view of themselves as women. The book is organized in a way that shows the relationship between women's art and the conditions of women's lives. Each section is introduced with an essay that explores and connects the book's themes, and each artist is introduced with a brief biography.

*Careers:* Female = 105 Male = 67 Neutral = 17
*Subject Categories:* American Ethnic Minority; Fine Arts; Anthologies; Literature by Women; Poetry/Rhyme; Women's Studies

**8.42 New Women in Medicine.** Kathleen Bowman. Mankato, MN: Creative Education, 1976. 47 p.

Brief biographies of seven notable women in the medical field: Mary Calderon, sex education expert; Kathryn Nichol, pediatrician; Anna Ellington, neurologist; Mary Louise Robbins, medical researcher; Estelle Rainey, endocrinologist; Margaret Hewitt, nurse-midwife; and Elisabeth Kubler-Ross, international consultant on death and dying. Unlike most of the exemplary books in the "New Woman" series, only one of the characters in this book, Anna Ellington, is an ethnic minority (black). Book provides portraits of excellent role models.

*Careers:* Female = 24 Male = 10 Neutral = 15
*Subject Categories:* Autobiography/Biography; Careers; Science/Technology; Women's Studies

**8.43 New Women in Entertainment.** Kathleen Bowman. Mankato, MN: Creative Education, 1976. 47 p.

Short biographies of seven women who have been highly successful in various fields of entertainment: Lily Tomlin, Buffy Sainte-Marie, Judy Collins, Cicely Tyson, Valerie Harper, Diana Ross, and Melvina Reynolds. The women presented are strong, positive role models who have contributed much to society as well as to art.

*Careers:* Female = 31 Male = 15 Neutral = 9
*Subject Categories:* American Ethnic Minority; Autobiography/ Biography; Careers; Fine Arts; Women's Studies

**8.44 Saturday's Child.** Suzanne Seed. Chicago: J. Philip O'Hara, 1973. 158 p. $4.95. Paper.

Interviews with women representing 37 careers in four areas: arts and communications; science and medicine; trades, services and businesses; and commerce and government. Women who work as sportswriters, oceanographers, carpenters and city planners tell how they got started, what they do on the job and why they enjoy their chosen careers. The book is illustrated with photographs and contains a section on where to write for more information. This is an excellent idea generator for students who are uncertain about a career.

*Careers:* Female = 93 Male = 40 Neutral = 37
*Subject Categories:* Careers; Women's Studies

# Reading Grade Level 9–Dale-Chall Formula

**9.1 Eloquent Crusader: Ernestine Rose.** Yuri Suhl. New York: Messner, 1970. 188 p. $3.34.

Biography of Ernestine Rose, who helped organize women of America into a powerful instrument for change. Born in a Polish ghetto, she rebelled against the traditional place of women in her society, emigrated to America and became active in the women's rights and antislavery movements.

*Careers:* Female = 2 Male = 18 Neutral = 5
*Subject Categories:* Biography; History

**9.2 Fanny Kemble's America.** John Anthony Scott. New York: Thomas Y. Crowell, 1973. 137 p. $6.95.

The story of Fanny Kemble, an actress, writer and remarkable woman who battled against slavery and injustices in human relations. Although her convictions cost her dearly, she left a record of her time which has enduring value for our own.

*Careers:* Female = 13 Male = 33 Neutral = 12
*Subject Categories:* Biography; Health/Human Development; History

**9.3 Four Women in a Violent Time.** Deborah Crawford. New York: Crown Publishers, 1970. 183 p. $6.95.

The biographies of four outstanding women of the seventeenth century—Mary Dyer, Anne Hutchinson, Lady Deborah Moody and Penelope Stout. Dyer and Hutchinson fought against religious intolerance; Lady Moody built a community based on equal rights; and Stout survived misfortune and a brutal beating to live and prosper until the age of 110.

*Careers:* Female = 11 Male = 64 Neutral = 42
*Subject Categories:* Biography; History

**9.4 MS.—M.D.** D.X. Fenten. Philadelphia, PA: Westminster Press, 1975. 121 p. $5.25.

This book provides a realistic description of how a young woman can prepare for a career in medicine. Included are case studies of women who are practicing physicians, descriptions of the various special fields in medicine and prejudices women who choose medicine for a career must face.

*Careers:* Female = 19 Male = 7 Neutral = 17
*Subject Categories:* Careers; Health/Human Development

**9.5 Martha Berry: Little Woman with a Big Dream.** Joyce Blackburn. Philadelphia, PA: J.B. Lippincott, 1968. 158 p. $5.95.

Biography of Martha Berry, founder of the Berry Schools, which were dedicated to improving education for the mountain children in Georgia. Shows her struggles in developing the schools, which grew from a one-room schoolhouse into an educational complex with grade school, high school, junior college and college. The book dwells on accomplishments of the male students.

*Careers:* Female = 21 Male = 53 Neutral = 35
*Subject Categories:* Biography; Health/Human Development; History

**9.6 Women in Music.** Barbara Stanford and Felicia Diamond. Portland, ME: J. Weston Walch, 1974. 19 p.

Biographical sketches of 18 prominent women in the field of music including opera, folk, blues and gospel singers; pianists; composers; and conductors. Each biography, with accompanying illustration, is on a separate 11 x 14 sheet.

*Careers:* Female = 15 Male = 6 Neutral = 2
*Subject Categories:* American Ethnic Minority; Biography; Careers; Fine Arts

**9.7 100 Greatest Women in Sports.** Phyllis Hollander. New York: Grosset & Dunlap, 1976. 142 p. $4.95.

A comprehensive survey of women's accomplishments in a wide variety of sports including basketball, bicycling, bowling, field hockey, figure and speed skating, golf, gymnastics, horseback riding, horse racing, skiing, softball, swimming, tennis, track and field and volleyball. Emphasis is on record setting as well as the barriers women had to overcome in order to gain professional equality with men. Included are women from many countries who are young, old, married, single, professionals and amateurs.

*Careers:* Female = 32 Male = 30 Neutral = 14
*Subject Categories:* Biography; Sports

**9.8 The Young Woman's Guide to Liberation.** Karen DeCrow. Indianapolis, IN: Bobbs-Merrill, 1971. 200 p.

This introduction to feminist issues and the liberation movement, written by a regional director of the National Organization of Women (NOW), tells of the various sources in our culture that have continued to make women feel, think and act like second-class citizens. Although it is rather "militant," this book is an invaluable aid for encouraging high school-aged young women and men to examine the influences deeply rooted in our culture for the past 6,000 years, which have tended to keep women from participating in society as fully equipped, competent and self-loving individuals.

*Careers:* Female = 82 Male = 63 Neutral = 51

*Subject Categories:* Behavioral Science; Cont. Issues/Curr. Events; Health/Human Development; Women's Studies

**9.9 Daughters of the Earth. (The Lives and Legends of American Indian Women).** Carolyn Niethammer. New York: Collier Books, 1977. 281 p. $7.95. Paper. (Originally published by Macmillan, 1977.)

This absorbing book presents a chronology of multi-ethnic Native American women's lives. Herbal remedies, childbirth and marriage rituals, sexuality, menstrual taboos, puberty rites, spiritual experiences and many other fundamental aspects of daily life are discussed in great detail.

*Careers:* Female = 38 Male = 17 Neutral = 5
*Subject Categories:* American Ethnic Minority; Behavioral Science; Cultural Heritage; History; Religion/Mythology; Women's Studies

**9.10 The Feminine Mystique.** Betty Friedan. New York: Dell, 1979. 420 p. $2.25. Paper. (Originally published by W.W. Norton, 1963.)

*The Feminine Mystique* is a sophisticated, comprehensive study articulating the essence of the women's movement in America. It is, therefore, rather intense reading, recommended for highly motivated young people. Selected excerpts may provide excellent impetus for class discussion and debate.

*Careers:* Female = 80 Male = 61 Neutral = 48
*Subject Categories:* Behavioral Science; Careers; Cont. Issues/ Curr. Events; Health/Human Development; Literature by Women; Women's Studies

**9.11 Gather Together in My Name.** Maya Angelou. New York: Bantam Books, 1979. 181 p. $2.25. Paper. (Originally published by Random House, 1974.)

Maya Angelou's second book is about her life as a young black woman growing up in America in the late 1940s. In it she traces her experiences from her seventeenth year—including a brief stint as a prostitute and raising a fatherless son—while maintaining her dignity and pride throughout. She presents all of her exploits with humor and warmth. Although the language is often explicit, it seems appropriate to the story and times and allows the reader a taste of life before "civil rights."

*Careers:* Female = 14 Male = 17 Neutral = 1
*Subject Categories:* American Ethnic Minority; Autobiography; Cultural Heritage; Literature by Women

**9.12 A Hero Ain't Nothin' but a Sandwich.** Alice Childress. New York: Avon, 1974. 128 p. $1.50. Paper. (Originally published by Coward, McCann and Geoghegan, 1973.)

A very readable book, written in dialect and slang, about a 13-year-old black junkie and the effect his addiction has on his family. Each chapter presents the first-person perspective of different characters: junkie, mother, stepfather, grandmother, pusher, friends and teachers. A warm and sensitive, yet realistic story. Excellent reading.

*Careers:* Female = 20 Male = 29 Neutral = 45
*Subject Categories:* American Ethnic Minority; Cultural Heritage; Families/Friendship; Health/Human Development

**9.13 Frontiers of Dance: The Life of Martha Graham.** Walter Terry. New York: Thomas Y. Crowell, 1975. 167 p.

The story of Martha Graham's dance career is told by Walter Terry, a dance critic, editor and lecturer. He begins with the childhood influences that steer Martha Graham toward dancing. Much of the chronology deals with Graham's relationships with her teachers in her early dancing years and with her contemporaries in dance throughout her lifetime. The reader is shown how Graham's growth and changes surface in her personality and in the dances she creates. Graham rejects ballet and looks to deep emotions and social issues as themes for her pioneering dance form. Terry emphasizes Graham's strengths—her conviction to dance in a radically new way and her almost superhuman physical power as a dancer.

*Careers:* Female = 15 Male = 20 Neutral = 3
*Subject Categories:* Biography; Fine Arts

**9.14 Blackberry Winter: My Earlier Years.** Margaret Mead. New York: William Morrow, 1972. 297 p. $8.95.

This is a fascinating autobiographical account of Margaret Mead's family, early influences and the years spent on field location at various places in the Pacific. Young women readers will be provided with the kind of role model that encourages one to seek high adventure and doesn't let societal conventions interfere with one's ambitions. Readers learn about the norms in the Mead family as Margaret was growing up and how her field studies of Pacific cultures reinforced her notions about child-rearing practices when she had her own daughter.

*Careers:* Female = 18 Male = 38 Neutral = 9
*Subject Categories:* Autobiography; Behavioral Science; Careers; Foreign Countries; Women's Studies

**9.15 Enterprising Women.** Caroline Bird. New York: W.W. Norton, 1976. 256 p. $12.95.

A fascinating chronicle of the economic achievements made by women during the last 200 years of American history. The short essays about little known women not mentioned in traditional history books keep the reader's interest and show women who have influenced the status of their sex for either better or worse. The careers portrayed cover a variety of fields, ranging from farming and canning to banking and publishing. This book provides a clear view of what women have accomplished and will continue to contribute to the economic makeup of America.

*Careers:* Female = 69 Male = 42 Neutral = 2
*Subject Categories:* Behavioral Science; Careers; History; Women's Studies

**9.16 Watching the Wild Apes: The Primate Studies of Goodall, Fossey, and Galdikas.** Bettyann Kevles. New York: E.P. Dutton, 1976. 164 p. $8.95.

This fascinating book is appropriate for free reading or as a resource or text supplement for classrooms studying the natural or behavioral sciences. The book focuses on the primate studies of Jane Goodall, Dian Fossey and Birute Galdikas, which involved observations of chimpanzees, mountain gorillas and orangutans in the primates' natural habitats. Their work opened up the field of primate ethology with startling new information that also had impact on the study of human behavior. The descriptions of the three women and their pioneering efforts, as well as the great apes themselves, provide informative and entertaining reading.

*Careers:* Female = 10 Male = 24 Neutral = 19
*Subject Categories:* Animals; Behavioral Science; Careers; Foreign Countries; Science/Technology

**9.17 I'm Running Away from Home but I'm Not Allowed to Cross the Street.** Gabrielle Burton. Pittsburgh, PA: KNOW, Inc., 1972. 206 p. $4.50.

This very readable book has been subtitled "A Primer of Women's Liberation." It will provide young women of all ages a gentle, humorous and thoughtful introduction to feminist issues as well as a guide for "learning to cross the street." Highly recommended.

*Careers:* Female = 24 Male = 25 Neutral = 11
*Subject Categories:* Families/Friendship; Health/Human Development; Women's Studies

**9.18 A Pictorial History of Women in America.** Ruth Warren. New York: Crown, 1975. 228 p. $7.95.

A very readable history that pays tribute to American women—from Jamestown and Plymouth colony settlers to twentieth century women active in sports, politics, the sciences and the performing arts. Although women are shown in a wide variety of careers and roles, the contributions of American ethnic minority women are only dealt with in two chapters: "Indian Women—the First American Women" and "The Black Revolution." The contributions of other ethnic minorities have been ignored.

*Careers:* Female = 201 Male = 80 Neutral = 53
*Subject Categories:* History; Women's Studies

**9.19 Bloomsday for Maggie.** May McNeer. Boston: Houghton Mifflin, 1976. 246 p. $7.95.

Spirited Maggie Murphy wants a career in journalism. But during the prohibition era in Florida, "ladies" were allowed only the opportunity to be society editors. Maggie's struggle to become a "front page girl" and her exposure to the scandals brewing around the town's most respectable elite make amusing reading.

*Careers:* Female = 20 Male = 41 Neutral = 22
*Subject Categories:* Families/Friendship; History

**9.20 Math Equals: Biographies of Women Mathematicians + Related Activities.** Teri Perl. Menlo Park, CA: Addison-Wesley, 1978. 250 p. Paper.

Biographies of nine women mathematicians with related math activities. The women range from Hypatia of Greece (370–415 A.D.) to Emmy Noether (1882–1935). The relatively brief biographies are fascinating; each one notes the particular problems that the mathematician faced by virtue of her sex. The mathematical activities are presented in original and thought-provoking ways. Appendices and solutions to the problems are included, and the book is well illustrated.

*Careers:* Female = 29 Male = 44 Neutral = 12
*Subject Categories:* Autobiography/Biography; Science/Technology

**9.21 Lawyers for the People: A New Breed of Defenders and Their Work.** Elizabeth Levy. New York: Dell, 1974. 128 p. $1.25. Paper.

Nine profiles of women and men in various organizations using a variety of approaches. They represent people who have traditionally been too poor or unorganized to obtain legal services. This book shows that a career in law and a desire to change society are not incompatible.

*Careers:* Female = 13 Male = 28 Neutral = 34
*Subject Categories:* Careers; Cont. Issues/Curr. Events

**9.22ˣ What Can She Be? A Computer Scientist.** Gloria and Esther Goldreich. New York: Lothrop, Lee & Shepard, 1979. 47 p. $ 5.95.

With black and white photographs and simple text, this work follows Linda Wong on the job as a computer scientist. Excellent introduction to the various opportunities associated with a career in the field of computer science. Ethnic minorities are well represented in the photographs. Format makes this book appropriate for upper intermediate-grade and junior high students.

*Careers:* Female = 9 Male = 8 Neutral = 6
*Subject Categories:* American Ethnic Minority; Careers; Science/Technology

**9.23 Black Foremothers: Three Lives.** Dorothy Sterling. Old Westbury, NY: The Feminist Press, 1979. 157 p. Paper.

This excellent classroom resource tells the stories of three black leaders: Ellen Craft, a renowned abolitionist; Ida B. Wells, a consciousness-raising journalist who led a crusade against lynching; and Mary Church Terrell, a leader in the suffrage movement, civil rights and world peace. All three women were exceedingly intelligent, well educated, independent and courageous. All were an important part of the history of the United States, and their fascinating lives should be common knowledge today.

*Careers:* Female = 41 Male = 91 Neutral = 34
*Subject Categories:* American Ethnic Minority; Autobiography/Biography; Cultural Heritage; History; Women's Studies

**9.24 Blue Collar Jobs for Women.** Muriel Lederer. New York: E.P. Dutton, 1979. 257 p. $7.95. Paper.

This work is an excellent introduction to blue collar jobs and an invaluable aid for a woman considering a position in the trades. The information is very well organized and readable.

*Careers:* Female = 55 Male = 0 Neutral = 0
*Subject Categories:* Careers; Women's Studies

**9.25 Famous American Women.** Hope Stoddard. New York: Thomas Y. Crowell, 1970. 440 p.

Forty-one biographies of famous American women of the nineteenth and twentieth centuries, from Jane Addams to Babe Didrikson Zaharias. The women included in this book represent a wide range of backgrounds and talents, but all have made a major contribution to the cultural and social progress of America. Each woman is viewed in terms of events and attitudes of her time so that the reader gains an understanding of history as well as a knowledge of the historical figure herself.

*Careers:* Female = 152 Male = 154 Neutral = 89
*Subject Categories:* Autobiography/Biography; History; Women's Studies

**9.26 Men's Bodies Men's Selves.** Sam Julty. New York: Dell, 1979. 453 p. $9.95. Paper.

An outstanding resource book; comes close to providing everything a male needs to know to gain an understanding of his maleness and, most importantly, his humanity. Written in a warm, supportive tone, the book explores such aspects as work, homosexuality, physical and emotional health, fathering, aging, sexuality, venereal diseases and rape. Throughout the book, the author explodes masculine myths and stereotypes. Women are viewed as partners in life experience rather than as sexual objects and/or second-class citizens. As such, women are encouraged to read this book. Each chapter contains an extensive list of other resource materials such as books, films, newsletters and organizations. The frankness of subject matter and sexually explicit language may make this book most appropriate for senior high students and above, but the book is an invaluable reference for every parent and teacher.

*Careers:* Female = 34 Male = 76 Neutral = 69
*Subject Categories:* Behavioral Science; Health/Human Development

**9.27 Dancer.** Suzanne Merry. New York: Charles Scribner's Sons, 1980. 59 p. $8.95.

Celeste Jabczenski began dancing with the Joffrey II ballet in New York at the age of 18. *Dancer,* which is about her life as a ballet professional, gives an inside look to the dancer's world. The constant self-discipline, exercises, classes, rehearsals and exhilaration of performances are all portrayed. The story of Celeste is the story of a young woman willing to sacrifice for her goals.

*Careers:* Female = 2 Male = 4 Neutral = 4
*Subject Categories:* Careers; Fine Arts

**9.28 Boys Have Feelings Too: Growing Up Male for Boys.** Dale Carson. New York: Atheneum, 1980. 165 p. $8.95.

This book emphasizes the idea that men are human beings first; men second. It urges young men not to fall into the "hero" or "macho" trap often assigned to the male sex but to learn who they are and what they really want rather than being defined by others.

*Careers:* Female = 6 Male = 47 Neutral = 5
*Subject Categories:* Behavioral Science; Health/Human Development

**9.29 Breakthrough: Women in Writing.** Diana Gleasner. New York: Walker, 1980. 143 p. $9.95.

An interesting book in which the author presents the personal insights of and the problems encountered by women writers: Judy Blume, Erica Jong, Erma Bombeck, Jessamyn West and Phyllis Whitney. This is a delightful book which will no doubt inspire aspiring writers, female and male.

*Careers:* Female = 12 Male = 14 Neutral = 5
*Subject Categories:* Autobiography/Biography; Health/Human Development; Women's Studies

**9.30 I Am the Fire of Time.** Jane B. Katz. New York: E.P. Dutton, 1977. 193 p. $6.95. Paper.

An anthology of Native American women's voices in song, poetry, prayer, narrative and oral history. Quietly explodes many myths about Native Americans in general and Native American women in particular. This is an awareness-raising view of history, the environment, cultural traditions and the family. Includes traditional and contemporary works. Excellent for research, free reading or selected oral reading.

*Careers:* Female = 44 Male = 27 Neutral = 14
*Subject Categories:* American Ethnic Minority; Cont. Issues/Curr. Events; Cultural Heritage; History; Anthologies; Literature by Women; Women's Studies

**9.31 Sports for the Handicapped.** Anne Allen. New York: Walker and Company, 1981. 80 p. $9.95.

A gold mine of information about the impressive variety of sports opportunities available for disabled persons of all ages. Participating, not winning, is the goal, but it's clear that the athletes gain in physical well-being, self-esteem and social contacts—the same benefits that attract their able-bodied counterparts. The book is excellent for describing and depicting males and females both as athletes and coach/trainers in such sports as skiing, swimming, horseback riding, track and field, football and wheelchair basketball. Includes an index of resource and sports organizations serving the handicapped, as well as numerous black and white photographs.

*Careers:* Female = 10 Male = 11 Neutral = 7
*Subject Categories:* The Handicapped; Health/Human Development; Sports

**9.32 Portraits of Chinese Women in Revolution.** Agnes Smedley. Old Westbury, NY: The Feminist Press, 1976. 203 p. $4.50. Paper.

A collection of published writings covering the 1930s in China by "a writer, a participant in revolutionary movements and a vigorous feminist." The women she writes about offer a real diversity of lives and consciousness, ranging from exponents of China's feudal regime to modern revolutionaries (including those caught up in the historical transition). The stories are somewhat propagandistic in tone—the good are without blemish, and the bad are without a single redeeming virtue—but Smedley does pay deserved tribute to the tremendous courage of Chinese women who sought not only to improve their own oppressed condition but that of society as a whole. A foreword and afterword provide considerable biographical material about Agnes Smedley, a remarkable woman in her own right.

*Careers:* Female = 33 Male = 49 Neutral = 23
*Subject Categories:* American Ethnic Minority; Cultural Heritage; Essays/Short Stories; Foreign Countries; History; Women's Studies

# Reading Grade Level 10–Dale-Chall Formula

**10.1 Ms. Attorney.** D.X. Fenten. Philadelphia, PA: The Westminster Press, 1974. 159 p. $5.50.

This is a comprehensive book for students contemplating a career in the legal profession. It not only describes the career role of an attorney, it also reviews coursework and tests that are required for preparation before entering the field. Book also discusses the realities of discrimination against women and explodes the fallacy about the appropriateness of "lady-lawyers."

*Careers:* Female = 2 Male = 6 Neutral = 2
*Subject Categories:* Careers

**10.2 African Rhythm—American Dance: A Biography of Katherine Dunham.** Terry Harnan. New York: Alfred A. Knopf, 1974.

Biography of the versatile and multitalented Katherine Dunham, a black dancer and choreographer noted for her dances drawn from African and Caribbean sources. After studying anthropology, she went to the Caribbean where she lived in isolated villages and used anthropological field techniques to trace the African sources in the people's dances and customs. The story of how she incorporated their dances into her choreography, the subsequent impact of her work on the theatrical and dance world, her efforts to help other black dancers and students, her involvement with Haiti and the Haitians, as well as her ensuing writing career, make fascinating reading of an outstanding woman and her times.

*Careers:* Female = 35 Male = 66 Neutral = 39
*Subject Categories:* American Ethnic Minority; Biography; Cultural Heritage; Fine Arts

**10.3 Our Hidden Heritage: Five Centuries of Women Artists.** Eleanor Tufts. New York: Paddington Press, 1974. 256 p. $7.95.

This collection of short biographies of 22 women artists from the Renaissance to the twentieth century provides fascinating portrayals and new insights into the lives and works, the frustrations and successes of these talented women. This book is highly commendable for redressing the collective and rather recent cultural neglect of women artists in basic art survey books used today. The author makes plain that in the past women were appointed as court painters, accepted as professionals and unstintingly appreciated by their contemporaries. More than 125 black and white reproductions are included in this work.

*Careers:* Female = 50 Male = 83 Neutral = 30

*Subject Categories:* Biography; Fine Arts; Foreign Countries; History; Women's Studies

**10.4 Sex & Birth Control.** E. James Lieberman and Ellen Peck. New York: Schocken Books, 1975. 287 p. $3.45. Paper.

An excellent, straightforward, nonjudgmental book that deals with the various forms of birth control, abortion, sterilization and venereal disease. Perhaps more importantly, it discusses attitudes toward sex and sexual behavior, "what's normal," "what's moral" and overpopulation. Case histories and questions from young people of both sexes are helpful. Sources for obtaining more help and information are also included. This is a responsible book on sex for young people, and it encourages a responsibility for individual action which can only be attained with adequate knowledge.

*Careers:* Female = 23 Male = 41 Neutral = 35
*Subject Categories:* Health/Human Development

**10.5 New Women in Politics.** Kathleen Bowman. Mankato, MN: Creative Education, 1976. 47 p.

An excellent book providing brief biographies of Bess Myerson, Elizabeth Holtzman, Dolores Huerta, Patsy Takemoto Mink, Barbara Jordan, Yvonne Burke and Ella Grasso. The short sketches of each of the women provide interesting glimpses into the lives and philosophies of these strong, capable and independent leaders who have become well-known names in politics.

*Careers:* Female = 29 Male = 16 Neutral = 15
*Subject Categories:* American Ethnic Minority; Autobiography/Biography; Careers; Cont. Issues/Curr. Events; Women's Studies

**10.6 Root of Bitterness.** Nancy F. Cott (ed.). New York: E.P. Dutton, 1972. 373 p. $ 5.95. Paper.

By the use of actual documents, either written, spoken, or read by women during the last 400 years, the editor presents a documentary on the social history of American women as it relates to the "root of bitterness" or "mistaken notion of the inequality of the sexes." In the introduction, the editor explains that the documents deal with the consciousness and self-consciousness of American women, not the history of the feminist movement. The book is divided into eight categories: (1) The Early Colonial Milieu: Goodwives, Shrews, and Witches; (2) An Achieving Society: The Eighteenth-Century; (3) The Cult of Domesticity Versus Social Change; (4) Slavery and Sex; (5) Nineteenth-Century Alternatives: Pioneers and Utopians; (6) Sexuality and Gynecology in the Nineteenth Century; (7) Industrialization and Women's Work; and (8)

Legacy of Leisure: Discontent. Appropriate as a supplementary text for a senior high history or women's studies course as well as an eye-opening experience for anyone interested in the history of women in America.

*Careers:* Female = 69 Male = 55 Neutral = 65
*Subject Categories:* Behavioral Science; History; Women's Studies

**10.7 Margaret Mead.** Edward Rice. New York: Harper & Row, 1979. 194 p. $10.00.

This account of the life and work of Margaret Mead, America's best known anthropologist, is well written and informative. Mead's professional achievements as well as her three marriages and her motherhood are explored. Mead's studies of other cultures shed light on understanding the lives of Westerners, especially young American women. Recommended nonsexist literature.

*Careers:* Female = 12 Male = 18 Neutral = 7
*Subject Categories:* Autobiography/Biography; Behavioral Science; Foreign Countries; Women's Studies

**10.8 Feminism: The Essential Historical Writings.** Miriam Schneir (ed.). New York: Random House, 1972. 355 p. $2.95. Paper.

This anthology of "essential historical writings" on feminist issues includes excerpts from works dating from 1776 (Abigail Adams) to 1929 (Virginia Woolf). A wide variety of selections (more than 40), accompanied by context-setting introductions by the editor, focus on feminist issues of relevance today. Contrary to popular belief, the "old" feminism concentrated on more than the suffrage issue. One section entitled "Men As Feminists" contains excerpts from ideological and literary works written by men who were sympathetic to the condition of womankind. An informative and thought-provoking introduction to the history of feminism, this book is appropriate for high school women's studies and history courses.

*Careers:* Female = 68 Male = 49 Neutral = 35
*Subject Categories:* History; Women's Studies

**10.9 Women See Women.** Cheryl Wiesenfeld, et al., (eds.). New York: Thomas Y. Crowell, 1976. 145 p. $7.95. Paper.

A collection of photographs by women photographers presenting varied images of women at work, at play, alone, young and old. Deliberate editorial exclusion of images expressive of self-hatred—cruel, mocking or grotesque. Interesting and thought-provoking photographs.

*Careers:* Female = 8 Male = 2 Neutral = 5
*Subject Categories:* Fine Arts; Women's Studies

**10.10 I Can Be Anything: Careers and Colleges for Young Women.** Joyce Slayton Mitchell. New York: College Entrance Examination Board, 1978. 294 p. Paper.

This guide to 108 careers provides a candid look at what each career is like, including on-the-job interviews with women from every part of the country. Includes required educational background, present employment opportunities, lists of colleges and sources for additional information. Readers should note that the book was published in 1978 making salary information inaccurate. Looks at many nontraditional careers for women in a positive manner.

*Careers:* Female = 144 Male = 6 Neutral = 6
*Subject Categories:* Careers

**10.11 Contemporary Women Scientists of America.** Iris Noble. New York: Julian Messner, 1979. 151 p.

This book presents profiles of seven twentieth century women who pioneered in the scientific field. These women recount how they started their careers and what obstacles and difficulties they encountered. They also offer advice for young women seeking careers in science.

*Careers:* Female = 36 Male = 9 Neutral = 23
*Subject Categories:* Autobiography/Biography; Careers; Science/Technology; Women's Studies

**10.12 The Language of Show Dancing.** Jacqueline Lowe and Charles Selber. New York: Charles Scribner's Sons, 1980. 35 p. $9.95.

This book is an exciting visual interpretation of some of the more colorful show dancing terms. Martha Swope's photographs are delightful.

*Careers:* Female = 1 Male = 1 Neutral = 0
*Subject Categories:* Careers; Fine Arts

# Reading Grade Level 11–Dale-Chall Formula

**11.1 Mirror Mirror: Images of Women Reflected in Popular Culture.** Kathryn Weibel. Garden City, NY: Anchor Press, 1977. 256 p. $3.95. Paper.

A well-researched, historical survey of the images of women reflected in popular culture. The author discusses how the myths and cultural norms for women have been defined and distorted by the popular images of women in fiction, television, movies, magazines, advertising and fashion. Although this book would be fairly heavy free reading for a high school student, it would provide a valuable resource for use in classes studying fiction, media and the culture and sociology of women and American society. The images of minority women are only briefly discussed.

*Careers:* Female = 81 Male = 76 Neutral = 62
*Subject Categories:* Behavioral Science; Women's Studies

**11.2 Popcorn Venus.** Marjorie Rosen. New York: Avon, 1974. 447 p. $1.95. Paper. (Originally published by Coward, McCann & Geoghegan, 1973.)

In this fascinating and somewhat "gossipy" retrospective on women in films—on camera and off—the author asks the question of whether "art" (pop culture) reflects life or life reflects "art." Although that judgment is left to the reader, the author suggests it is time to reinterpret the American Dream and the fantasy roles movies define for women as part of that dream. This book provides an excellent resource for a student or class studying the sociology of women and American pop culture by contrasting the lives of women as they were and are in reality versus the lives of women portrayed on the silver screen. Especially commendable is the emphasis placed on labor statistics and the variety of careers and jobs performed by women in "real life" since the turn of the century.

*Careers:* Female = 134 Male = 83 Netural = 39
*Subject Categories:* Behavioral Science; Fine Arts; History; Women's Studies

**11.3 Single and Pregnant.** Ruth I. Pierce. Boston: Beacon Press, 1970. 214 p. $5.95.

Without the traditional moralizing, this book answers questions and provides information for the single, pregnant girl on abortion, adoption, marriage and single parenthood. A wealth of information is offered, including facts on contraceptives, conception, physical changes during pregnancy, relationships with family and friends, maternity homes, community resources, medical care and counseling and therapy. The appendix includes abortion referrals, planned parenthood affiliates and maternity and infant care projects. However, some of the information is out-of-date, particularly regarding the legality of abortion and the treatment of minors. It is also geared toward white, middle class girls, and some of the careers are stereotyped. With these cautions in mind, this book should provide an acceptable resource for young women.

*Careers:* Female = 11 Male = 8 Neutral = 43
*Subject Categories:* Health/Human Development; Women's Studies

**11.4 Psychology and the New Woman.** Mary McHugh. New York: Franklin Watts, 1976. 114 p.

This book is part of a series designed to help young women choose lifestyles and careers suited to their interests and abilities. This volume contains a comprehensive study of the field of psychology from graduate training to its many specialty areas: clinical, environmental, developmental, educational, experimental, counseling and the psychology of women. The author frankly discusses salaries and how this type of career can be coordinated with having a family. A very good book for a young person looking at career choices.

*Careers:* Female = 18 Male = 5 Neutral = 31
*Subject Categories:* Behavioral Science; Careers; Women's Studies

**11.5 Women Artists: Recognition and Reappraisal from the Early Middle Ages to the Twentieth Century.** Karen Petersen and J.J. Wilson. New York: Harper Colophon, 1976. 212 p. $5.95. Paper.

A chronological history of women's art, beginning with the fifth century A.D. and continuing through to the present. Its focus is on art that women have created rather than the form women took in other people's art. The book is very complete with numerous black and white reproductions. It is specific, detailed and an excellent resource for reference on women artists.

*Careers:* Female = 47 Male = 18 Neutral = 7
*Subject Categories:* Fine Arts; History; Women's Studies

**11.6 The Jewish Woman: New Perspectives.** Elizabeth Koltun (ed.). New York: Schocken Books, 1976. 282 p. $6.95. Paper.

An anthology of essays dealing with what it means to be a Jewish woman in terms of religion, marriage, parenthood and feminism. It explores cultural stereotypes and the role of women in the Old Testament, history and literature and discusses possible changes and alternatives necessary to allow the modern Jewish woman to achieve full personhood and Jewish identity. The book is very scholarly in tone and may intimidate all but the serious reader. It also assumes that the reader possesses a good deal of knowledge about Jewish history, religion and the Hebrew language. High school students may find the essays on alternative wedding, birth and bar/bas mitzvah cermonies of particular interest.

*Careers:* Female = 50 Male = 20 Neutral = 13
*Subject Categories:* Behavioral Science; Cultural Heritage; Religion/Mythology; Women's Studies

**11.7 Beautiful, Also, Are the Souls of My Black Sisters.** Jeanne Noble. Englewood Cliffs, NJ: Prentice-Hall, 1978. 346 p.

A powerful history of the black woman in America written by a black female historian. This is not a dry history book, rather, it is a history of black women from African queens who were engineers and city planners to women in the current women's movement. Again and again their strength, capacity to endure and to do much more than endure is emphasized. The preslave history is particularly fascinating, but the entire book will grip the reader.

*Careers:* Female = 75 Male = 75 Neutral = 59
*Subject Categories:* American Ethnic Minority; Cont. Issues/Curr. Events; Cultural Heritage; History; Women's Studies

**11.8 Self-Defense & Assault Prevention for Girls & Women.** Bruce Tegner and Alice McGrath. Ventura, CA: Thor Publishing Company, 1977. 123 p. Paper.

A book of instruction in basic, practical self-defense for girls and women. The text is accompanied by photographs to illustrate various techniques. The book teaches women and girls not to view themselves as helpless victims without being militant in tone. Self-defense is presented as an aspect of general competence and self-reliance. A teacher's guide to accompany the book is available from the publisher.

*Careers:* Female = 0 Male = 3 Neutral = 5
*Subject Categories:* Health/Human Development; Sports

**11.9 What Are Little Girls Made of? The Roots of Feminine Stereotypes.** Elena Gianini Belotti. New York: Schocken Books, 1978. 158 p. $4.95. Paper.

A book on feminine stereotypes which focuses on the infant and young child who learn so very early the "shoulds" and "should nots" pertaining to sex role stereotypes. Belotti, an Italian Montessori educator, speaks from an Italian point of view, and as Margaret Mead points out in her excellent introduction, she is somewhat biased and strident. Nevertheless, Belotti's points are well taken, and her description of the role teachers play in enforcing stereotypes makes this book a "must" for educators and an excellent resource for secondary students.

*Careers:* Female = 18 Male = 42 Neutral = 10
*Subject Categories:* Behavioral Science; Health/Human Development; Women's Studies

**11.10 Chemistry Careers.** L.B. Taylor. New York: Franklin Watts, 1978. 62 p.

Excellent introduction for junior and senior high school students to careers available in the field of chemistry, from chemists and chemical engineers to technical writers and patent agents. Included is salary information and required educational preparation. The book is exemplary in its use of nonsexist language, and women and ethnic minorities are represented in the photographs.

*Careers:* Female = 4 Male = 8 Neutral = 64
*Subject Categories:* Careers; Science/Technology

# Reading Grade Level 12 and Above–Dale-Chall Formula

**12.1 Masculine/Feminine: Readings in Sexual Mythology and the Liberation of Women.** Betty Roszak and Theodore Roszak (eds.). New York: Harper & Row, 1969. 316 p. $4.50. Paper.

An anthology of readings viewing the subjugation of women from a variety of perspectives—sociological, psychological and anthropological. The contents are organized into four major sections: (1) a brief survey of sexual stereotypes as promulgated by playwrights, philosophers, sociologists and psychologists, which have been integrated in the pedagogy, psychotherapy and mass media imagery of today; (2) excerpts from the writings of male allies of feminism over the last half-century; (3) feminist writings from the 1930s up to the present, including readings from the "new militancy"; and (4) a collection of women's liberation manifestos. Provides a variety of materials which teachers may use to supplement texts, build units around, provide background information or use as take-off points for discussion.

*Careers:* Female = 58 Male = 52 Neutral = 32
*Subject Categories:* Behavioral Science; Health/Human Development; History; Women's Studies

**12.2 Witches, Midwives and Nurses: A History of Women Healers.** Barbara Ehrenreich and Deirdre English. Old Westbury, NY: The Feminist Press, 1973. 48 p. $1.95. Paper.

This brief, fascinating and well-researched history of women healers chronicles the participation of women in the healing arts. It also details their suppression by an elitist medical establishment composed of upper-class, white males from the middle ages to the present century. The first section of the book, "Witchcraft and Medicine in the Middle Ages," discusses the witchhunt craze (fourteenth to seventeenth centuries) during which time thousands of women were burned at the stake, accused not only of murdering and poisoning, sex crimes and conspiracy, but also of helping and healing. The second section of the book, "Women and the Rise of the American Medical Profession," discusses the Popular Health Movement and the political confrontation between the "regular" doctor (in a time when there was little medical "science") and the lay-practitioners, many of whom were women, blacks and poor white males.

*Careers:* Female = 18 Male = 13 Neutral = 13
*Subject Categories:* Health/Human Development; History; Science/Technology; Women's Studies

**12.3 Persuasion.** Jane Austen. New York: New American Library, 1964. 256 p. $1.75. Paper. (Originally published by John Murray, 1818.)

A nineteenth-century novel about the world of country gentry in Regency England. The hero, Anne Elliot, is a woman of perfect breeding, profound depth of emotion and unswerving integrity. While Anne exhibits remarkable strength and understanding, her aspirations do not go beyond the traditional role of wife. The characters are highly stereotyped and in many instances reveal the shallowness and hypocrisy of that society.

*Careers:* Female = 3 Male = 9 Neutral = 2
*Subject Categories:* Foreign Countries; Health/Human Development; History; Literature by Women

**12.4 Looking Forward to a Career: Veterinary Medicine.** Helen L. Gillum. Minneapolis, MN: Dillon Press, 1976. 107 p.

This book explains what a veterinarian does and what preparation is needed for the career of veterinary medicine as well as related careers. Print size and use of photographs make this book appropriate for junior high readers.

*Careers:* Female = 5 Male = 2 Neutral = 21
*Subject Categories:* Careers; Science/Technology

**12.5 Contraception, Abortion, Pregnancy.** Alice L. Fleming. Nashville, TN: Thomas Nelson, 1974. 92 p. $5.95.

Factual information about sexual intercourse, contraception, pregnancy, childbirth and abortion. Although the lack of illustrations and the author's practice of referring to doctors as "he" and nurses as "she" could be improved upon, this book is a readable, informative resource.

*Careers:* Female = 5 Male = 4 Neutral = 12
*Subject Categories:* Health/Human Development; Science/Technology

**12.6 Man's World, Woman's Place: A Study in Social Mythology.** Elizabeth Janeway. New York: William Morrow, 1971. 307 p. $8.95.

A discussion on women and their relationship to the world from several perspectives: historical, biological, psychological, sexual, sociological and economic. The author examines social myths and roles—where and how they developed—and makes comparisons between American values and norms and those of other cultures. An interesting discussion on proposed differences between the sexes runs throughout the book, which looks at biological, intellectual and social differences and possible explanations for their existence. This work is stimulating and probing—a useful and complete introduction to women's issues.

*Careers:* Female = 45 Male = 52 Neutral = 30
*Subject Categories:* Behavioral Science; History; Women's Studies

**12.7 Women and Womanhood in America.** Ronald W. Hogeland (ed.). Lexington, MA: D.C. Heath, 1973. 183 p. Paper.

A collection of essays from Cotton Mather in colonial times to Alice S. Rossi, a contemporary sociologist, which illustrate a historical view of woman's role in America. The book does not dwell on the accomplishments or contributions of women. Rather, women as a group are seen in American history through the eyes of their male and female contemporaries,. Not all of the selections are easy to read, and the flow of selections is somewhat disjointed. The teacher should note that the last essay was written in 1964. However, the book is a good supplement to the study of periods of American history.

*Careers:* Female = 72 Male = 42 Neutral = 36
*Subject Categories:* Behavioral Science; Cultural Heritage; History; Women's Studies

**12.8 Commonsense Sex.** Ronald M. Mazur. Boston: Beacon Press, 1968. 110 p. $2.95. Paper.

Mazur's book is exactly what it purports to be: common sense about sex. Starting with the idea that sex should be a positive, rewarding collaboration between women and men, the author questions hypocritical attitudes and damaging feelings of shame and guilt. He explores such topics as petting, mutual masturbation, contraception, premarital intercourse, homosexuality and extramarital relationships matter-of-factly. He emphasizes responsibility for one's sexual activity again and again. Mazur says, "Today, chastity means acting with integrity." In a gentle, reasonable and sensitive manner, this book gives young people a context in which to make their own decisions about sexual behavior. An excellent book to spark thoughtful discussion.

*Careers:* Female = 1 Male = 3 Neutral = 17
*Subject Categories:* Cont. Issues/ Curr. Events; Health/Human Development

**12.9 Rights and Wrongs: Women's Struggle for Legal Equality.** Susan Cary Nicholas, Alice M. Price, and Rachel Rubin. New York: Feminist Press, 1979. 84 p. Paper.

A very readable book about women's struggles for legal equality. Covers four areas of major concern to women: constitutional law, the family, employment and the right to have control over one's body. Clear and calm narrative, supplemented by excerpts from trials, court opinions and historical statements of protest and persuasion provide fascinating reading.

*Careers:* Female = 34 Male = 30 Neutral = 10
*Subject Categories:* Cont. Issues/Curr. Events; History; Women's Studies

# Appendix 1: Resource Bibliographies

Books appearing in this bibliography were selected for analysis by the Center for Sex Equity staff from several existing nonsexist bibliographies. The following resources were consulted:

Adell, Judith and Klein, Hilary Dole. *A Non-Sexist Guide to Children's Books*. Chicago: Academy Press Limited, 1976.

*Advisory List of Instructional Media for Reduction of Sex Bias*. North Carolina State Department of Education, 1977. ED 149 755.

Bryne, Kathy. "Little Girls and Picture Books: Problem and Solution." *Reading Teacher* 29 (7) (April 1976): 671–74.

*By-For-About-Women*. Portland, OR: Multnomah County Library, 1975.

Davis, Enid. *Liberty Cap*. Chicago: Academy Press Limited, 1978.

Easley, Ann. *Elements of Sexism in a Selected Group of Picture Books Recommended for Kindergarten Use*. 1973. ED 104 559.

Feminist Book Mart Newsletters. Flushing, NY: Feminist Book Mart. Geisler, Harlynne. *A Bibliography of Non-Sexist Books for Junior and Senior High Readers*. Champaign, IL: National Organization of Women, 1973.

*General Resources for Sex Stereotyping*. San Francisco, CA: WEECN, Far West Laboratory for Research and Development, May 1979.

Hulme, Marilyn. *Fair Play, A Bibliography of Non-Stereotyped Materials (Volume II)*. New Brunswick, NJ: Training Institute for Sex Desegregation of the Public Schools, September 1977.

*Human and Anti-Human Values in Children's Books*. New York: Council on Interracial Books for Children, Inc., 1976.

Johnson, Laurie Olson. *Non-Sexist Curricular Materials for Elementary Schools*. Old Westbury, NY: The Feminist Press, 1974.

Labakow-Rudman, Masha. *Children's Literature: An Issues Approach*. Lexington, MA: D.C. Heath, 1976.

*Little Miss Muffet Fights Back*. New York: Feminists on Children's Media, n.d.

*Materials for Sex Equality Education for Use by Teachers, Parents and Young People*. Champaign, IL: National Organization of Women, 1974.

Matomatsu, Nancy R. *A Selected Bibliography of Bias-Free Materials: Grades 1–12*. Olympia, WA: Washington Office of the State Superintendent of Public Instruction, November 1977.

Millstein, Beth, et al. *Women Studies: Women in American History or HERstory: Changing Roles of American Women*. Brooklyn, NY: New York City Board of Education, Bureau of Social Studies. ED 071 754.

*Minority Women: A Sample Bibliography*. St. Paul, MN: Highland Park Elementary School, August 1978.

"New Kinds of Books for New Kinds of Girls." *Elementary English* 5 (7) (October 1973): 1035–38.

*Non-Sexist Books for Children*. Portland, OR: Multnomah County Library, n.d.

Non-Sexist Child Development Project. *Sex-Stereotyping in Child Care*. New York: Women's Action Alliance, 1973.

Olin, Ferris. *Fair Play, A Bibliography of Non-Stereotyped Materials (Volume I)*. New Brunswick, NJ: Training Institute for Sex Desegregation of the Public Schools, June 1976.

*180 Plus: A Framework for Non-Stereotyped Human Roles in Elementary Media Center Materials*. Michigan: Kalamazoo Public Schools, 1976.

Pastine, Maureen. *Articles on Non-Sexist, Non-Racist Children's Literature*. 1975. ED 117 654.

Reid, Virginia M., ed. *Reading Ladders*. Washington, DC: American Council on Education, 1972.

Resource Center for Sex Roles in Education, National Foundation for the Improvement of Education. *A Resource List of Non-Sexist Education* . Washington, DC: National Education Association, 1976.

Rosenfelt, Deborah Silverton. *Strong Women: An Annotated Bibliography of Literature for the High*

*School Classroom*. Old Westbury, NY: The Feminist Press, 1976.

*A Selected Bibliography of Bias-Free Print and Non-Print Materials* . Vancouver, WA: Vancouver Public Schools, n.d.

"Sexism in Education." *Joint Task Force Report*. Harrisburg, PA: Pennsylvania State Board of Education, 1975.

Smith, Margot and Pasternak, Carol, eds. *Breaking the Mould*. Toronto, Canada: The Ontario Institute for Studies in Education, 1977.

Sprung, Barbara. *Guide to Non-Sexist Early Childhood Education*. New York: Women's Action Alliance, 1974.

*Teaching About Women in the Social Studies: Concepts, Methods and Materials (Bulletin 48)*. Washington, DC: National Council for the Social Studies, 1976.

*Up the Hill with Jack and Jill*. Portland, OR: Portland Public Schools, n.d.

# Appendix 2: Analysis Procedures

Each book appearing in this bibliography was read by the Center for Sex Equity Program staff to determine the following:

- sex and ethnicity of the major character(s)
- specific careers listed by sex for all races
- specific careers listed by sex for ethnic groups designated in the 1970 Bureau of Census, including Black, Native American, Mexican, Puerto Rican, Chinese, Japanese, Filipino and other nonidentifiable ethnic minorities
- qualitative information to aid teachers in selecting books for their students

The determination of sex, race and particularly career bias was facilitated by the use of analysis forms developed by Britton and Associates* and adapted by program staff. (Copies of these forms are included at the end of this appendix.)

A breakdown of the total number of careers into female, male and neutral categories is noted for each book. Britton and Associates have defined "career" as providing either directly or indirectly to a person's financial support. "Mother" and "father" are counted as careers only if the person is not shown in any other career. Children's careers are not counted unless they provide a significant amount of financial support for the child or family. Careers not specifically designated in the story or its illustrations as either female or male are assigned to a neutral category (even though many of these "neutral" words evoke an image of one sex or the other to the reader, e.g., "soldier" and "nurse").

Although all of the books analyzed were selected from an existing nonsexist reading list or publishers' recommendations, very few show females in an equal or greater number of careers when compared to males. In fact, many books present females only in the traditional careers of wife, mother, nurse and teacher. Therefore, the *manner* in which female and male characters are portrayed is particularly important, and additional criteria for including a book in the bibliography had to be generated. A book was included if it generally met the following criteria:

- Girls and women portrayed in a positive manner (e.g., active, capable, independent)
- Girls and women portrayed in positive, nonstereotypic roles or with positive, nonstereotypic behaviors (e.g., overcoming obstacles, solving problems)
- Biography of a woman or women who have made a significant contribution to society
- Story about an average girl (to balance out books about average boys)
- Boys and men shown in positive, nonstereotypic roles or with positive, nonstereotypic behaviors (e.g., baking cookies, caring for children)
- Families shown in many configurations, including single parent and extended families
- Girls and boys and/or women and men shown working together effectively
- Girls and boys and/or women and men portrayed in equal friendships
- A positive portrayal of minority major characters and/or minorities well represented

It should be noted that many books portraying a female major character in a positive or nontraditional role contain language and/or secondary or peripheral characters reflecting sex bias and sex role stereotyping. Examples of this taken from books appearing in the bibliography follow:

1. "'If she were a boy...' he said longingly to himself. With that light body and grand heart he would get her into a racing stable....She'd be a great jockey some day." *National Velvet*. Enid Bagnold, 1935. p. 96.
2. "How does Margaret Mead, or any person, find the road he wishes to follow in life? A child explores many paths while he grows. But the ways that are open to him depend on the place of his birth and the era in which he is born." *Women of Courage*. Dorothy Nathan, 1964. p. 158.
3. "She was glad Rod would not be there to see her carried from the ambulance. He'd only look down

---

* Britton, Gwyneth and Lumpkin, Margaret. *A Consumer's Guide to Sex, Race and Career Bias in Public Schools Textbooks*. Corvallis, OR: Britton and Associates, 1977.

his nose at her helplessness and make it further proof of what he'd always said. Girls should never be allowed." *Tall and Proud*. Vian Smith, 1967. p. 44.

4. "Mary was glad, too, that he had seen and was proud of her little one-man show." *American Painter in Paris: A Life of Mary Cassatt*. Ellen Wilson, 1971. p. 152.

5. "Fishing is no sissy sport. Fishing is for men. That's why we have this contest for boys....We voted to open this contest to all kids. And this little girl, well, she's something special." *Rod-n-Reel Trouble*. Bobbi Katz, 1974. pp. 50, 52.

In these five books, each major character is a girl or woman in a positive and/or nonstereotypic role. Although some sex bias is virtually impossible to avoid, examples of sex role stereotypes can be used by teachers to generate class discussion.

A number of books were reviewed and not included in the bibliography because they failed to meet the previously listed criteria. Few books were rejected, however, since they were originally selected from nonsexist bibliographies and publishers' recommendations.

# CAREER, RACE AND SEX BIAS ANALYSIS FORM

TITLE: _____

TOTAL STORIES: _____

**MAJOR CHARACTERS**

Boy(s) _____

Girl(s) _____

Adult Male(s) _____

Adult Female(s) _____

Male(s) & Female(s) _____

Male Animal(s) _____

Female Animal(s) _____

Male Biography(s) _____

Female Biography(s) _____

Other _____

RACE AND/OR ETHNICITY OF MAJOR CHARACTER(S)*

## CAREER ROLES: ALL RACES

FEMALE
1.
2.
3.
4.
5.
6.
7.

MALE
1.
2.
3.
4.
5.
6.
7.

NEUTRAL
1.
2.
3.
4.
5.

## CAREER ROLES: ETHNIC GROUPS *

FEMALE
*
1.
2.
3.
4.
5.

MALE
*
1.
2.
3.
4.
5.

NEUTRAL
*
1.
2.
3.

*Write in applicable Bureau of Census ethnic group category(s), including Black, Native American, Mexican, Puerto Rican, Chinese, Japanese, Filipino and other ( identify if possible ).

## CAREER ROLES: ALL RACES

Female _____ Male _____ Neutral _____ Total _____

## CAREER ROLES: ETHNIC GROUPS

Female _____ Male _____ Neutral _____ Total _____

Adapted from: Britton, Gwyneth and Lumpkin, Margaret. *A Consumer's Guide to Sex, Race and Career Bias in Public School Textbooks.* Corvallis, Oregon: Britton & Associates, 1977, by the Center for Sex Equity, Northwest Regional Educational Laboratory, Portland, Oregon. pp. 37-45.

# Appendix 3: Readability

The books in this bibliography are organized by grade level readability. Researchers and publishers have developed readability formulas in order to determine how difficult a piece of written narrative is to read and understand. The level of difficulty is normally expressed in terms of school grade equivalents. (For example: a book with a fourth grade reading level is labeled "4.") The primary function of readability labels is to enable educators to match a student's skills to a story's level of difficulty and, as a result, to provide a more successful reading experience for the student.

Each book appearing in the bibliography was subjected to a computerized readability assessment developed by Britton and Associates.* Five formulas were used to analyze sample passages from the materials to determine a grade rating. Samples were taken in accordance with a plan designed to eliminate sampling bias. The formulas selected for the computerized program by Britton and Associates are as follows:

- Spache (range: pre-primary through grade 3)
- Harris-Jacobson (range: pre-primary through grade 8)
- Fry (range: grades 1 through 13)
- Dale-Chall (range: grades 4 through 16)
- Flesch (range: grades 5 through 17)

Britton and Associates offer several reasons why they chose to use these particular formulas, including (1) the formulas have been validated by extensive research; (2) they are objective; (3) they can be computerized; and (4) they are most frequently cited by publishers and therefore familiar to many people.

In determining a book's reading grade level for this bibliography, greater emphasis was given to the results of the following *vocabulary-based* formulas: Spache (for grades 1 and 2); Harris-Jacobson (for grades 3 and 4); and Dale-Chall (for grades 5 and above).

---

* Britton, Gwyneth and Lumpkin, Margaret. *Reading, A Consumer's Guide. Computerized Analysis: Reading Perspectives.* D.C. Heath, 1975. Corvallis, OR: Britton and Associates, 1978.

# Appendix 4: Subject Definitions

1. AMERICAN ETHNIC MINORITY. Stories whose major characters are members of American ethnic minority groups, as identified by the 1970 Bureau of the Census, including Black, Native American, Mexican, Puerto Rican, Chinese, Japanese, Filipino and other nonidentifiable ethnic minorities; stories that deal with topics relevant to American ethnic minority groups.
2. ANIMALS. Stories about animals or with animal characters.
3. AUTOBIOGRAPHY/BIOGRAPHY. Books containing the life history of one or more individuals.
4. BEHAVIORAL SCIENCE. Books focusing on the behavior of human beings in society from an anthropological, sociological or psychological perspective.
5. CAREERS. Books exploring careers and career choices.
6. CONTEMPORARY ISSUES/CURRENT EVENTS. Books dealing with issues and events of the latter half of the twentieth century (1950 to the present), such as civil rights, politics, environmental concerns and the modern women's movement.
7. CULTURAL HERITAGE. Books portraying the culture, social traditions, behavior patterns or beliefs particular to a specific population group in America or abroad.
8. FAMILIES/FRIENDSHIP. Stories about individual relationships among friends and family members.
9. FINE ARTS. Stories about art, dance, film and music and individuals in these fields.
10. FOREIGN COUNTRIES. Stories about or set in countries other than the United States.
11. THE HANDICAPPED. Stories whose characters confront problems of physical or mental impairment.
12. HEALTH/HUMAN DEVELOPMENT. Stories about the emotional, mental and physical growth and development of human beings; stories about "growing up."
13. HISTORY. Stories relating to or based on events or people in history (pre–1950).
14. INFORMATION BOOK. Books conveying factual information about a place, thing, event or phenomenon, which are not included under any of the other subject matter categories.
15. LANGUAGE ARTS. Books that focus on the creative expression of language in prose and poetry.

*Anthologies*: A collection of literary works which may include poems, short stories, essays and plays, written by a variety of authors.
*Drama*: Prose or verse written for performance by actors.
*Essays/Short Stories*: Short literary composition(s) on a single subject, usually presenting the personal views of the author; short prose fiction aiming at unity of characterization, theme and effect.
*Fantasy, Folk & Fairy Tales*: Stories characterized by highly fanciful or supernatural elements; stories handed down from earlier times which are culturally based.
*Literature by Women*: Literary works, usually poetry or prose fiction, that are written by women and are generally considered to be "classics"—part of the body of great literature taught and studied in high school and college; literature by women generally considered to be "important" or "classic" authors.
*Poetry/Rhyme*: Stories in verse, including anthologies and rhyming tales; biographies of poets.

16. MYSTERY/ADVENTURE. Stories having elements of suspense, excitement and risk, or dealing with unexplained, secret or unknown phenomena.
17. PICTURE BOOK. Books with approximately 50 pages or less, having more pictures than text.
18. RELIGION/MYTHOLOGY. Stories dealing with a character's relationship to his or her church, or stories based on or about a particular religion's beliefs or philosophy.
19. SCIENCE FICTION. Fiction in which scientific discoveries and development form an element of plot or background, particularly fiction based on prediction of future scientific possibilities.
20. SCIENCE/TECHNOLOGY. Books about the observation, identification, description, experimental investigation and theoretical explanation of natural phenomena; books about the application of science to industrial or commercial objectives.
21. SPORTS. Stories about athletic competition, team and individual sport events and the players.
22. WOMEN'S STUDIES. Books focusing on women and society from an anthropological, biological, cultural, historical, psychological and/or sociological perspective; books about women's lives—their day-to-day hopes, dreams, problems and struggles.

# Title Index

ABC Play with Me, 4.61
ABC Workbook, 4.12
Abigail Adams: "Dear Partner," 3.9
About Dying, 2.73
Adventures of B.J., The Amateur Detective, 6.21
Aekyung's Dream, 2.86
African Rhythm—American Dance: A Biography of Katherine Dunham, 10.2
After the Wedding, 6.53
Against Rape, 8.38
Album of Women in American History, An, 7.24
Alesia, 5.57
All Kinds of Families, 2.39
Along Sandy Trails, 4.34
Amazing Miss Laura, The, 3.40
Amelia Earhart, 2.55
America's First Woman Astronomer: Maria Mitchell, 6.42
America's First Woman Chemist: Ellen Richards, 6.77
American Painter in Paris: A Life of Mary Cassatt, 8.1
American Women in Sports, 8.7
Amigo, 2.47
Amy and the Cloud Basket, 5.5
And All Her Paths Were Peace, 8.20
And I Mean It, Stanley, 1.2
Andrea Jaeger Tennis Champion, 4.62
Animal Daddies and My Daddy, 2.68
Animals Should Definitely *Not* Wear Clothing, 3.2
Ann Aurelia and Dorothy, 3.36
Ann Can Fly, 1.5
Annie and the Old One, 5.13
Annie Sullivan, 2.50
Anywhere Else But Here, 4.83
Are You in the House Alone?, 6.54
Are You There God? It's Me, Margaret, 4.7
Ariel: Poems by Sylvia Plath, 6.52
Arthur Mitchell, 4.63
Autobiography of Miss Jane Pittman, The, 4.60

Balancing Girl, The, 2.87
Ballet Shoes, 5.22

Barefoot in the Grass: The Story of Grandma Moses, 6.78
Beautiful, Also, Are the Souls of My Black Sisters, 11.7
Beckoner, The, 4.76
Becky and the Bear, 2.7
Before the Supreme Court: The Story of Belva Ann Lockwood, 4.19
Bell Jar, The, 6.55
Bella Abzug, 8.29
Best Friends for Frances, 2.40
Billie Jean, 7.41
Billie Jean King: Queen of the Courts, 4.65
Birthday for Frances, A, 2.37
Bitter Herbs and Honey, 5.35
Black Artists of the New Generation, 7.50
Black Cow Summer, 6.93
Black Foremothers: Three Lives, 9.23
Black Is Brown Is Tan, 2.8
Black Stallion and the Girl, The, 7.3
Blackberry Winter: My Earlier Years, 9.14
Bloomsday for Maggie, 9.19
Blue Collar Jobs for Women, 9.24
Blue Trees, Red Sky, 2.22
Blueberries for Sal, 3.24
Bluest Eye, The, 7.42
Bodies, 2.4
Book about Us, A, 3.50
Borrowers, The, 4.29
Bouquets for Brimbal, 6.80
Boy Who Wanted a Family, The, 4.79
Boys Have Feelings Too: Growing Up Male for Boys, 9.28
Breakthrough: Women in Religion, 8.36
Breakthrough: Women in Writing, 9.29
By and about Women: An Anthology of Short Fiction, 6.74
By the Highway Home, 4.68

Cameras and Courage: Margaret Bourke-White, 7.62
Cancer Lady: Maud Slye and Her Heredity Studies, The, 8.23
Careers in Conservation, 8.27

Carlotta and the Scientist, 3.20
Cat Ate My Gymsuit, The, 5.42
Chair for My Mother, A, 2.88
Changeling, The, 4.43
Charlotte Forten: Free Black Teacher, 6.34
Charlotte's Web, 3.38
Chemistry Careers, 11.10
Chief Sarah: Sarah Winnemucca's Fight for Indian Rights, 6.76
Child of the Dark: The Diary of Carolina Maria de Jesus, 3.45
Childtimes: A Three Generation Memoir, 6.61
Chris Evert: Tennis Pro, 4.37
Christmas Memory, A, 6.87
Clara Barton: Founder of the American Red Cross, 6.40
Clara Barton: Soldier of Mercy, 3.6
Classmates by Request, 6.37
Claudia, Where Are You, 6.43
Clever Gretchen and Other Forgotten Folktales, 5.47
Clever Princess, The, 4.79
Clock Book, The, 2.63
Clowning Around, 2.51
Cold Feet, 2.69
Coleen the Question Girl, 3.16
Come by Here, 5.24
Commonsense Sex, 12.8
Contraception, Abortion, Pregnancy, 12.5
Contributions of Women: Education, 7.23
Contributions of Women: Labor, 6.96
Contributions of Women: Sports, 7.26
Country Bunny and the Little Golden Shoes, The, 5.2
Country of Broken Stone, 7.72
Cowgirls: Women of the American West, 6.102
Cowslip, 4.25
Crazy Salad: Some Things about Women, 7.47
Cross Fox, 3.47
Cry of the Crow, The, 3.57
Cuckoo Tree, The, 4.26
Curious Missie, 3.3

Daddy, 3.12
Daddy and Ben Together, 2.85
Daddy Is a Monster...Sometimes, 6.94
Daddy Was a Number Runner, 4.70
Dancer, 9.27
Darlene, 2.82
Daughter of Discontent, 7.31
Daughter of Earth, 6.50
Daughter of the Mountains, 7.11
Daughters of the Earth: Lives and Legends of American Indian Women, 9.9
Deadline, 8.21
Delilah, 2.29
Did You Ever?, 6.12
Dinky Hocker Shoots Smack!, 4.57
Doctor Mary's Animals, 7.7
Doctors for the People, 8.22
Dollmaker, The, 8.39
Don't Forget Tom, 3.49
Don't Play Dead before You Have to, 6.62
Don't Put Vinegar in the Copper, 5.56
Don't Ride the Bus on Monday: The Rosa Parks Story, 2.38
Don't You Remember?, 2.9
Dorothea L. Dix: Hospital Founder, 2.15
Dorothy Day: Friend of the Poor, 6.64
Downright Dencey, 7.28
Dragon and the Doctor, The, 3.22
Dragonwings, 5.45
Dreams in Harrison Railroad Park, 7.51
Dumb Old Casey Is a Fat Tree, 2.65
Dust of the Earth, 6.32

Early Rising, 5.37
Egypt Game, The, 6.33
Eleanor Roosevelt: First Lady of the World, 2.57
Elizabeth Blackwell, Pioneer Doctor, 4.64
Eliza's Daddy, 3.21
Eloquent Crusader: Ernestine Rose, 9.1
Emma Tupper's Diary, 6.3
Emmeline and Her Daughters: The Pankhurst Suffragettes, 6.25
Empty Schoolhouse, The, 4.31
Enchantress from the Stars, 8.16
Endless Steppe: A Girl in Exile, The, 6.14
Enterprising Women, 9.15
Eskimo Birthday, An, 4.73
Evan's Corner, 2.34

Famous American Women, 9.25
Famous Modern American Women Athletes, 7.27
Famous Spies, 8.3
Fannie Lou Hamer, 4.30
Fanny Kemble's America, 9.2
Fanshen, the Magic Bear, 8.19

Farewell to Manzanar, 6.4
Fat Jack, 6.60
Feast of Light, A, 6.38
Feminine Mystique, The, 9.10
Feminine Plural: Stories by Women about Growing Up, 6.59
Feminism: The Essential Historical Writings, 10.8
Fifth Chinese Daughter, 6.57
Fighting Shirley Chisholm, 7.30
Firegirl, 4.47
First Snow, 5.12
First Woman Ambulance Surgeon: Emily Barringer, 6.46
Flat on My Face, 4.5
Forge and the Forest, The, 7.1
Four Women in a Violent Time, 9.3
Four Women of Courage, 3.27
Frankie and the Fawn, 3.26
Free to Be...You and Me, 8.34
Free to Choose: Decision Making for Young Men, 7.37
Fresh Fish...and Chips, 7.8
From Parlor to Prison, 7.66
Frontiers of Dance: The Life of Martha Graham, 9.13

Gather Together in My Name, 9.11
Gaudy Night, 8.32
Gender Trap: A Closer Look at Sex Roles (Book 1: Education and Work), The, 8.24
George Sand, 8.15
Girl Sports, 6.72
Girl Who Loved Wild Horses, The, 3.66
Girl Who Would Rather Climb Trees, The, 2.11
Girls of Huntington House, The, 4.51
Go Well, Stay Well, 7.67
Going to the Sun, 5.55
Golda Meir Story, The, 6.92
Good Morrow, The, 2.16
Grandma Didn't Wave Back, 2.26
Granny's Fish Story, 2.6
Grownups Cry Too, 2.32

Hannah Senesh: Her Life and Diary, 8.40
Happy Endings Are All Alike, 3.60
Harriet and the Promised Land, 3.5
Harriet and the Runaway Book, 2.31
Harriet the Spy, 3.29
Harriet Tubman: Conductor on the Underground Railroad, 6.23
Haunted Summer, 5.46
He Bear, She Bear, 2.46
Headless Cupid, The, 6.39
Heart Is a Lonely Hunter, The, 5.41
Heart-of-Snowbird, 3.13
Heidi, 5.29
Helen Keller: Toward the Light, 2.56
Hello, Aurora, 3.8
Hero Ain't Nothing but a Sandwich, A, 9.12

Heroines of '76, 2.53
Hey, Dollface, 4.66
Hideaway Summer, The, 5.53
Higher than the Arrow, 3.55
Hiroshima No Pika, 3.72
Hole Is to Dig, A, 1.4
House for Jonnie O., A, 3.53
House without a Christmas Tree, The, 6.36
How Many Miles to Sundown?, 4.54
Howie Helps Himself, 2.25

I Always Wanted to be Somebody, 6.70
"I Am Cherry Alive," the Little Girl Sang, 6.95
I Am the Fire of Time, 9.30
I Am the Running Girl, 4.72
I Can Be Anything: Careers and Colleges for Young Women, 10.10
I Can Help Too, 1.3
I Carve Stone, 6.82
I, Charlotte Forten, Black and Free, 8.4
I Climb Mountains, 4.11
I Know Why the Caged Bird Sings, 6.81
I Love Gram, 2.41
I Love Myself When I Am Laughing, 7.55
I Never Promised You a Rose Garden, 8.26
I Was So Mad!, 2.20
I Wish Laura's Mommy Was My Mommy, 2.75
Ida Early Comes over the Mountain, 5.58
Iggie's House, 4.16
Ikwa of the Temple Mounds, 3.18
I'll Get There: It Better Be Worth the Trip, 4.55
I'm Deborah Sampson: A Soldier in the War of the Revolution, 5.54
I'm Nobody! Who Are You?, 7.25
I'm Running Away from Home but I'm Not Allowed to Cross the Street, 9.17
In Her Own Image: Women Working in the Arts, 8.41
Ira Sleeps Over, 3.7
Island of the Blue Dolphins, 3.4
Israel's Golda Meir: Pioneer to Prime Minister, 6.47
It Can't Hurt Forever, 3.54
It's Not the End of the World, 2.62
It's Not What You Expect, 5.30

Jacob Have I Loved, 7.53
Jane Addams, 2.35
Jane Addams, 3.61
Jellybeans for Breakfast, 2.49
Jemmy, 4.75
Jennifer, Hecate, MacBeth, William McKinley and Me, Elizabeth, 4.15
Jenny Kimura, 7.63

Jewish Woman: New Perspectives, The, 11.6
Jim Meets The Thing, 2.81
Jo, Flo and Yolanda, 4.1
Joshua's Day, 2.30
Journey of the Shadow Bairns, The, 6.99
Journey to America, 4.36
Jubilee, 7.34
Judy's Journey, 5.4
Julie of the Wolves, 6.27
Just Think!, 2.36

Kathe Kollwitz: Life in Art, 8.13
Kids Are Natural Cooks, 4.42
Kristy's Courage, 4.27

Lady Ellen Grae, 6.2
Lady for the Defense: A Biography of Belva Lockwood, 6.63
Lady Sings the Blues, 5.33
Lancelot Closes at Five, The, 3.55
Language of Show Dancing, The, 10.12
Lark and the Laurel, The, 7.2
Law and the New Woman, 8.12
Lawyers for the People: A New Breed of Defenders and Their Work, 9.21
Leap before You Look, 6.45
Leaving Home, 5.50
Legends of American Indian Women, 9.9
Lemon and a Star, A, 6.7
Leo the Lioness, 6.30
Liberation of Clementine Tipton, The, 6.26
Life in the Iron Mills, 8.37
Life with Working Parents: Practical Hints for Everyday Situations, 7.29
Liking Myself, 5.48
Linda Richards: First American Trained Nurse, 2.59
Lion, the Witch and the Wardrobe, The, 5.23
Lisa, Bright and Dark, 4.56
Listen for the Fig Tree, 7.44
Listen to Your Kitten Purr, 6.85
Little Lion, A, 4.4
Liza Lou and the Yeller Belly Swamp, 4.10
Long Way from Verona, A, 6.91
Look at Divorce, A, 2.80
Looking Forward to a Career: Veterinary Medicine, 12.4
Loon Feather, The, 7.48
Lordy, Aunt Hattie, 5.1
Lucille, 2.24
Ludell, 6.79
Ludell's New York Time, 7.54
Lupita Manana, 5.59

Maggie Rose: Her Birthday Christmas, 7.21
Magic at Wynchwood, 7.4
Magic Hat, The, 5.14
Mahalia: Gospel Singer, 4.39

Maid of the North: Feminist Folktales from around the World, The, 6.100
Making Our Way, 5.32
Male & Female under 18, 8.28
Man Who Didn't Wash His Dishes, The, 5.7
Mandy and the Flying Map, 3.14
Man's World, Woman's Place: A Study in Social Mythology, 12.6
Margaret Mead, 10.7
Margaret Sanger: Pioneer of Birth Control, 6.84
Maria Looney and the Remarkable Robot, 4.59
Maria Luisa, 4.6
Maria Montessori: Knight of the Child, 7.56
Maria Sanford: Pioneer Professor, 7.5
Maria Tallchief, 5.8
Maria Teresa, 3.62
Marian Anderson, 2.14
Marie Curie, 8.25
Marly the Kid, 3.42
Martha Berry: Little Woman with a Big Dream, 9.5
Martha Quest, 8.31
Martin's Father, 5.17
Mary Jane, 5.18
Mary Jo's Grandmother, 2.3
Mary McLeod Bethune, 3.32
Mary McLeod Bethune, 4.71
Mary's Monster, 6.17
Masculine/Feminine: Readings in Social Mythology and the Liberation of Women, 12.1
Master Rosalind, 6.6
Math Equals: Biographies of Women + Related Activities, 9.20
Maude Reed Tale, The, 5.34
Max, 2.2
Me Too, 4.78
Member of the Wedding, The, 5.31
Memoirs of an Ex-Prom Queen, 4.50
Men's Bodies Men's Selves, 9.26
Millicent the Magnificent, 3.59
Min-Min, The, 5.36
Mirror Mirror: Images of Women Reflected in Popular Culture, 11.1
Miss Bianca, 8.2
Miss Hickory, 6.20
Mixed Marriage Daughter, 3.43
Mom, the Wolfman and Me, 3.44
Monday I Was an Alligator, 2.66
Moon Eyes, 5.19
Motherlove: Stories by Women about Motherhood, 7.61
Mothers Can Do Anything, 2.31
Mouse, the Monster and Me, The, 6.73
Moy Moy, 4.14
Mrs. Dalloway, 6.71
Mrs. Frisby and the Rats of NIMH, 5.27
Ms. Attorney, 10.1
Ms.—M.D., 9.4

Mulberry Music, The, 3.25
Mumbet: The Story of Elizabeth Freeman, 4.38
My Antonia, 7.36
My Daddy Don't Go to Work, 2.76
My Doctor, 4.2
My Doctor Bag Book, 2.64
My Little Book of Cats, 6.83
My Mom Travels a Lot, 2.83
My Mother and I Are Growing Strong, 3.69
My Mother the Mail Carrier, 4.35

Nancy Ward, Cherokee, 2.60
Nannabah's Friend, 3.11
Naomi, 5.28
National Velvet, 7.13
Nectar in a Sieve, 6.49
Never Jam Today, 3.39
New Women in Entertainment, 8.43
New Women in Medicine, 8.42
New Women in Politics, 10.5
Nice Little Girls, 2.45
Nick Joins In, 2.79
Night Journey, The, 7.71
Nilda, 6.8
Nine Lives of Moses: On the Oregon Trail, 6.9
Nobody's Family Is Going to Change, 2.18
Noisy Nora, 2.19
Notes on the Hauter Experiment: A Journey through the Inner World of Evelyn B. Chestnut, 4.45
Nothing but a Dog, 7.60
Nothing Is Impossible: The Story of Beatrix Potter, 4.23
Now One Foot, Now the Other, 2.84

O Pioneers!, 5.52
Of Life and Death and Other Journeys, 6.90
Oh, Boy! Babies!, 3.67
Oh, Lizzie! The Story of Elizabeth Cady Stanton, 7.10
Oh, Lord, I Wish I Was a Buzzard, 2.5
Once at the Weary Way, 6.65
100 Greatest Women in Sports, 9.7
Only Love, 6.98
Ostrich Chase, The, 4.46
Other Choices for Becoming a Woman, 7.38
Our Cup Is Broken, 4.53
Our Hidden Heritage: Five Centuries of Women Artists, 10.3
Over the Hills and Far Away, 3.10

Patriots in Petticoats, 8.5
Pearl in the Egg, 4.82
Penelope and the Mussels, 4.9
Persuasion, 12.3
Phillis Wheatley: America's First Black Poetess, 6.28
Phoebe's Revolt, 5.15

Pictorial History of Women in America, A, 9.18
Pigman, The, 5.39
Pioneer Women: Voices from the Kansas Frontier, 5.62
Pippa Mouse, 2.13
Plants in Winter, 2.27
Plays by and about Women, 6.66
Pony for Linda, A, 2.52
Popcorn Venus, 11.2
Portraits of Chinese Women in Revolution, 9.32
Practical Princess and Other Liberating Fairy Tales, The, 4.8
Preacher's Kid, The, 4.13
Prime of Miss Jean Brodie, The, 8.11
Princess and the Admiral, The, 7.22
Promise Is a Promise, A, 3.15
Proud Taste for Scarlet and Miniver, A, 6.13
Psychology and the New Woman, 11.4

Queenie Peavy, 6.11
Quiet on Account of Dinosaur, 2.44

Rabbit Finds a Way, 1.7
Rabbit Is Next, The, 2.77
Rachel Carson: Who Loved the Sea, 2.21
Rachel Pushes Back, 3.52
Rafiki, 4.18
Ramona Quimby, Age 8, 5.60
Ramona the Pest, 3.1
Real Me, The, 3.30
Rebecca of Sunnybrook Farm, 7.15
Red Rock over the River, 3.31
Rice Cakes and Paper Dragons, 3.51
Rights and Wrongs: Women's Struggle for Equality, 12.9
Rod-and-Reel Trouble, 2.43
Roll of Thunder, Hear My Cry, 7.59
Room of One's Own, A, 8.17
Root of Bitterness, 10.6
Rosa Parks, 2.42
Rose Kennedy: No Time for Tears, 7.58
Rosie and Michael, 4.24
Ruby, 6.86
Runaway Summer, The, 5.6
Runaway to Freedom: A Story of the Underground Railway, 5.20

Sacagawea: The Story of an American Indian, 5.3
Sam, 6.88
Saturday's Child, 8.44
Science Experiments You Can Eat, 6.69
Sea and Earth: The Life of Rachel Carson, 8.30
Search for Charlie, The, 6.16
Secret Castle, 5.25
Secret Garden, The, 7.16
Self-Defense and Assault Prevention for Girls and Women, 11.8

Self-Portrait: Margot Zemach, 4.81
Selma, Lord, Selma, 6.75
Senator from Maine: Margaret Chase Smith, The, 7.17
Sex and Birth Control, 10.4
Sexes: Male/Female Roles and Relationships, The, 4.58
She Never Looked Back: Margaret Mead in Samoa, 7.70
She Shoots, She Scores!, 6.1
She Wanted to Read: The Story of Mary McLeod Bethume, 4.17
Shirley Chisholm: A Biography, 7.19
Shoeshine Girl, 2.28
Sidewalk Story, 2.23
Silent Storm, The, 7.35
Silver Whistle, The, 3.17
Sing to the Dawn, 7.14
Single and Pregnant, 11.3
Skull in the Snow and Other Folktales, The, 6.101
Snow, 1.6
Sojourner Truth: Fearless Crusader, 4.32
Some Lose Their Way, 3.65
Some Things You Just Can't Do by Yourself, 5.49
Somebody's Angel Child: The Story of Bessie Smith, 7.32
Song of Sedna, 7.69
Soul Brothers and Sister Lou, The, 3.41
Sports for the Handicapped, 9.31
Squire's Bride, The, 6.18
Stand Up Lucy, 4.52
Star Ka'ats and the Plant People, 3.56
Steffie and Me, 2.58
Stories for Free Children, 4.84
Story of Ferdinand, The, 4.33
Story of Helen Keller, The, 4.3
Street, The, 6.44
Stubborn Old Woman, The, 2.71
Sue Ellen, 3.19
Sumi's Prize, 3.34
Summer of My German Soldier, 6.68
Sunflower Garden, The, 5.11
Sunshine, 1.9
Sunshine Family and the Pony, The, 2.17
Susan B. Anthony: Pioneer in Women's Rights, 5.9
Susannah and the Blue House Mystery, 6.97
Susette La Flesche: Voice of the Omaha Indians, 6.41
Sweet Whispers, Brother Rush, 3.68

Tall and Proud, 6.19
Tamarack Tree, The, 6.35
Taste of Spruce Gum, The, 6.31
Tatterhood and Other Tales, 5.26
Tell Me a Riddle, 6.58
Terrible Thing that Happened at Our House, The, 5.10
Thank You All Very Much, 7.43
That Is That, 2.72

They Wouldn't Quit: Stories of Handicapped People, 7.12
This Time of Darkness, 5.51
This Time, Tempe Wick?, 6.22
Three Days on a River in a Red Canoe, 3.70
Three Stalks of Corn, 7.9
Through Grandpa's Eyes, 2.74
Thunder at Gettysburg, 3.23
Tiger Eyes, 3.71
Time at the Top, 7.18
Time for Everything, A, 8.33
Tisha, 5.44
To the Barricades: The Anarchist Life of Emma Goldman, 7.20
Tommy and Sarah Dress Up, 4.20
Train, The, 1.1
Train for Jane, A, 3.28
Transport 7-41-R, 6.51
Tree Grows in Brooklyn, A, 6.48
Trouble with Princesses, The, 7.73
Trouble with Thirteen, The, 3.46
True Grit, 5.21
Try and Catch Me, 2.48
Two Piano Tuners, 4.41
Two Tickets to Freedom: The True Story of Ellen and William Craft, Fugitive Slaves, 4.22

Umbrella, 2.33

Very Easy Death, A, 8.14

Waiting for Johnny Miracle, 3.58
Watching the Wild Apes: The Primate Studies of Goodall, Fossey and Galdikas, 9.16
We Are Mesquakie, We Are One, 2.70
What Are Little Girls Made Of? The Roots of Feminine Stereotypes, 11.9
What Can She Be? A Computer Scientist, 9.22
What Can She Be? A Farmer, 5.43
What Can She Be? A Geologist, 7.64
What Can She Be? A Lawyer, 4.28
What Can She Be? A Legislator, 6.67
What Can She Be? A Newscaster, 4.67
What Can She Be? A Police Officer, 4.77
What Can She Be? A Veterinarian, 4.21
What Can She Be? An Architect, 7.45
What Is a Girl? What Is a Boy?, 1.8
What Mary Jo Wanted, 2.54
What Will I Be?, 3.63
Where Is Daddy? The Story of a Divorce, 2.67
Where the Lilies Bloom, 4.44
Why Am I Different?, 2.1

Why Am I So Miserable If These Are the Best Years of My Life?, 8.8

Wife of Martin Guerre, The, 7.33

Wild Animals, Gentle Women, 8.35

Wilderness Challenge, 5.61

Will I Have a Friend?, 2.12

William's Doll, 3.33

Wind Is Not a River, The, 4.74

Window Wishing, 4.69

Winter Wheat, 3.48

Witch of Blackbird Pond, The, 5.38

Witches, Midwives and Nurses: A History of Women Healers, 12.2

Witch's Daughter, The, 6.5

Woman Chief, 5.40

Woman Warrior: Memoirs of a Girlhood among Ghosts, The, 7.65

Women and Fiction: Short Stories by and about Women, 7.52

Women and Womanhood in America, 12.7

Women Artists: Recognition and Reappraisal from the Early Middle Ages to the Twentieth Century, 11.5

Women at Their Work, 6.15

Women in Music, 9.6

Women in Sports: Swimming, 7.68

Women in Television, 7.40

Women of Courage, 6.10

Women of Crisis: Lives of Struggle and Hope, 6.89

Women of the West, 6.24

Women of Wonder: Science Fiction Stories by Women about Women, 8.10

Women See Women, 10.9

Women Who Dared to Be Different, 2.61

Women Who Shaped History, 7.57

Women Who Win, 8.6

Women with a Cause, 5.16

Women Working: An Anthology of Stories and Poems, 7.49

Womenfolk and Fairy Tales, 4.49

Women's Rights, 7.39

Wonder Women of Sports, 3.69

Words in Our Hands, 2.78

World of Mary Cassatt, The, 7.46

Wrinkle in Time, A, 6.29

Year in the Life of Rosie Bernard, A, 4.40

Yellow Wallpaper, The, 8.18

Young and Female, 8.9

Young Woman's Guide to Liberation, The, 9.8

Zanballer, 7.6

Zeely, 4.48

Zia, 3.37

# Author Index

Adams, Carol, 8.24
Adoff, Arnold, 2.8, 4.72
Aiken, Joan, 4.26
Aldis, Dorothy, 4.23
Allen, Anne, 9.31
Allinson, Beverley, 2.51, 3.14, 7.7
Anderson, C.W., 2.52
Anderson, Margaret J., 6.99
Andrews, Jan, 7.8
Angelou, Maya, 6.81, 9.11
Anticaglia, Elizabeth, 2.53
Archer, Marion Fuller, 6.9
Armstrong, William H., 6.78
Arnow, Harriette, 8.39
Asbjornsen, P.C., 6.18
Atkinson, Mary, 3.62
Austin, Jane, 12.3

Babbitt, Natalie, 5.15
Bach, Alice, 3.58, 3.59
Bagnold, Enid, 7.13
Bailey, Carolyn Sherwin, 6.20
Baker, Joanna Merlen, 6.42
Baker, Rachel, 6.42
Barrett, Judi, 3.2
Barth, Edna, 7.25
Bauer, Caroline Feller, 2.83
Bawden, Nina, 5.6, 6.5
Beatty, Jerome Jr., 4.59
Beatty, John, 6.6
Beatty, Patricia, 3.31, 4.54, 5.59, 6.6
Begley, Kathleen A., 8.21
Belotti, Elena Gianini, 11.9
Berenstain, Jan, 2.46
Berenstain, Stan, 2.46
Biddle, Marcia McKenna, 6.96
Bird, Caroline, 9.15
Blackburn, Joyce, 9.5
Blaine, Marge, 5.10
Blair, Ruth VanNess, 6.17
Blos, Joan, 2.36
Blue, Rose, 2.26, 4.13
Blume, Judy, 2.62, 3.71, 4.7, 4.16
Boccaccio, Shirley, 4.9
Boegehold, Betty, 2.13
Bolton, Carole, 3.39
Bond, Nancy, 7.72
Bonsall, Crosby, 1.2
Bottner, Barbara, 2.65
Bowman, Kathleen, 8.42, 8.43, 10.5
Boylston, Helen Dore, 6.40
Brenner, Barbara, 2.4, 4.40

Brown, Marion Marsh, 7.35
Brownmiller, Susan, 7.19
Buckmaster, Henrietta, 7.57
Bulla, Clyde Robert, 2.28, 2.71
Burch, Robert, 5.58, 6.11
Burgess, Mary W., 7.23
Burnett, Frances Hodgson, 7.16
Burton, Gabrielle, 9.17

Cahill, Susan (ed.), 7.52
Caines, Jeannette, 3.12, 4.69
Capote, Truman, 6.87
Carlson, Dale, 9.29
Carlson, Natalie Savage, 3.36, 4.31
Carruth, Ella Kaiser, 4.7
Cather, Willa, 5.52, 7.36
Cavanna, Betty, 7.63
Chapman, Kim Westsmith, 5.14
Childress, Alice, 9.12
Church, Carol Bauer, 4.65, 6.64, 7.58
Clapp, Patricia, 5.54
Clark, Ann Nolan, 4.34
Clark, Mavis Thorpe, 5.36
Clarke, Joan, 5.37
Cleary, Beverly, 3.1, 5.60
Cleaver, Bill, 4.44, 4.78, 6.2, 6.32
Cleaver, Vera, 4.44, 4.78, 6.2, 6.32
Clements, Bruce, 4.83
Clifton, Lucille, 2.9
Clyne, Patricia Edwards, 8.5
Cobb, Vicki, 6.69
Cohen, Barbara, 5.35, 6.60
Cohen, Miriam, 2.12, 2.81
Cole, Joanna, 2.27
Coles, Jane Hallowell, 6.89
Coles, Robert, 6.89
Collins, David R., 2.59
Colman, Hila, 3.40, 3.43, 6.37, 6.43, 6.53, 7.31
Colver, Ann, 5.25
Cone, Molly, 3.15
Coolidge, Olivia, 5.24
Corcoran, Barbara, 6.88
Cott, Nancy F. (ed.), 10.6
Coutant, Helen, 5.12
Cowles, Kathleen Krull, 3.63
Crary, Margaret, 6.41
Crawford, Deborah, 9.3
Crone, Ruth, 7.35

D'Adamo, Anthony, 2.55
Daly, Kathleen N., 2.64
Danish, Barbara, 3.22
Danziger, Paula, 5.42
Davidson, Margaret, 6.92
Davis, Rebecca Harding, 8.37
de Beauvoir, Simone, 8.14
de Jesus, Carolina Maria, 3.45
de Paola, Tomie, 2.84
DeCrow, Karen, 9.8
Degens, T., 6.51
Delton, Judy, 1.7
dePoix, Carol, 4.1
Diamond, Felicia, 9.6
Dickinson, Peter, 6.3
Dixon, Paige, 6.16
Donnelly, Linda, 7.8
Donovan, John, 4.55
Douty, Esther M., 6.34, 6.77
Drabble, Margaret, 7.43
Dunnahoo, Terry, 4.19

Eagan, Andrea Boroff, 8.8
Eastman, P.D., 1.6
Ehrenreich, Barbara, 12.2
Eichler, Margrit, 5.17
Elfman, Blossom, 3.53, 4.51
Elmore, Patricia, 6.97
Engdahl, Sylvia Louise, 8.16
English, Betty Lou, 6.15
English, Deirdre, 12.2
Ephron, Nora, 7.47
Epstein, Beryl, 7.70
Epstein, Sam, 7.70

Faber, Doris, 7.10, 8.29
Facklam, Margery, 8.35
Farley, Walter, 7.3
Fassler, Joan, 2.25
Felton, Harold W., 2.60, 4.38
Fenten, D.X., 9.4, 10.1
Fine, Joan, 6.82
First, Julia, 4.5
Fitzhugh, Louise, 2.18, 3.29
Fleming, Alice, 7.17, 12.5
Flory, Jane, 6.26
Fogel, Julianna A., 4.62
Fox, Elton C., 7.50
Fox, Mary Virginia, 6.63
Freedman, Florence B., 4.22
Friedan, Betty, 9.10
Friis, Babbis, 4.27

Fuller, Iola, 7.48
Fuller, Miriam Morris, 6.28

Gaines, Ernest J., 4.60
Gardam, Jane, 6.91
Gauch, Patricia Lee, 3.23, 6.22
Gelfand, Ravina, 7.12
George, Jean Craighead, 3.57, 5.55, 6.27
Gibson, Althea, 6.70
Gillum, Helen L., 12.4
Gilman, Charlotte Perkins, 8.18
Gleasner, Diana C., 7.68, 9.30
Gluck, Sherna (ed.), 7.66
Goble, Paul, 3.66
Goff, Beth, 2.67
Goffstein, M.B., 4.41
Goldreich, Esther, 4.21, 4.28, 4.67, 4.77, 5.43, 6.67, 7.45, 7.64, 9.22
Goldreich, Gloria, 4.21, 4.28, 4.67, 4.77, 5.43, 6.67, 7.45, 7.64, 9.22
Goldsmid, Paula, 6.12
Gordon, Shirley, 4.79
Graber, Richard, 6.93
Graff, Polly Anne, 2.56
Graff, Stewart, 2.56
Graham, Ada, 8.27
Graham, Frank, 8.27
Grant, Matthew G., 3.61, 4.64
Graves, Charles P., 2.57
Greenberg, Joanne, 8.26
Greenburg, Polly, 2.5
Greene, Bette, 6.68
Greene, Constance C., 6.30
Greenfield, Eloise, 2.42, 2.82, 4.71, 5.57, 6.61
Greiner, N. Gretchen, 6.83
Griese, Arnold A., 4.74
Grohskopf, Bernice, 4.45
Guy, Rosa, 6.86

Hall, Elizabeth, 4.52
Hamilton, Virginia, 3.68, 4.48
Harnan, Terry, 10.2
Harris, Christie, 7.73
Hart, Carole, 2.29
Hartley, Lucie, 7.5
Haskins, James, 7.30
Hassler, Jon, 4.75
Hatch, James (ed.), 6.66
Hautzig, Deborah, 4.66
Hautzig, Esther, 4.18, 7.29
Haynes, Betsy, 4.25
Hazen, Barbara Shook, 2.68
Hazen, Nancy, 2.32
Hedges, Elaine (ed.), 8.41
Herzig, Alison Cragin, 3.67
Hess, Lilo, 6.85
Heyward, DuBose, 5.2
Hickok, Lorena A., 4.3
Hill, Elizabeth Starr, 2.34
Ho, Minfong, 7.14
Hoban, Russell, 2.37, 2.40
Hochschild, Arlie Russell, 3.16
Hoffman, Nancy (ed.), 7.49
Hoffman, Phyllis, 2.58
Hogeland, Ronald W. (ed.), 12.7
Holiday, Billie, 5.33

Holland, Isabelle, 6.90
Hollander, Phyllis, 8.7, 9.7
Hoover, H. M., 5.51
Houston, James D., 6.4
Houston, Jeanne Wakatsuki, 6.4
Howard, Moses L., 4.46
Howe, Florence (ed.), 7.49
Hunter, Edith, 3.19
Hunter, Kristin, 3.41

Ingraham, Claire, 7.24
Ingraham, Leonard W., 7.24
Irwin, Hadley, 2.70
Isadora, Rachel, 2.2

Jackson, Jacqueline, 6.31
Jacobs, Helen Hull, 7.27
Jacobs, Karen Folger, 6.72
Jacobs, Linda, 4.37
Janeway, Elizabeth, 12.6
Jewell, Nancy, 2.48
Johnston, Johanna, 3.5
Jones, Adrienne, 4.76
Jones, Betty Millsaps, 3.69
Jones, Toeckey, 7.67
Jordan, Hope Dahle, 5.46
Jordan, June, 4.30
Jordan, Ruth, 8.15
Jordan, Teresa, 6.102
Julty, Sam, 9.27

Kalmus, Yvonne (ed.), 10.9
Kandell, Alice S., 2.85
Katchian, Sonia (ed.), 10.9
Katz, Bobbi, 2.43, 7.60
Katz, Jacqueline Hunt, 5.32
Katz, Jane B., 9.31
Katz, William Loren, 5.32
Keller, Gail Faithfull, 2.35
Kellerhals-Stewart, Heather, 6.1
Kelly, Donna, 2.63, 4.61
Kerr, M.E., 4.57
Kevles, Bettyann, 9.16
King, Billie Jean, 7.41
Kingston, Maxine Hong, 7.65
Klein, H. Arthur, 8.13
Klein, Mina C., 8.13
Klein, Norma, 2.22, 3.28, 3.44, 5.30
Klever, Anita, 7.40
Knudson, R.R., 7.6
Koltun, Elizabeth (ed.), 11.6
Konigsburg, E.L., 4.15, 6.13
Krasilovsky, Phyllis, 5.7
Kraus, Ruth, 1.4

Lader, Lawrence, 6.84
LaFarge, Phyllis, 2.6
Langner, Nola, 4.18
Larrick, Nancy (ed.), 8.28
Larsen, Hanne, 3.49
Lasker, Joe, 2.31, 2.79
Lasky, Kathryn, 7.71
Latham, Jean Lee, 2.21
Laurikietis, Rae, 8.24
Lawrence, Jacob, 2.10
Lawrence, Judith, 2.51
Lawrence, Mildred, 6.65
Leaf, Munro, 4.33

Lederer, Muriel, 9.25
Leithauser, Gladys, 2.77
L'Engle, Madeleine, 6.29
Lengyel, Emil, 8.20
Lenski, Lois, 5.4
Lenthall, Patricia Riley, 3.20
Leone, Bruno, 7.56
LeRoy, Gen, 2.69
Lessing, Doris, 8.31
Levenson, Dorothy, 6.24
Levitin, Sonia, 4.36
Levy, Elizabeth, 2.45, 8.22, 9.21
Lewis, C.S., 5.23
Lewis, Janet, 7.33
Lieberman, E. James, 10.4
Lipp, Frederick J., 3.65
Litchfield, Ada B., 2.78
Little, Lessie Jones, 6.61
Lobel, Arnold, 2.24
Lofts, Norah, 5.34
Longsworth, Polly, 8.4
Loree, Sharron, 2.17
Lorenzo, Carol Lee, 3.13
Lowe, Jacqueline, 10.12
Lurie, Alison, 5.47

MacLachlan, Patricia, 2.74
Madison, Winifred, 4.6
Madlee, Dorothy, 3.56
Mali, Jane Lawrence, 3.67
Malone, Mary, 2.15, 2.50
Mangi, Jean, 4.12
Markandaya, Kamala, 6.49
Maruki, Toshi, 3.72
Mathis, Sharon Bell, 2.23, 7.43
Maury, Inez, 3.64, 4.35
Mayer, Mercer, 4.10
Mazur, Ronald M., 12.8
McCarty, Toni, 6.101
McCloskey, Robert, 3.24
McCoy, J.J., 8.23
McCullers, Carson, 5.31, 5.41
McDearmon, Kay, 4.39
McGrath, Alice, 11.8
McHugh, Mary, 8.12, 11.4
McKie, Roy, 1.6
McKown, Robin, 7.46
McNeer, May, 9.19
Mead, Margaret, 9.14
Means, Florence Crannell, 4.53
Medea, Andra, 8.38
Meltzer, Milton, 6.84
Meriwether, Louise, 2.38, 4.70
Merriam, Eve (ed.), 8.28
Merry, Suzanne, 9.28
Miels, Miska, 5.13
Miles, Betty, 2.36, 3.30, 3.46
Miller, Mara, 8.22
Minard, Rosemary, 4.49
Mitchell, Joyce Slayton, 7.37, 7.38, 10.10
Mohr, Nicholasa, 6.8
Moore, Carman, 7.32
Morrison, Dorothy Nafus, 6.76
Morrison, Toni, 7.42

Nathan, Dorothy, 6.10
National Geographic Society, 5.61

Nelson, Rachel West, 6.75
Neufeld, John, 4.56
New Seed Collective, 3.50, 5.49
Nicholas, Susan Cary, 12.9
Niethammer, Carolyn, 9.9
Noble, Iris, 6.25, 6.46, 6.47, 7.62, 10.11
Noble, Jeanne, 11.7
Nolan, Madeena Spray, 2.76
Norris, Gunilla B., 2.16, 6.38
Norton, Andre, 3.56
Norton, Mary, 4.29

O'Brien, Robert C., 5.27
O'Dell, Scott, 3.4, 3.37
Olsen, Tillie, 6.58, 8.31
Orgel, Doris, 3.25
Ormerod, Jan, 1.9
Ormondroyd, Edward, 7.18

Paek, Min, 2.86
Palmer, Pat, 5.48, 6.73
Parents' Nursery School, 4.42
Paterson, Katherine, 7.53
Patterson, Letha, 7.12
Pearson, Susan, 2.66
Peck, Ellen, 10.4
Peck, Richard, 6.54
Perl, Teri, 9.20
Perrine, Mary, 3.11
Petersen, Karen, 11.5
Peterson, Helen Stone, 3.9, 4.32, 5.9
Peterson, Jeanne Whitehouse, 2.72
Petry, Ann, 6.44
Petry, Elisabeth Ann, 6.23
Pfeffer, Susan Beth, 3.42
Phelps, Ethel Johnston, 5.26, 6.100
Phleger, Fred, 1.5
Pierce, Ruth I., 11.3
Plath, Sylvia, 6.52, 6.55
Pogrebin, Letty Cottin (ed.), 4.84
Polese, Marcia, 3.26
Politi, Leo, 4.14, 7.9
Pomerantz, Charlotte, 7.22
Poole, Josephine, 5.19
Portis, Charles, 5.21
Power, Barbara, 2.75
Pratt, Ellen, 5.5
Price, Alice M., 12.9
Pursell, Margaret Sanford, 2.80

Rabe, Berniece, 2.87, 5.28
Radford, Ruby L., 3.32
Rankin, Louise, 7.11
Reading, J.P., 6.80
Reid, Robert, 8.25
Reit, Seymour, 3.51
Renner, Beverly Hollett, 5.53
Revis, Alesia, 5.57
Rice, Edward, 10.7
Rich, Gibson, 4.47
Richards, Arlene Kramer, 5.50
Ripp, Rikki (ed.), 10.9
Robinson, Tom D., 4.73
Rock, Gail, 6.36
Rockwell, Harlow, 4.2
Rose, Mary Catherine, 3.6
Rosen, Marjorie, 11.2

Ross, Pat, 8.9
Roszak, Betty, 12.1
Roszak, Theodore, 12.1
Rubin, Rachel, 12.9
Russ, Lavinia, 3.10
Ryan, Betsy, 4.50
Ryan, Joan, 7.26

Sabin, Francene, 8.6
Sallis, Susan, 6.98, 8.33
SanSouci, Robert D., 7.69
Sarah, Becky, 8.19
Sargent, Pamela, 8.10
Sawyer, Ruth, 7.21
Sayers, Dorothy L., 8.32
Saylor, Mildred D., 7.59
Schlein, Miriam, 2.11
Schneiderman, Beth Kline (ed.), 6.74
Schneir, Miriam, 10.8
Schwartz, Delmore, 6.95
Schweitzer, Byrd Baylor, 2.47
Scoppettone, Sandra, 3.60
Scott, Jane, 3.47
Scott, John Anthony, 9.2
Searcy, Margaret Zehmer, 3.18
Seed, Suzanne, 8.44
Segner, Bruce, 11.8
Selber, Charles, 10.12
Senesh, Hannah, 8.40
Sharmat, Marjorie Weinman, 3.35
Sharp, Margery, 8.2
Shulman, Alix Kates, 4.50, 7.20
Simon, Norma, 2.1, 2.20, 2.39
Singer, Marilyn, 3.54
Skold, Betty Westrom, 5.3
Smedley, Agnes, 6.50, 9.32
Smith, Betsy Covington, 8.36
Smith, Betty, 6.48
Smith, Vian, 6.19
Smucker, Barbara, 5.20
Snedeker, Caroline Dale, 7.28
Snyder, Zilpha Keatley, 4.43, 6.33, 6.39
Sobol, Rose, 5.40
Sonneborn, Ruth A., 2.41
Sorensen, Virginia, 3.3
Sortor, Toni, 6.21
Spark, Muriel, 8.11
Speare, Elizabeth George, 5.38
Specht, Robert, 5.44
Spinner, Stephanie (ed.), 6.59, 7.61
Spykman, E.C., 6.7
Spyri, Johanna, 5.29
Stanford, Barbara, 9.6
Stecher, Miriam B., 2.85
Stein, Sara Bonnetl, 2.73
Steptoe, John, 6.94
Sterling, Dorothy, 5.18, 9.24
Sterling, Philip, 8.30
Stevenson, Janet, 7.39
Stoddard, Hope, 9.26
Stolz, Mary, 4.68, 6.45
Stratton, Joanna L., 5.62
Streatfield, Noel, 5.22
Suhl, Yuri, 9.1
Sullivan, Victoria (ed.), 6.66
Surge, Frank, 8.3
Surowiecki, Sandra Lucas, 2.30

Taylor, Barbara, 4.11
Taylor, L.B., 11.10
Taylor, Mildred D., 7.59
Tegner, Bruce, 11.8
Terry, Walter, 9.13
Thayer, Jane, 2.44
Thomas, Ianthe, 3.21, 5.1
Thomas, Marlo, 8.34
Thompson, Kathleen, 8.38
Tobias, Tobi, 2.14, 4.63, 5.8
Tompert, Ann, 4.79
Tufts, Eleanor, 10.3

Uchida, Yoshiko, 3.34
Udry, Janice May, 2.3, 2.54, 5.11
Underwood, Betty, 6.35, 7.1

Van der Veer, Judy, 3.55
Van Woerkom, Dorothy, 2.7, 4.82
Vestly, Anne-Catherine, 3.8
Viorst, Judith, 4.24

Waber, Bernard, 3.7
Walker, Alice (ed.), 7.55
Walker, Margaret, 7.34
Walker, Mildred, 3.48
Warren, Ruth, 9.18
Watkins, Mary S., 4.62
Watson, Sally, 7.4
Waxman, Stephanie, 1.8
Wayne, Bennett (ed.), 2.61, 3.27, 5.16
Webb, Sheyann, 6.75
Weibel, Kathryn, 11.1
Welber, Robert, 1.1
Wells, Rosemary, 2.19
Wender, Dorothy, 3.26
Wendt, Ingrid (ed.), 8.41
Westerberg, Christine, 4.4
White, E.B., 3.38
Wiesenfeld, Cheryl (ed.), 10.9
Wiggin, Kate Douglas, 7.15
Wikland, Ilon, 1.3
Wilkinson, Brenda, 6.79, 7.54
Willard, Barbara, 7.2
Williams, Jay, 3.17, 4.8
Williams, Vera B., 2.88, 3.70
Willis, Irene, 5.50
Willow, Samantha, 3.52
Wilson, Ellen, 8.1
Wilson, J.J., 11.5
Wojciechowska, Maia, 6.62
Wolde, Gunilla, 4.20
Wong, Jade Snow, 6.57
Wong, Kat, 5.56
Wong, Nellie, 7.51
Woolf, Virginia, 6.71, 8.17

Yashima, Taro, 2.33
Yep, Lawrence, 5.45
Young, Miriam, 2.49

Zemach, Margot, 4.81
Zindel, Paul, 5.39
Zolotow, Charlotte, 3.33

# Subject Index

An "x" indicates the book may be inappropriate for the grade level at which it is written because of its format or subject matter.

## AMERICAN ETHNIC MINORITY

### General *

The Train, 1.1
Why Am I Different?, 2.1
Black Is Brown Is Tan, 2.8
Aekyung's Dream, 2.86
A Book About Us, 3.50
Wonder Women of Sports, 3.69
Jo, Flo and Yolanda, 4.1ˣ
ABC Play with Me, 4.61ˣ
The Clever Princess, 4.79
First Snow, 5.12ˣ
Martin's Father, 5.17ˣ
Making Our Way, 5.32ˣ
Some Things You Just Can't Do by Yourself, 5.49
Women at Their Work, 6.15
Julie of the Wolves, 6.27
The Egypt Game, 6.33
Girl Sports, 6.72
Women of Crisis: Lives of Struggle and Hope, 6.89ˣ
The Maid of the North: Feminist Folktales from around the World, 6.100
The Skull in the Snow and Other Folktales, 6.101
An Album of Women in American History, 7.24
Women and Fiction: Short Stories by and about Women, 7.52
Male & Female under 18, 8.28
In Her Own Image: Women Working in the Arts, 8.41
New Women in Entertainment, 8.43

_____

* Variety of ethnic minorities represented.

Women in Music, 9.6
New Women in Politics, 10.5

### Black

Mary Jo's Grandmother, 2.3
Oh Lord, I Wish I Was a Buzzard, 2.5
Don't You Remember?, 2.9
Harriet and the Promised Land, 2.10
Marian Anderson, 2.14
The Good Morrow, 2.16ˣ
Nobody's Family Is Going to Change, 2.18ˣ
Sidewalk Story, 2.23
Grownups Cry Too, 2.32
Evan's Corner, 2.34
Don't Ride the Bus on Monday: The Rosa Parks Story, 2.38
I Love Gram, 2.41
Rosa Parks, 2.42
Heroines of '76, 2.53ˣ
What Mary Jo Wanted, 2.54
Steffie and Me, 2.58
My Daddy Don't Go to Work, 2.76
Darlene, 2.82
Harriet and the Runaway Book, 3.5
Daddy, 3.12
Eliza's Daddy, 3.21
Mary McLeod Bethune, 3.32
Ann Aurelia and Dorothy, 3.36
The Soul Brothers and Sister Lou, 3.41ˣ
Star Ka'ats and the Plant People, 3.56
Sweet Whispers, Brother Rush, 3.68ˣ
Liza Lou and the Yeller Belly Swamp, 4.10
The Preacher's Kid, 4.13
Jennifer, Hecate, MacBeth, William McKinley and Me, Elizabeth, 4.15
Iggie's House, 4.16
She Wanted to Read: The Story of Mary McLeod Bethune, 4.17
Two Tickets to Freedom: The True Story of Ellen and William Craft, Fugitive Slaves, 4.22

Cowslip, 4.25
Fannie Lou Hamer, 4.30ˣ
The Empty Schoolhouse, 4.31
Sojourner Truth: Fearless Crusader, 4.32
Mumbet: The Story of Elizabeth Freeman, 4.38
Mahalia: Gospel Singer, 4.39
Zeely, 4.48
The Autobiography of Miss Jane Pittman, 4.60
Arthur Mitchell, 4.63
What Can She Be? A Newscaster, 4.67
Window Wishing, 4.69ˣ
Daddy Was a Number Runner, 4.70ˣ
Mary McLeod Bethune, 4.71
Lordy, Aunt Hattie, 5.1ˣ
Mary Jane, 5.18
Runaway to Freedom: A Story of the Underground Railway, 5.20
Come by Here, 5.24
The Member of the Wedding, 5.31ˣ
Lady Sings the Blues, 5.33ˣ
The Heart Is a Lonely Hunter, 5.41ˣ
Alesia, 5.57ˣ
Women of Courage, 6.10
Harriet Tubman: Conductor on the Underground Railroad, 6.23
Phillis Wheatley: America's First Black Poetess, 6.28ˣ
Charlotte Forten: Free Black Teacher, 6.34
Classmates by Request, 6.37
The Street, 6.44ˣ
Hey, White Girl!, 6.56
Childtimes: A Three Generation Memoir, 6.61
Plays by and about Women, 6.66ˣ
I Always Wanted to Be Somebody, 6.70
Selma, Lord, Selma, 6.75
Ludell, 6.79
I Know Why the Caged Bird Sings, 6.81
Ruby, 6.86ˣ
Daddy Is a Monster...Sometimes, 6.94ˣ

Contributions of Women: Labor, 6.96

Susannah and the Blue House Mystery 6.97

Shirley Chisholm: A Biography, 7.19

Contributions of Women, Education, 7.23

Contributions of Women, Sports, 7.26

Fighting Shirley Chisholm, 7.30

Somebody's Angel Child: The Story of Bessie Smith, 7.32

Jubilee, 7.34

The Bluest Eye, 7.42[x]

Listen for the Fig Tree, 7.44

Black Artists of the New Generation, 7.50

Ludell's New York Time, 7.54

I Love Myself When I Am Laughing, 7.55

Women Who Shaped History, 7.57

Roll of Thunder, Hear My Cry, 7.59

I, Charlotte Forten, Black and Free, 8.4

Gather Together in My Name, 9.11

A Hero Ain't Nothin' but a Sandwich, 9.12

Black Foremothers: Three Lives, 9.23

African Rhythm—American Dance: A Biography of Katherine Dunham, 10.2

Beautiful Also, Are the Souls of My Black Sisters, 11.7

### Native American

Nancy Ward, Cherokee, 2.60

We Are Mesquakie, We Are One, 2.70[x]

That Is That, 2.72

Island of the Blue Dolphins, 3.4[x]

Nannabah's Friend, 3.11

Heart-of-Snowbird, 3.13[x]

Ikwa of the Temple Mounds, 3.18

Red Rock over the River, 3.31[x]

Zia, 3.37[x]

Higher than the Arrow, 3.55

The Girl Who Loved Wild Horses, 3.66

Along Sandy Trails, 4.34

Our Cup Is Broken, 4.53[x]

An Eskimo Birthday, 4.73

The Wind Is Not a River, 4.74

Jemmy, 4.75[x]

Sacajawea, 5.3

Maria Tallchief, 5.8[x]

The Sunflower Garden, 5.11[x]

Annie and the Old One, 5.13

Woman Chief, 5.40

Tisha, 5.44[x]

Susette La Flesche: Voice of the Omaha Indians, 6.41

Chief Sarah: Sarah Winnemucca's Fight for Indian Rights, 6.76

The Loon Feather, 7.48

Song of Sedna, 7.69[x]

The Trouble with Princesses, 7.73

Daughters of the Earth, 9.9

I Am the Fire of Time, 9.30

### Mexican

Amigo, 2.47

Higher than the Arrow, 3.55

Maria Teresa, 3.62

My Mother and I Are Growing Strong, 3.64

Maria Luisa, 4.6

My Mother the Mail Carrier, 4.35

Lupita Manana, 5.59

Three Stalks of Corn, 7.9[x]

### Puerto Rican

Nilda, 6.8

### Chinese

Rice Cakes and Paper Dragons, 3.51

Moy Moy, 4.14

Dragonwings, 5.45

Don't Put Vinegar in the Copper, 5.56[x]

Fifth Chinese Daughter, 6.57

Dreams in Harrison Railroad Park, 7.51

The Woman Warrior: Memoirs of a Girlhood among Ghosts, 7.65

What Can She Be? A Computer Scientist, 9.22[x]

Portraits of Chinese Women in Revolution, 9.32

### Japanese

Umbrella, 2.33

Hiroshima No Pika, 3.72

Farewell to Manzanar, 6.4

Jenny Kimura, 7.63

## ANIMALS

Rabbit Finds a Way, 1.7

Pippa Mouse, 2.13

The Sunshine Family and the Pony, 2.17

Noisy Nora, 2.19

Lucille, 2.24

A Birthday for Frances, 2.37

Best Friends for Frances, 2.40

Quiet on Account of Dinosaur, 2.44

He Bear, She Bear, 2.46

Amigo, 2.47

A Pony for Linda, 2.52

What Mary Jo Wanted, 2.54

Animal Daddies and My Daddy, 2.68

The Rabbit Is Next, 2.77

Animals Should Definitely *Not* Wear Clothing, 3.2

Carlotta and the Scientist, 3.20

The Dragon and the Doctor, 3.22

Blueberries for Sal, 3.24

Frankie and the Fawn, 3.26[x]

Charlotte's Web, 3.38

Cross Fox, 3.47[x]

Higher than the Arrow, 3.55

The Cry of the Crow, 3.57

Millicent the Magnificent, 3.59

Some Lose Their Way, 3.65[x]

Penelope and the Mussels, 4.9

Rafiki, 4.18[x]

What Can She Be? A Veterinarian, 4.21

Nothing Is Impossible: The Story of Beatrix Potter, 4.23

The Story of Ferdinand, 4.33[x]

The Country Bunny and the Little Golden Shoes, 5.2[x]

Mrs. Frisby and the Rats of NIMH, 5.27

Going to the Sun, 5.55

Nine Lives of Moses: On the Oregon Trail, 6.9

Tall and Proud, 6.19

Miss Hickory, 6.20

Julie of the Wolves, 6.27

My Little Book of Cats, 6.83[x]

Listen to Your Kitten Purr, 6.85

Sam, 6.88

The Black Stallion and the Girl, 7.3

Doctor Mary's Animals, 7.7[x]

Fresh Fish...and Chips, 7.8[x]

Daughter of the Mountains, 7.11

National Velvet, 7.13

Nothing but a Dog, 7.60[x]

Miss Bianca, 8.2[x]

Wild Animals, Gentle Women, 8.35

Watching the Wild Apes: The Primate Studies of Goodall, Fossey and Galdikas, 9.16

## AUTOBIOGRAPHY/ BIOGRAPHY

Harriet and the Promised Land, 2.10

Marian Anderson, 2.14

Dorothea L. Dix: Hospital Founder, 2.15

Rachel Carson: Who Loved the Sea, 2.21

Jane Addams, 2.35

Don't Ride the Bus on Monday: The Rosa Parks Story, 2.38

Rosa Parks, 2.42

Annie Sullivan, 2.50

Heroines of '76, 2.53[x]

Amelia Earhart, 2.55

Helen Keller: Toward the Light, 2.56
Eleanor Roosevelt: First Lady of the World, 2.57
Linda Richards: First American Trained Nurse, 2.59
Nancy Ward, Cherokee, 2.60$^x$
Women Who Dared to Be Different, 2.61
Harriet and the Runaway Book, 3.5
Clara Barton: Soldier of Mercy, 3.6
Abigail Adams: "Dear Partner," 3.9
Four Women of Courage, 3.27
Mary McLeod Bethune, 3.32
Child of the Dark: The Diary of Carolina Maria de Jesus, 3.45$^x$
Jane Addams, 3.61
Wonder Women of Sports, 3.69
The Story of Helen Keller, 4.3
She Wanted to Read: The Story of Mary McLeod Bethune, 4.17
Before the Supreme Court: The Story of Belva Ann Lockwood, 4.19
Two Tickets to Freedom: The True Story of Ellen and William Craft, Fugitive Slaves, 4.22
Nothing Is Impossible: The Story of Beatrix Potter, 4.23
Fannie Lou Hamer, 4.30$^x$
Sojourner Truth: Fearless Crusader, 4.32
Chris Evert: Tennis Pro, 4.37
Mumbet: The Story of Elizabeth Freeman, 4.38
Mahalia: Gospel Singer, 4.39
Andrea Jaeger Tennis Champion, 4.62
Arthur Mitchell, 4.63
Elizabeth Blackwell, Pioneer Doctor, 4.64
Billie Jean King: Queen of the Courts, 4.65
Mary McLeod Bethune, 4.71
Self Portrait, 4.81
Sacajawea, 5.3
Maria Tallchief, 5.8$^x$
Susan B. Anthony: Pioneer in Women's Rights, 5.9
Women with a Cause, 5.16
Making Our Way, 5.32$^x$
Lady Sings the Blues, 5.33$^x$
Woman Chief, 5.40
Alesia, 5.57$^x$
Women of Courage, 6.10
A Proud Taste for Scarlet and Miniver, 6.13
Mary's Monster, 6.17$^x$
Harriet Tubman: Conductor on the Underground Railroad, 6.23
Emmeline and Her Daughters: The Pankhurst Suffragettes, 6.25
Phillis Wheatley: America's First Black Poetess, 6.28$^x$
Charlotte Forten: Free Black Teacher, 6.34
Clara Barton: Founder of the American Red Cross, 6.40

Susette La Flesche: Voice of the Omaha Indians, 6.41
America's First Woman Astronomer: Maria Mitchell, 6.42
First Woman Ambulance Surgeon: Emily Barringer, 6.46
Israel's Golda Meir: Pioneer to Prime Minister, 6.47
The Bell Jar, 6.55$^x$
Lady for the Defense: A Biography of Belva Lockwood, 6.63
Dorothy Day: Friend of the Poor, 6.64
I Always Wanted to Be Somebody, 6.70
Chief Sarah: Sarah Winnemucca's Fight for Indian Rights, 6.76
America's First Woman Chemist: Ellen Richards, 6.77
Barefoot in the Grass: The Story of Grandma Moses, 6.78
I Know Why the Caged Bird Sings, 6.81
Margaret Sanger: Pioneer of Birth Control, 6.84
A Christmas Memory, 6.87
The Golda Meir Story, 6.92
Contributions of Women: Labor, 6.96
Cowgirls: Women of the American West, An Oral History, 6.102$^x$
Maria Sanford: Pioneer Professor, 7.5
Oh, Lizzie! The Story of Elizabeth Cady Stanton, 7.10
They Wouldn't Quit: Stories of Handicapped People, 7.12
The Senator from Maine: Margaret Chase Smith, 7.17
Shirley Chisholm: A Biography, 7.19
To the Barricades: The Anarchist Life of Emma Goldman, 7.20
Contributions of Women, Education, 7.23
I'm Nobody! Who Are You?, 7.25
Contributions of Women, Sports, 7.26
Famous Modern American Women Athletes, 7.27
Fighting Shirley Chisholm, 7.30
Somebody's Angel Child: The Story of Bessie Smith, 7.32
The Silent Storm, 7.35
The World of Mary Cassatt, 7.46
Black Artists of the New Generation, 7.50
I Love Myself When I Am Laughing, 7.55
Maria Montessori: Knight of the Child, 7.56
Women Who Shaped History, 7.57
Rose Kennedy: No Time For Tears, 7.58
Cameras and Courage: Margaret Bourke-White, 7.62
From Parlor to Prison, 7.66
She Never Looked Back: Margaret Mead in Samoa, 7.70

American Painter in Paris: A Life of Mary Cassatt, 8.1
Famous Spies, 8.3
I, Charlotte Forten, Black and Free, 8.4
Patriots in Petticoats, 8.5
Women Who Win, 8.6
American Women in Sports, 8.7
Young and Female, 8.9
Kathe Kollwitz: Life in Art, 8.13
George Sand, 8.15
And All Her Paths Were Peace, 8.20
The Cancer Lady: Maud Slye and Her Heredity Studies, 8.23
Marie Curie, 8.25
Bella Abzug, 8.29
Sea and Earth: The Life of Rachel Carson, 8.30
Wild Animals, Gentle Women, 8.35
Life in the Iron Mills, 8.37
Hannah Senesh: Her Life and Diary, 8.40
New Women in Medicine, 8.42
New Women in Entertainment, 8.43
Eloquent Crusader: Ernestine Rose, 9.1
Fanny Kemble's America, 9.2
Four Women in a Violent Time, 9.3
Martha Berry: Little Woman with a Big Dream, 9.5
Women in Music, 9.6
100 Greatest Women in Sports, 9.7
Gather Together in My Name, 9.11
Frontiers of Dance: The Life of Martha Graham, 9.13
Blackberry Winter: My Earlier Years, 9.14
Math Equals: Biographies of Women + Related Activities, 9.20
Black Foremothers: Three Lives, 9.23
Famous American Women, 9.25
Breakthrough: Women in Writing, 9.29
African Rhythm—American Dance: A Biography of Katherine Dunham, 10.2
Our Hidden Heritage: Five Centuries of Women Artists, 10.3
New Women in Politics, 10.5
Margaret Mead, 10.7
Contemporary Women Scientists of America, 10.11

## BEHAVIORAL SCIENCE

Child of the Dark: The Diary of Carolina Maria de Jesus, 3.45$^x$
Our Cup Is Broken, 4.53$^x$
Lisa, Bright and Dark, 4.56$^x$
The Sexes: Male/Female Roles and Relationships, 4.58$^x$
The Beckoner, 4.76$^x$

Making Our Way, 5.32[x]
The Min-Min, 5.36
Leaving Home, 5.50[x]
The Street, 6.44[x]
Leap before You Look, 6.45[x]
Nectar in a Sieve, 6.49
Ariel: Poems by Sylvia Plath, 6.52
Are You in the House Alone?, 6.54[x]
Women of Crises: Lives of Struggle and Hope, 6.89[x]
Free to Choose: Decision Making for Young Men, 7.37
Other Choices for Becoming a Woman, 7.38
Billie Jean, 7.41
She Never Looked Back: Margaret Mead in Samoa, 7.70
A Very Easy Death, 8.14
The Yellow Wallpaper, 8.18
The Gender Trap: A Closer Look at Sex Roles (Book I: Education and Work), 8.24
I Never Promised You a Rose Garden, 8.25
The Dollmaker, 8.39
The Young Woman's Guide to Liberation, 9.8
Daughters of the Earth, 9.9
Blackberry Winter: My Earlier Years, 9.14
Enterprising Women, 9.15
Watching the Wild Apes: The Primate Studies of Goodall, Fossey and Galdikas, 9.16
Men's Bodies Men's Selves, 9.26
Boys Have Feelings Too: Growing Up Male for Boys, 9.28
Root of Bitterness, 10.6
Margaret Mead, 10.7
Mirror Mirror: Images of Women Reflected in Popular Culture, 11.1
Popcorn Venus, 11.2
Psychology and the New Woman, 11.4
The Jewish Woman: New Perspectives, 11.6
What Are Little Girls Made Of? The Roots of Feminine Stereotypes, 11.9
Masculine/Feminine: Readings in Sexual Mythology and the Liberation of Women, 12.1
Man's World, Woman's Place: A Study in Social Mythology, 12.6
Women and Womanhood in America, 12.7

## CAREERS

Mothers Can Do Anything, 2.31
He Bear, She Bear, 2.46
My Doctor Bag Book, 2.64

The Rabbit Is Next, 2.77
What Will I Be?, 3.63
My Doctor, 4.2[x]
What Can She Be? A Veterinarian, 4.21
What Can She Be? A Lawyer, 4.28
What Can She Be? A Newscaster, 4.67
What Can She Be? A Police Officer, 4.77
Self Portrait: Margot Zemach, 4.81
What Can She Be? A Farmer, 5.43
Did You Ever?, 6.12[x]
Women at Their Work, 6.15
First Woman Ambulance Surgeon: Emily Barringer, 6.46
What Can She Be? A Legislator, 6.67
America's First Woman Chemist: Ellen Richards, 6.77
I Carve Stone, 6.82
Doctor Mary's Animals, 7.7[x]
Free to Choose: Decision Making for Young Men, 7.37
Other Choices for Becoming a Woman, 7.38
Women in Television, 7.40
What Can She Be? An Architect, 7.45
Black Artists of the New Generation, 7.50
Cameras and Courage: Margaret Bourke-White, 7.62
What Can She Be? A Geologist, 7.64
Young and Female, 8.9
Law and the New Woman, 8.12
Deadline, 8.21
Doctors for the People, 8.22
The Cancer Lady: Maud Slye and Her Heredity Studies, 8.23
The Gender Trap: A Closer Look at Sex Roles (Book I: Education and Work), 8.24
Careers in Conservation, 8.27
Free to Be...You and Me, 8.34[x]
Wild Animals, Gentle Women, 8.35
New Women in Medicine, 8.42
New Women in Entertainment, 8.43
Saturday's Child, 8.44
Ms.—M.D., 9.4
Women in Music, 9.6
Blackberry Winter: My Earlier Years, 9.14
Enterprising Women, 9.16
Lawyers for the People: A New Breed of Defenders and Their Work, 9.21
What Can She Be? A Computer Scientist, 9.22[x]
Blue Collar Jobs for Women, 9.24
Dancer, 9.27
Ms. Attorney, 10.1
New Women in Politics, 10.5
I Can Be Anything: Careers and Colleges for Young Women, 10.10

Contemporary Women Scientists of America, 10.11
The Language of Show Dancing, 10.12
Psychology and the New Woman, 11.4
Chemistry Careers, 11.10
Looking Forward to a Career: Veterinary Medicine, 12.4[x]

## CONTEMPORARY ISSUES/CURRENT EVENTS

Nobody's Family Is Going to Change, 2.18[x]
Don't Ride the Bus on Monday: The Rosa Parks Story, 2.38
Rosa Parks, 2.42
The Preacher's Kid, 4.13
Fannie Lou Hamer, 4.30[x]
The Empty Schoolhouse, 4.31
The Autobiography of Miss Jane Pittman, 4.60
Mary Jane, 5.18
Classmates by Request, 6.37
Hey, White Girl!, 6.56
Plays by and about Women, 6.66[x]
Selma, Lord, Selma, 6.75
Margaret Sanger: Pioneer of Birth Control, 6.84
Contributions of Women: Labor, 6.96
The Black Stallion and the Girl, 7.3
The Senator from Maine: Margaret Chase Smith, 7.17
Crazy Salad: Some Things about Women, 7.47
Go Well, Stay Well, 7.67
Male & Female under 18, 8.28
Sea and Earth: The Life of Rachel Carson, 8.30
The Young Woman's Guide to Liberation, 9.8
The Feminine Mystique, 9.10
Lawyers for the People: A New Breed of Defenders and Their Work, 9.21
I Am the Fire of Time, 9.30
New Women in Politics, 10.5
Beautiful, Also, Are the Souls of My Black Sisters, 11.7
Rights and Wrongs: Women's Struggle for Equality, 12.9

## CULTURAL HERITAGE

We Are Mesquakie, We Are One, 2.70[x]
Aekyung's Dream, 2.86

The Soul Brothers and Sister Lou, 3.41ˣ
Mixed Marriage Daughter, 3.43ˣ
Child of the Dark: The Diary of Carolina Maria de Jesus, 3.45ˣ
Winter Wheat, 3.48ˣ
Rice Cakes and Paper Dragons, 3.51
Higher than the Arrow, 3.55
Maria Teresa, 3.62
The Girl Who Loved Wild Horses, 3.66
Sweet Whispers, Brother Rush, 3.68ˣ
Our Cup Is Broken, 4.53
The Autobiography of Miss Jane Pittman, 4.60
Mary McLeod Bethune, 4.71
The Wind Is Not a River, 4.74
Making Our Way, 5.32ˣ
Lady Sings the Blues, 5.33ˣ
Bitter Herbs and Honey, 5.35
The Min-Min, 5.36
Tisha, 5.44ˣ
Dragonwings, 5.45
O Pioneers!, 5.52ˣ
Don't Put Vinegar in the Copper, 5.56ˣ
Lupita Manana, 5.59
Pioneer Women: Voices from the Kansas Frontier, 5.62ˣ
Nectar in a Sieve, 6.49
Hey, White Girl!, 6.56
Fifth Chinese Daughter, 6.57
Childtimes: A Three Generation Memoir, 6.61
Chief Sarah: Sarah Winnemucca's Fight for Indian Rights, 6.76
Women of Crises: Lives of Struggle and Hope, 6.89ˣ
The Skull in the Snow and Other Folktales, 6.101
Somebody's Angel Child: The Story of Bessie Smith, 7.32
Jubilee, 7.34
The Bluest Eye, 7.42ˣ
Listen for the Fig Tree, 7.44
The Loon Feather, 7.48
Black Artists of the New Generation, 7.50
Dreams in Harrison Railroad Park, 7.51
I Love Myself When I Am Laughing, 7.55
Jenny Kimura, 7.63
The Woman Warrior: Memoirs of a Girlhood among Ghosts, 7.65
Go Well, Stay Well, 7.67
Song of Sedna, 7.69ˣ
She Never Looked Back: Margaret Mead in Samoa, 7.70
The Night Journey, 7.71
The Trouble with Princesses, 7.73
The Dollmaker, 8.39
Hannah Senesh: Her Life and Diary, 8.40
Daughters of the Earth, 9.9
Gather Together in My Name, 9.11

A Hero Ain't Nothin' but a Sandwich, 9.12
Black Foremothers: Three Lives, 9.23
I Am the Fire of Time, 9.30
Portraits of Chinese Women in Revolution, 9.32
African Rhythm—American Dance: A Biography of Katherine Dunham, 10.2
The Jewish Woman: New Perspectives, 11.6
Beautiful, Also, Are the Souls of My Black Sisters, 11.7
Women and Womanhood in America, 12.7

## FAMILIES/FRIENDSHIP

The Train, 1.1
I Can Help Too, 1.3
A Hole Is to Dig, 1.4
Ann Can Fly, 1.5
Snow, 1.6
Sunshine, 1.9
Why Am I Different?, 2.1
Mary Jo's Grandmother, 2.3
Oh Lord, I Wish I Was a Buzzard, 2.5
Granny's Fish Story, 2.6
Becky and the Bear, 2.7
Black Is Brown Is Tan, 2.8
Don't You Remember?, 2.9
The Girl Who Would Rather Climb Trees, 2.11
Will I Have a Friend?, 2.12
Pippa Mouse, 2.13
Marian Anderson, 2.14
The Good Morrow, 2.16ˣ
The Sunshine Family and the Pony, 2.17
Nobody's Family Is Going to Change, 2.18ˣ
Noisy Nora, 2.19
I Was So Mad!, 2.20
Blue Trees, Red Sky, 2.22
Sidewalk Story, 2.23
Howie Helps Himself, 2.25
Grandma Didn't Wave Back, 2.26ˣ
Shoeshine Girl, 2.28
Delilah, 2.29
Joshua's Day, 2.30
Grownups Cry Too, 2.32
Evan's Corner, 2.34
Just Think!, 2.36
A Birthday for Frances, 2.37
All Kinds of Families, 2.39
Best Friends for Frances, 2.40
I Love Gram, 2.41
Rod-and-Reel Trouble, 2.43ˣ
Quiet on Account of Dinosaur, 2.44
Nice Little Girls, 2.45
Amigo, 2.47
Try and Catch Me, 2.48

Jellybeans for Breakfast, 2.49
A Pony for Linda, 2.52
What Mary Jo Wanted, 2.54
Steffie and Me, 2.58
It's Not the End of the World, 2.62ˣ
The Clock Book, 2.63
Monday I Was an Alligator, 2.66
Where Is Daddy? The Story of a Divorce, 2.67
Animal Daddies and My Daddy, 2.68
Cold Feet, 2.69ˣ
We Are Mesquakie, We Are One, 2.70ˣ
The Stubborn Old Woman, 2.71
That Is That, 2.72
Through Grandpa's Eyes, 2.74
I Wish Laura's Mommy Was My Mommy, 2.75
My Daddy Don't Go to Work, 2.76
Words in Our Hands, 2.78
Nick Joins In, 2.79
A Look at Divorce, 2.80
Jim Meets the Thing, 2.81
Darlene, 2.82
My Mom Travels a Lot, 2.83
Now One Foot, Now the Other, 2.84
Daddy and Ben Together, 2.85
A Chair for My Mother, 2.88
Ramona the Pest, 3.1
Curious Missie, 3.3
Harriet and the Runaway Book, 3.5
Ira Sleeps Over, 3.7
Hello, Aurora, 3.8
Abigail Adams: "Dear Partner," 3.9
Over the Hills and Far Away, 3.10ˣ
Nannabah's Friend, 3.11
Daddy, 3.12
Heart-of-Snowbird, 3.13ˣ
Mandy and the Flying Map, 3.14
A Promise Is a Promise, 3.15ˣ
Coleen the Question Girl, 3.16
Sue Ellen, 3.19
Carlotta and the Scientist, 3.20
Eliza's Daddy, 3.21
The Dragon and the Doctor, 3.22
Blueberries for Sal, 3.24
The Mulberry Music, 3.25ˣ
Frankie and the Fawn, 3.26ˣ
A Train for Jane, 3.28
Harriet the Spy, 3.29ˣ
The Real Me, 3.30ˣ
Red Rock over the River, 3.31ˣ
The Lancelot Closes at Five, 3.35
Ann Aurelia and Dorothy, 3.36
Zia, 3.37ˣ
Charlotte's Web, 3.38
Never Jam Today, 3.39ˣ
The Amazing Miss Laura, 3.40ˣ
The Soul Brothers and Sister Lou, 3.41ˣ
Marly the Kid, 3.42ˣ
Mixed Marriage Daughter, 3.43ˣ
Mom, the Wolfman and Me, 3.44ˣ
The Trouble with Thirteen, 3.46ˣ

Cross Fox, 3.47ˣ
Winter Wheat, 3.48ˣ
Don't Forget Tom, 3.49
A Book about Us, 3.50
Rice Cakes and Paper Dragons, 3.51
Rachel Pushes Back, 3.52
A House for Jonnie O., 3.53ˣ
It Can't Hurt Forever, 3.54
Higher than the Arrow, 3.55
The Cry of the Crow, 3.57
Waiting for Johnny Miracle, 3.58ˣ
Happy Endings Are All Alike, 3.60ˣ
Maria Teresa, 3.62
My Mother and I Are Growing Strong, 3.64
Some Lose Their Way, 3.65ˣ
Sweet Whispers, Brother Rush, 3.68ˣ
Three Days on a River in a Red Canoe, 3.70
Tiger Eyes, 3.71ˣ
Hiroshima No Pika, 3.72
Jo, Flo and Yolanda, 4.1ˣ
The Story of Helen Keller, 4.3
A Little Lion, 4.4ˣ
Flat on My Face, 4.5
Maria Luisa, 4.6
Are You There God? It's Me, Margaret, 4.7
Penelope and the Mussels, 4.9
I Climb Mountains, 4.11
The Preacher's Kid, 4.13
Moy Moy, 4.14
Jennifer, Hecate, MacBeth, William McKinley and Me, Elizabeth, 4.15
Iggie's House, 4.16
Tommy and Sarah Dress Up, 4.20ˣ
Nothing Is Impossible: The Story of Beatrix Potter, 4.23
Rosie and Michael, 4.24
Kristy's Courage, 4.27
The Borrowers, 4.29
The Empty Schoolhouse, 4.31
Along Sandy Trails, 4.34
My Mother the Mail Carrier, 4.35
Journey to America, 4.36
A Year in the Life of Rosie Bernard, 4.40
Two Piano Tuners, 4.41
The Changeling, 4.43
Where the Lilies Bloom, 4.44
The Ostrich Chase, 4.46
Zeely, 4.48
The Girls of Huntington House, 4.51ˣ
Stand Up Lucy, 4.52
How Many Miles to Sundown?, 4.54
I'll Get There. It Better Be Worth the Trip, 4.55ˣ
Lisa, Bright and Dark, 4.56ˣ
Dinky Hocker Shoots Smack! 4.57
ABC Play with Me, 4.61ˣ
Hey, Dollface, 4.66
By the Highway Home, 4.68
Window Wishing, 4.69ˣ
An Eskimo Birthday, 4.73

Jemmy, 4.75ˣ
The Beckoner, 4.76ˣ
Me Too, 4.78
The Boy Who Wanted a Family, 4.79
Self Portrait: Margot Zemach, 4.81
Pearl in the Egg, 4.82
Anywhere Else but Here, 4.83
Stories for Free Children, 4.84
Lordy, Aunt Hattie, 5.1ˣ
Judy's Journey, 5.4
The Runaway Summer, 5.6
The Terrible Thing that Happened at Our House, 5.10ˣ
The Sunflower Garden, 5.11ˣ
First Snow, 5.12ˣ
Annie and the Old One, 5.13
The Magic Hat, 5.14ˣ
Phoebe's Revolt, 5.15
Martin's Father, 5.17ˣ
Moon Eyes, 5.19
Runaway to Freedom: A Story of the Underground Railway, 5.20
True Grit, 5.21
Ballet Shoes, 5.22
Come by Here, 5.24
Secret Castle, 5.25
Mrs. Fisby and the Rats of NIMH, 5.27
Naomi, 5.28
Heidi, 5.29
It's Not What You Expect, 5.30ˣ
The Member of the Wedding, 5.31ˣ
Bitter Herbs and Honey, 5.35
The Min-Min, 5.36
Early Rising, 5.37
The Witch of Blackbird Pond, 5.38
The Pigman, 5.39
The Heart Is a Lonely Hunter, 5.41ˣ
The Cat Ate My Gymsuit, 5.42
Dragonwings, 5.45
Haunted Summer, 5.46ˣ
Liking Myself, 5.48
Some Things You Just Can't Do by Yourself, 5.49
Leaving Home, 5.50ˣ
This Time of Darkness, 5.51
The Hideaway Summer, 5.53
Going to the Sun, 5.55
Don't Put Vinegar in the Copper, 5.56ˣ
Alesia, 5.57ˣ
Ida Early Comes over the Mountain, 5.58
Lupita Manana, 5.59
Ramona Quimby, Age 8, 5.60ˣ
She Shoots, She Scores!, 6.1
Lady Ellen Grae, 6.2
Emma Tupper's Diary, 6.3
Farewell to Manzanar, 6.4
The Witch's Daughter, 6.5
A Lemon and a Star, 6.7
Nilda, 6.8
Nine Lives of Moses: On the Oregon Trail, 6.9
Women of Courage, 6.10
Queenie Peavy, 6.11

The Endless Steppe: A Girl in Exile, 6.14
The Search for Charlie, 6.16
Mary's Monster, 6.17ˣ
Adventures of B.J., The Amateur Detective, 6.21
This Time, Tempe Wick?, 6.22ˣ
Emmeline and Her Daughters: The Pankhurst Suffragettes, 6.25
The Liberation of Clementine Tipton, 6.26
Leo the Lioness, 6.30
The Taste of Spruce Gum, 6.31
Dust of the Earth, 6.32
The Egypt Game, 6.33
The Tamarack Tree, 6.35
The House without a Christmas Tree, 6.36
Classmates by Request, 6.37
A Feast of Light, 6.38
The Headless Cupid, 6.39
Susette La Flesche: Voice of the Omaha Indians, 6.41
Claudia, Where Are You?, 6.43
The Street, 6.44ˣ
Leap before You Look, 6.45ˣ
A Tree Grows in Brooklyn, 6.48
Nectar in a Sieve, 6.49
Daughter of Earth, 6.50ˣ
Transport 7-41-R, 6.51
After the Wedding, 6.53
Are You in the House Alone?, 6.54ˣ
The Bell Jar, 6.55ˣ
Hey, White Girl!, 6.56
Fifth Chinese Daughter, 6.57
Tell Me a Riddle, 6.58
Fat Jack, 6.60
Childtimes: A Three Generation Memoir, 6.61
Don't Play Dead before You Have to, 6.62
Once at the Weary Way, 6.65
Summer of My German Soldier, 6.68
Ludell, 6.79
Bouquets for Brimbal, 6.80
I Know Why the Caged Bird Sings, 6.81
Ruby, 6.86ˣ
A Christmas Memory, 6.87
Sam, 6.88
Of Life and Death and Other Journeys, 6.90
A Long Way from Verona, 6.91
Black Cow Summer, 6.93
Daddy Is a Monster...Sometimes, 6.94ˣ
Susannah and the Blue House Mystery, 6.97
Only Love, 6.98
The Journel of the Shadow Bairns, 6.99
The Forge and the Forest, 7.1
The Lark and the Laurel, 7.2
The Black Stallion and the Girl, 7.3
Zanballer, 7.6
Fresh Fish...and Chips, 7.8ˣ

Three Stalks of Corn, 7.9ˣ
National Velvet, 7.13
Sing to the Dawn, 7.14
Rebecca of Sunnybrook Farm, 7.15
The Secret Garden, 7.16
Shirley Chisholm: A Biography 7.19
Maggie Rose: Her Birthday Christmas, 7.21
I'm Nobody! Who Are You?, 7.25
Contributions of Women: Sports, 7.26
Downright Dencey, 7.28
Life with Working Parents: Practical Hints for Everyday Situations, 7.29
Daughter of Discontent, 7.31
Jubilee, 7.34
My Antonia, 7.36
The Bluest Eye, 7.42ˣ
Listen for the Fig Tree, 7.44
Jacob Have I Loved, 7.53
Ludell's New York Time, 7.54
Rose Kennedy: No Time for Tears, 7.58
Roll of Thunder, Hear My Cry, 7.59
Motherlove: Stories by Women about Motherhood, 7.61
Jenny Kimura, 7.63
The Night Journey, 7.71
Country of Broken Stone, 7.72
Why Am I So Miserable If These Are the Best Years of My Life?, 8.8
A Very Easy Death, 8.14
I Never Promised You a Rose Garden, 8.26
A Time for Everything, 8.33
Free to Be...You and Me, 8.34ˣ
A Hero Ain't Nothin' but a Sandwich, 9.12
I'm Running Away from Home but I'm Not Allowed to Cross the Street, 9.17 Bloomsday for Maggie, 9.19

## FINE ARTS

Max, 2.2
Marian Anderson, 2.14
Dumb Old Casey Is a Fat Tree, 2.65
Two Piano Tuners, 4.41
Arthur Mitchell, 4.63
Ballet Shoes, 5.22
Lady Sings the Blues, 5.33ˣ
Barefoot in the Grass: The Story of Grandma Moses, 6.78
I Carve Stone, 6.82
I'm Nobody! Who Are You?, 7.25
Somebody's Angel Child: The Story of Bessie Smith, 7.32
Women in Television, 7.40
The World of Mary Cassatt, 7.46
Black Artists of the New Generation, 7.50
Cameras and Courage: Margaret Bourke-White, 7.62
American Painter in Paris: A Life of Mary Cassatt, 8.1
Kathe Kollwitz: Life in Art, 8.13
In Her Own Image: Women Working in the Arts, 8.41
New Women in Entertainment, 8.43
Women in Music, 9.6
Frontiers of Dance: The Life of Martha Graham, 9.13
Dancer, 9.27
African Rhythm—American Dance: A Biography of Katherine Dunham, 10.2
Our Hidden Heritage: Five Centuries of Women Artists, 10.3
Women See Women, 10.9
The Language of Show Dancing, 10.12
Popcorn Venus, 11.2
Women Artists: Recognition and Reappraisal from the Early Middle Ages to the Twentieth Century, 11.5

## FOREIGN COUNTRIES

Hello Aurora, 3.8
Sumi's Prize, 3.34
Child of the Dark: The Diary of Carolina Maria de Jesus, 3.45ˣ
Hiroshima No Pika, 3.72
Rafiki, 4.18ˣ
Nothing Is Impossible: The Story of Beatrix Potter, 4.23
The Cuckoo Tree, 4.26ˣ
The Story of Ferdinand, 4.33ˣ
Journey to America, 4.36
The Ostrich Chase, 4.46
Pearl in the Egg, 4.82
The Runaway Summer, 5.6
Moon Eyes, 5.19
Heidi, 5.29
The Maude Reed Tale, 5.34
The Min-Min, 5.36
Early Rising, 5.37
Lupita Manana, 5.59
Emma Tupper's Diary, 6.3
The Witch's Daughter, 6.5
Master Rosalind, 6.6
A Proud Taste for Scarlet and Miniver, 6.13
The Endless Steppe: A Girl in Exile, 6.14
Mary's Monster, 6.17ˣ
Tall and Proud, 6.19
Emmeline and Her Daughters: The Pankhurst Suffragettes, 6.25
Israel's Golda Meir: Pioneer to Prime Minister, 6.47
Nectar in a Sieve, 6.49
Transport 7-41-R, 6.51
A Long Way from Verona, 6.91
The Golda Meir Story, 6.92
The Journey of the Shadow Bairns, 6.99
The Skull in the Snow and Other Folktales, 6.101
The Lark and the Laurel, 7.2
Daughter of the Mountains, 7.11
National Velvet, 7.13
Sing to the Dawn, 7.14
The Princess and the Admiral, 7.22ˣ
The Wife of Martin Guerre, 7.33
Thank You All Very Much, 7.43
The Woman Warrior: Memoirs of a Girlhood among Ghosts, 7.65
Go Well, Stay Well, 7.67
She Never Looked Back: Margaret Mead in Samoa, 7.70
The Night Journey, 7.71
Country of Broken Stone, 7.72
Famous Spies, 8.3
The Prime of Miss Jean Brodie, 8.11
Kathe Kollwitz: Life in Art, 8.13
George Sand, 8.15
And All Her Paths Were Peace, 8.20
Martha Quest, 8.31
Gaudy Night, 8.32
A Time for Everything, 8.33
Hannah Senesh: Her Life and Diary, 8.40
Blackberry Winter: My Earlier Years, 9.14
Portraits of Chinese Women in Revolution, 9.32
Our Hidden Heritage: Five Centuries of Women Artists, 10.3
Margaret Mead, 10.7
Persuasion, 12.3

## THE HANDICAPPED

Dorothea L. Dix: Hospital Founder, 2.15
Howie Helps Himself, 2.25
Annie Sullivan, 2.50
Helen Keller: Toward the Light, 2.56
Through Grandpa's Eyes, 2.74
Words in Our Hands, 2.78
Nick Joins In, 2.79
Darlene, 2.82
Now One Foot, Now the Other, 2.84
The Balancing Girl, 2.87
Sue Ellen, 3.19
Four Women of Courage, 3.27
Don't Forget Tom, 3.49
Waiting for Johnny Miracle, 3.58ˣ
Wonder Women of Sports, 3.69
The Story of Helen Keller, 4.3

Flat on My Face, 4.5
Kristy's Courage, 4.27
Lisa, Bright and Dark, 4.56ˣ
Dinky Hocker Shoots Smack! 4.57
Me Too, 4.78
The Heart Is a Lonely Hunter,
    5.41ˣ
Alesia, 5.57ˣ
The Witch's Daughter, 6.5
Tall and Proud, 6.19
Only Love, 6.98
They Wouldn't Quit: Stories of
    Handicapped People, 7.12
The Silent Storm, 7.35
Listen for the Fig Tree, 7.44
Cameras and Courage: Margaret
    Bourke-White, 7.62
Sports for the Handicapped, 9.31

## HEALTH/HUMAN DEVELOPMENT

The Train, 1.1
What Is a Girl? What Is a Boy?,
    1.8
Why Am I Different?, 2.1
Bodies, 2.4
Dorothea L. Dix: Hospital Founder,
    2.15
The Good Morrow, 2.16ˣ
I Was So Mad!, 2.20
Blue Trees, Red Sky, 2.22
Howie Helps Himself, 2.25
Grandma Didn't Wave Back, 2.26ˣ
Shoeshine Girl, 2.28
Grownups Cry Too, 2.32
Evan's Corner, 2.34
Linda Richards: First American
    Trained Nurse, 2.59
It's Not the End of the World,
    2.62ˣ
My Doctor Bag Book, 2.64
Dumb Old Casey Is a Fat Tree,
    2.65
Where Is Daddy? The Story of a
    Divorce, 2.67
Cold Feet, 2.69ˣ
The Stubborn Old Woman, 2.71
That Is That, 2.72
About Dying, 2.73
I Wish Laura's Mommy Was My
    Mommy, 2.75
Words in Our Hands, 2.78
Nick Joins In, 2.79
A Look at Divorce, 2.80
Clara Barton: Soldier of Mercy, 3.6
Over the Hills and Far Away,
    3.10ˣ
Heart-of-Snowbird, 3.13ˣ
A Promise Is a Promise, 3.15ˣ
Ikwa of the Temple Mounds, 3.18
Sue Ellen, 3.19
The Mulberry Music, 3.25ˣ
Four Women of Courage, 3.27

The Real Me, 3.30ˣ
Ann Aurelia and Dorothy, 3.36
Never Jam Today, 3.39ˣ
The Amazing Miss Laura, 3.40ˣ
The Soul Brothers and Sister Lou,
    3.41ˣ
Marly the Kid, 3.42ˣ
Mixed Marriage Daughter, 3.43ˣ
Mom, the Wolfman and Me, 3.44ˣ
Child of the Dark: The Diary of
    Carolina Maria de Jesus, 3.45ˣ
The Trouble with Thirteen, 3.46ˣ
Cross Fox, 3.47ˣ
Don't Forget Tom, 3.49
Rachel Pushes Back, 3.52
A House for Jonnie O., 3.53ˣ
It Can't Hurt Forever, 3.54
The Cry of the Crow, 3.57
Waiting for Johnny Miracle, 3.58ˣ
Millicent the Magnificent, 3.59
Happy Endings Are All Alike,
    3.60ˣ
Some Lose Their Way, 3.65ˣ
Oh, Boy! Babies!, 3.67ˣ
Sweet Whispers, Brother Rush,
    3.68ˣ
Tiger Eyes, 3.71ˣ
My Doctor, 4.2ˣ
The Story of Helen Keller, 4.3
Flat on My Face, 4.5
Maria Luisa, 4.6
Are You There God? It's Me, Mar-
    garet, 4.7
The Preacher's Kid, 4.13
Iggie's House, 4.16
Nothing Is Impossible: The Story of
    Beatrix Potter, 4.23
Cowslip, 4.25
Kristy's Courage, 4.27
Mahalia: Gospel Singer, 4.39
A Year in the Life of Rosie Ber-
    nard, 4.40
Two Piano Tuners, 4.41
The Changeling, 4.43
Where the Lilies Bloom, 4.44
Zeely, 4.48
Memoirs of an Ex-Prom Queen,
    4.50ˣ
The Girls of Huntington House,
    4.51ˣ
Our Cup Is Broken, 4.53ˣ
I'll Get There. It Better Be Worth
    the Trip, 4.55ˣ
Lisa, Bright and Dark, 4.56ˣ
Dinky Hocker Shoots Smack!, 4.57
The Sexes: Male/Female Roles and
    Relationships, 4.58ˣ
ABC Play with Me, 4.61ˣ
Elizabeth Blackwell, Pioneer Doctor,
    4.64
Hey, Dollface, 4.66
By the Highway Home, 4.68
Daddy Was a Number Runner,
    4.70ˣ
Jemmy, 4.75ˣ
The Beckoner, 4.76ˣ
Me Too, 4.78
Anywhere Else but Here, 4.83

Stories for Free Children, 4.84
The Runaway Summer, 5.6
Annie and the Old One, 5.13
Ballet Shoes, 5.22
Come by Here, 5.24
Naomi, 5.28
It's Not What You Expect, 5.30ˣ
The Member of the Wedding, 5.31ˣ
Lady Sings the Blues, 5.33ˣ
The Maude Reed Tale, 5.34
Bitter Herbs and Honey, 5.35
The Min-Min, 5.36
Early Rising, 5.37
The Pigman, 5.39
The Heart Is a Lonely Hunter,
    5.41ˣ
The Cat Ate My Gymsuit, 5.42
Haunted Summer, 5.46ˣ
Liking Myself, 5.48
Leaving Home, 5.50ˣ
Going to the Sun, 5.55
Alesia, 5.57ˣ
The Witch's Daughter, 6.5
Nilda, 6.8
Queenie Peavy, 6.11
The Endless Steppe: A Girl in Exile,
    6.14
The Search for Charlie, 6.16
Tall and Proud, 6.19
The Liberation of Clementine Tip-
    ton, 6.26
Julie of the Wolves, 6.27
Leo the Lioness, 6.30
The Taste of Spruce Gum, 6.31
The Egypt Game, 6.33
The Tamarack Tree, 6.35
The House without a Christmas
    Tree, 6.36
Classmates by Request, 6.37
A Feast of Light, 6.38
The Headless Cupid, 6.39
Clara Barton: Founder of the Amer-
    ican Red Cross, 6.40
Claudia, Where Are You?, 6.43
The Street, 6.44ˣ
Leap before You Look, 6.45ˣ
First Woman Ambulance Surgeon:
    Emily Barringer, 6.46
A Tree Grows in Brooklyn, 6.48
Nectar in a Sieve, 6.49
Daughter of Earth, 6.50ˣ
Ariel: Poems by Sylvia Plath, 6.52
After the Wedding, 6.53
Are You in the House Alone?,
    6.54ˣ
The Bell Jar, 6.55ˣ
Hey, White Girl!, 6.56
Fifth Chinese Daughter, 6.57
Tell Me a Riddle, 6.58
Feminine Plural: Stories by Women
    about Growing Up, 6.59
Fat Jack, 6.60
Don't Play Dead before You Have
    to, 6.62
Once at the Weary Way, 6.65
Summer of My German Soldier,
    6.68
Girl Sports, 6.72

The Mouse, the Monster and Me, 6.73
Ludell, 6.79
Bouquets for Brimbal, 6.80
Margaret Sanger: Pioneer of Birth Control, 6.84
Ruby, 6.86ˣ
Sam, 6.88
Of Life and Death and Other Journeys, 6.90
Black Cow Summer, 6.93
"I Am Cherry Alive," the Little Girl Sang, 6.95ˣ
Only Love, 6.98
The Forge and the Forest, 7.1
Rebecca of Sunnybrook Farm, 7.15
The Secret Garden, 7.16
Contributions of Women: Sports, 7.26
Daughter of Discontent, 7.31
Jubilee, 7.34
The Silent Storm, 7.35
Free to Choose: Decision Making for Young Men, 7.37
Other Choices for Becoming a Woman, 7.38
The Bluest Eye, 7.42ˣ
Thank You All Very Much, 7.43
Listen for the Fig Tree, 7.44
Women and Fiction: Short Stories by and about Women, 7.52
Jacob Have I Loved, 7.53
Ludell's New York Time, 7.54
Maria Montessori: Knight of the Child, 7.56
Motherlove: Stories by Women about Motherhood, 7.61
Jenny Kimura, 7.63
She Never Looked Back: Margaret Mead in Samoa, 7.70
Country of Broken Stone, 7.72
I, Charlotte Forten, Black and Free, 8.4
Why Am I So Miserable If These Are the Best Years of My Life?, 8.8
The Prime of Miss Jean Brodie, 8.11
A Very Easy Death, 8.14
The Yellow Wallpaper, 8.18
Doctors for the People, 8.22
I Never Promised You a Rose Garden, 8.26
Male & Female Under 18, 8.28
A Time for Everything, 8.33
Free to Be...You and Me, 8.34ˣ
Against Rape, 8.38
Fanny Kemble's America, 9.2
Ms.—M.D., 9.4
Martha Berry: Little Woman with a Big Dream, 9.5
The Young Woman's Guide to Liberation, 9.8
The Feminine Mystique, 9.10
A Hero Ain't Nothin' but a Sandwich, 9.12
I'm Running Away from Home, but I'm Not Allowed to Cross the Street, 9.17

Men's Bodies Men's Selves, 9.26
Boys Have Feelings Too: Growing Up Male for Boys, 9.28
Breakthrough: Women in Writing, 9.29
Sports for the Handicapped, 9.31
Sex & Birth Control, 10.4
Single and Pregnant, 11.3
Self-Defense and Assault Prevention for Girls and Women, 11.8
What Are Little Girls Made Of? The Roots of Feminine Stereotypes, 11.9
Masculine/Feminine: Readings in Sexual Mythology and the Liberation of Women, 12.1
Witches, Midwives and Nurses: A History of Women Healers, 12.2
Persuasion, 12.3
Contraception, Abortion, Pregnancy, 12.5
Commonsense Sex, 12.8

# HISTORY

Becky and the Bear, 2.7
Harriet and the Promised Land, 2.10
Dorothea L. Dix: Hospital Founder, 2.15
Jane Addams, 2.35
Annie Sullivan, 2.50
Heroines of '76, 2.53ˣ
Eleanor Roosevelt: First Lady of the World, 2.57
Linda Richards: First American Trained Nurse, 2.59
Nancy Ward, Cherokee, 2.60ˣ
Women Who Dared to Be Different, 2.61
We Are Mesquakie, We Are One, 2.70ˣ
Island of the Blue Dolphins, 3.4ˣ
Harriet and the Runaway Book, 3.5
Clara Barton: Soldier of Mercy, 3.6
Abigail Adams: "Dear Partner," 3.9
Over the Hills and Far Away, 3.10ˣ
Ikwa of the Temple Mounds, 3.18
Thunder at Gettysburg, 3.23
Four Women of Courage, 3.27
Red Rock over the River, 3.31ˣ
Mary McLeod Bethune, 3.32
Zia, 3.37ˣ
Never Jam Today, 3.39ˣ
Jane Addams, 3.61
Hiroshima No Pika, 3.72
She Wanted to Read: The Story of Mary McLeod Bethune, 4.17
Before the Supreme Court: The Story of Belva Ann Lockwood, 4.19

Two Tickets to Freedom: The True Story of Ellen and William Craft, Fugitive Slaves, 4.22
Cowslip, 4.25
The Cuckoo Tree, 4.26ˣ
Sojourner Truth: Fearless Crusader, 4.32
Journey to America, 4.36
Mumbet: The Story of Elizabeth Freeman, 4.38
Stand Up Lucy, 4.52
How Many Miles to Sundown?, 4.54
The Autobiography of Miss Jane Pittman, 4.60
Elizabeth Blackwell, Pioneer Doctor, 4.64
Mary McLeod Bethune, 4.71
The Wind Is Not a River, 4.74
Pearl in the Egg, 4.82
Sacajawea, 5.3
Susan B. Anthony: Pioneer in Women's Rights, 5.9
Women with a Cause, 5.16
Runaway to Freedom: A Story of the Underground Railway, 5.20
True Grit, 5.21
Come by Here, 5.24
Making Our Way, 5.32ˣ
The Maude Reed Tale, 5.34
Bitter Herbs and Honey, 5.35
Early Rising, 5.37
The Witch of Blackbird Pond, 5.38
Woman Chief, 5.40
Dragonwings, 5.45
O Pioneers!, 5.52ˣ
I'm Deborah Sampson: A Soldier in the War of the Revolution, 5.54
Pioneer Women: Voices from the Kansas Frontier, 5.62ˣ
Farewell to Manzanar, 6.4
Master Rosalind, 6.6
Nine Lives of Moses: On the Oregon Trail, 6.9
Women of Courage, 6.10
A Proud Taste for Scarlet and Miniver, 6.13
The Endless Steppe: A Girl in Exile, 6.14
Mary's Monster, 6.17ˣ
This Time, Tempe Wick?, 6.22ˣ
Harriet Tubman: Conductor on the Underground Railroad, 6.23
Women of the West, 6.24
Emmeline and Her Daughters: The Pankhurst Suffragettes, 6.25
The Liberation of Clementine Tipton, 6.26
Phillis Wheatley: America's First Black Poetess, 6.28ˣ
The Taste of Spruce Gum, 6.31
Charlotte Forten: Free Black Teacher, 6.34
The Tamarack Tree, 6.35
Clara Barton: Founder of the American Red Cross, 6.40
Susette La Flesche: Voice of the Omaha Indians, 6.41

America's First Woman Astronomer: Maria Mitchell, 6.42
First Woman Ambulance Surgeon: Emily Barringer, 6.46
Israel's Golda Meir: Pioneer to Prime Minister, 6.47
Transport 7-41-R, 6.51
Lady for the Defense: A Biography of Belva Lockwood, 6.63
Dorothy Day: Friend of the Poor, 6.64
Chief Sarah: Sarah Winnemucca's Fight for Indian Rights, 6.76
America's First Woman Chemist: Ellen Richards, 6.77
Margaret Sanger: Pioneer of Birth Control, 6.84
Contributions of Women: Labor, 6.96
The Journey of the Shadow Bairns, 6.99
The Forge and the Forest, 7.1
The Lark and the Laurel, 7.2
Maria Sanford: Pioneer Professor, 7.5
Oh, Lizzie! The Story of Elizabeth Cady Stanton, 7.10
Time at the Top, 7.18
To the Barricades: The Anarchist Life of Emma Goldman, 7.20
Contributions of Women: Education, 7.23
An Album of Women in American History, 7.24
The Wife of Martin Guerre, 7.33
Jubilee, 7.34
The Silent Storm, 7.35
My Antonia, 7.36
Women's Rights, 7.39
The Loon Feather, 7.48
Women Who Shaped History, 7.57
From Parlor to Prison, 7.66
I, Charlotte Forte, Black and Free, 8.4
Patriots in Petticoats, 8.5
Kathe Kollwitz: Life in Art, 8.13
George Sand, 8.15
And All Her Paths Were Peace, 8.20
Marie Curie, 8.25
Martha Quest, 8.31
Life in the Iron Mills, 8.37
The Dollmaker, 8.39
Hannah Senesh: Her Life and Diary, 8.40
Eloquent Crusader: Ernestine Rose, 9.1
Fanny Kemble's America, 9.2
Four Women in a Violent Time, 9.3
Martha Berry: Little Woman with a Big Dream, 9.5
Daughters of the Earth, 9.9
Enterprising Women, 9.15
A Pictorial History of Women in America, 9.18
Bloomsday for Maggie, 9.19
Black Foremothers: Three Lives, 9.23

Famous American Women, 9.25
I Am the Fire of Time, 9.30
Portraits of Chinese Women in Revolution, 9.32
Our Hidden Heritage: Five Centuries of Women Artists, 10.3
Root of Bitterness, 10.6
Feminism: The Essential Historical Writings, 10.8
Popcorn Venus, 11.2
Women Artists: Recognition and Reappraisal from the Early Middle Ages to the Twentieth Century, 11.5
Beautiful, Also, Are the Souls of My Black Sisters, 11.7
Masculine/Feminine: Readings in Sexual Mythology and the Liberation of Women, 12.1
Witches, Midwives and Nurses: A History of Women Healers, 12.2
Persuasion, 12.3
Man's World, Woman's Place: A Study in Social Mythology, 12.6
Woman and Womanhood in America, 12.7
Rights and Wrongs: Women's Struggle for Equality, 12.9

## INFORMATION BOOK

Oh, Boy! Babies!, 3.67ˣ
Three Days on a River in a Red Canoe, 3.70
Kids Are Natural Cooks, 4.42
Wilderness Challenge, 5.61
Life with Working Parents: Practical Hints for Everyday Situations, 7.29

## LANGUAGE ARTS

### Anthologies

Stories for Free Children, 4.84
Feminine Plural: Stories by Women about Growing Up, 6.59
Plays by and about Women, 6.66ˣ
By and about Women: An Anthology of Short Fiction, 6.74ˣ
Women Working: An Anthology of Stories and Poems, 7.49
Women and Fiction: Short Stories by and about Women, 7.52
Motherlove: Stories by Women about Motherhood, 7.61
Women of Wonder: Science Fiction Stories by Women about Women, 8.10

In Her Own Image: Women Working in the Arts, 8.41
I Am the Fire of Time, 9.30

### Drama

Plays by and about Women, 6.66ˣ

### Essays/Short Stories

Tell Me a Riddle, 6.58
Feminine Plural: Stories by Women about Growing Up, 6.59
By and About Women: An Anthology of Short Fiction, 6.74ˣ
Crazy Salad: Some Things about Women, 7.47
Women Working: An Anthology of Stories and Poems, 7.49
Women and Fiction: Short Stories by and about Women, 7.52
I Love Myself When I Am Laughing, 7.55
Motherlove: Stories by Women about Motherhood, 7.61
The Woman Warrior: Memoirs of a Girlhood among Ghosts, 7.65
Women of Wonder: Science Fiction Stories by Women about Women, 8.10
Portraits of Chinese Women in Revolution, 9.32

### Fantasy, Folk & Fairy Tales

Rabbit Finds a Way, 1.7
Pippa Mouse, 2.13
Lucille, 2.24
He Bear, She Bear, 2.46
Amigo, 2.47
Jellybeans for Breakfast, 2.49
Animals Should Definitely *Not* Wear Clothing, 3.2
Mandy and the Flying Map, 3.14
The Silver Whistle, 3.17
Carlotta and the Scientist, 3.20
The Dragon andthe Doctor, 3.21
William's Doll, 3.33
Charlotte's Web, 3.38
The Practical Princess and Other Liberating Tales, 4.8
Penelope and the Mussels, 4.9
Liza Lou and the Yeller Belly Swamp, 4.10
Rafiki, 4.18ˣ
The Borrowers, 4.29
The Story of Ferdinand, 4.33ˣ
The Changeling, 4.43
Womenfolk and Fairy Tales, 4.49
The Clever Princess, 4.79
The Country Bunny and the Little Golden Shoes, 5.2ˣ
Amy and the Cloud Basket, 5.5
Mary Jane, 5.18

The Lion, the Witch and the Wardrobe, 5.23
Tatterhood and Other Tales, 5.26
Mrs. Frisby and the Rats of NIMH, 5.27
Clever Gretchen and Other Forgotten Folktales, 5.47
The Squire's Bride, 6.18ˣ
Miss Hickory, 6.20
The Maid of the North: Feminist Folktales from around the World, 6.100
The Skull in the Snow and Other Folktales, 6.101
Magic at Wychwood, 7.4
Fresh Fish...and Chips, 7.8ˣ
Time at the Top, 7.18
The Princess and the Admiral, 7.22ˣ
Song of Sedna, 7.69ˣ
The Trouble with Princesses, 7.73
Miss Bianca, 8.2ˣ
Fanshen, the Magic Bear, 8.19ˣ
Free to Be...You and Me, 8.34ˣ

**Literature by Women**

Daddy Was a Number Runner, 4.70ˣ
The Member of the Wedding, 5.31ˣ
The Heart Is a Lonely Hunter, 5.41ˣ
O Pioneers!, 5.52ˣ
A Tree Grows in Brooklyn, 6.48
Nectar in a Sieve, 6.49
Ariel: Poems by Sylvia Plath, 6.52
The Bell Jar, 6.55ˣ
Tell Me a Riddle, 6.58
Feminine Plural: Stories by Women about Growing Up, 6.59
Mrs. Dalloway, 6.71ˣ
By and about Women: An Anthology of Short Fiction, 6.74ˣ
I Know Why the Caged Bird Sings, 6.81
My Antonia, 7.36
The Bluest Eye, 7.42ˣ
Thank You All Very Much, 7.43
Women Working: An Anthology of Stories and Poems, 7.49
Women and Fiction: Short Stories by and about Women, 7.52
I Love Myself When I Am Laughing, 7.55
Motherlove: Stories by Women about Motherhood, 7.61
Women of Wonder: Science Fiction Stories by Women about Women, 8.10
The Prime of Miss Jean Brodie, 8.11
A Very Easy Death, 8.14
George Sand, 8.15
A Room of One's Own, 8.17
The Yellow Wallpaper, 8.18
Martha Quest, 8.31
Gaudy Night, 8.32
Life in the Iron Mills, 8.37

The Dollmaker, 8.39
In Her Own Image: Women Working in the Arts, 8.41
The Feminine Mystique, 9.10
Gather Together in My Name, 9.11
I Am the Fire of Time, 9.31
Persuasion, 12.3

**Poetry/Rhyme**

Snow, 1.6
Black Is Brown Is Tan, 2.8
Harriet and the Promised Land, 2.10
Noisy Nora, 2.19
Amigo, 2.47
A Train for Jane, 3.28
Penelope and the Mussels, 4.9
Amy and the Cloud Basket, 5.5
Phoebe's Revolt, 5.15
Phillis Wheatley: America's First Black Poetess, 6.28ˣ
Ariel: Poems by Sylvia Plath, 6.52
Fresh Fish...and Chips, 7.8ˣ
I'm Nobody! Who Are You?, 7.25
Women Working: An Anthology of Stories and Poems, 7.49
Dreams in Harrison Railroad Park, 7.51
Male & Female under 18, 8.28
Free to Be...You and Me, 8.34ˣ
In Her Own Image: Women Working in the Arts, 8.41

# MYSTERY/ADVENTURE

Becky and the Bear, 2.7
Harriet and the Promised Land, 2.10
Rod-and-Reel Trouble, 2.43ˣ
Heroines of '76, 2.53ˣ
Amelia Earhart, 2.55
Island of the Blue Dolphins, 3.4ˣ
Coleen the Question Girl, 3.16
Thunder at Gettysburg, 3.23
Harriet the Spy, 3.29ˣ
Red Rock over the River, 3.31ˣ
The Lancelot Closes at Five, 3.35
Penelope and the Mussels, 4.9
Liza Lou and the Yeller Belly Swamp, 4.10
Jennifer, Hecate, MacBeth, William McKinley and Me, Elizabeth, 4.15
Two Tickets to Freedom: The True Story of Ellen and William Craft, Fugitive Slaves, 4.22
The Cuckoo Tree, 4.26ˣ
The Borrowers, 4.29
Journey to America, 4.36
Notes on the Hauter Experiment: A Journey through the Inner World of Evelyn B. Chestnut, 4.45
The Ostrich Chase, 4.46

Firegirl, 4.47
Womenfolk and Fairy Tales, 4.49
How Many Miles to Sundown?, 4.54
Maria Looney and the Remarkable Robot, 4.59
The Wind Is Not a River, 4.74
Pearl in the Egg, 4.82
The Runaway Summer, 5.6
Moon Eyes, 5.19
Runaway to Freedom: A Story of the Underground Railway, 5.20
True Grit, 5.21
The Lion, the Witch and the Wardrobe, 5.23
Secret Castle, 5.25
Heidi, 5.29
The Maude Reed Tale, 5.34
The Min-Min, 5.36
The Witch of Blackbird Pond, 5.38
Woman Chief, 5.40
Tisha, 5.44ˣ
This Time of Darkness, 5.51
The Hideaway Summer, 5.53
I'm Deborah Sampson: A Soldier in the War of the Revolution, 5.54
Wilderness Challenge, 5.61
Emma Tupper's Diary, 6.3
The Witch's Daughter, 6.5
Master Rosalind, 6.6
Nine Lives of Moses: On the Oregon Trail, 6.9
Women of Courage, 6.10
The Endless Steppe: A Girl in Exile, 6.14
The Search for Charlie, 6.16
Mary's Monster, 6.17ˣ
Adventures of B.J., The Amateur Detective, 6.21
This Time, Tempe Wick?, 6.22ˣ
Harriet Tubman: Conductor on the Underground Railroad, 6.23
Julie of the Wolves, 6.27
A Wrinkle in Time, 6.29
The Egypt Game, 6.33
The Headless Cupid, 6.39
Transport 7-41-R, 6.51
Susannah and the Blue House Mystery, 6.97
The Lark and the Laurel, 7.2
Daughter of the Mountains, 7.11
Time at the Top, 7.18
To the Barricades: The Anarchist Life of Emma Goldman, 7.20
The Princess and the Admiral, 7.22ˣ
Downright Dencey, 7.28
The Night Journey, 7.71
Country of Broken Stone, 7.72
The Trouble with Princesses, 7.73
Miss Bianca, 8.2ˣ
Famous Spies, 8.3
Patriots in Petticoats, 8.5
Enchantress from the Stars, 8.16
Gaudy Night, 8.32

# PICTURE BOOK

And I Mean It, Stanley, 1.2
I Can Help Too, 1.3
A Hole Is to Dig, 1.4
Ann Can Fly, 1.5
Snow, 1.6
What Is a Girl? What Is a Boy?, 1.8
Sunshine, 1.9
Why Am I Different, 2.1
Max, 2.2
Bodies, 2.4
Black Is Brown Is Tan, 2.8
Don't You Remember?, 2.9
Harriet and the Promised Land, 2.10
The Girl Who Would Rather Climb Trees, 2.11
The Sunshine Family and the Pony, 2.17
Noisy Nora, 2.19
I Was So Mad!, 2.20
Lucille, 2.24
Howie Helps Himself, 2.25
Plants in Winter, 2.27
Joshua's Day, 2.30
Mothers Can Do Anything, 2.31
Umbrella, 2.33
Evan's Corner, 2.34
Just Think!, 2.36
A Birthday for Frances, 2.37
Don't Ride the Bus on Monday: The Rosa Parks Story, 2.38
All Kinds of Families, 2.39
Best Friends for Frances, 2.40
I Love Gram, 2.41
Quiet on Account of Dinosaur, 2.44
Nice Little Girls, 2.45
He Bear, She Bear, 2.46
Try and Catch Me, 2.48
Annie Sullivan, 2.50
Clowning Around, 2.51
A Pony for Linda, 2.52
What Mary Jo Wanted, 2.54
Steffie and Me, 2.58
My Doctor Bag Book, 2.64
Monday I Was an Alligator, 2.66
Where Is Daddy? The Story of a Divorce, 2.67
Animal Daddies and My Daddy, 2.68
The Stubborn Old Woman, 2.71
That Is That, 2.72
About Dying, 2.73
Through Grandpa's Eyes, 2.74
I Wish Laura's Mommy Was My Mommy, 2.75
My Daddy Don't Go to Work, 2.76
The Rabbit Is Next, 2.77
Nick Joins In, 2.79
A Look at Divorce, 2.80
Jim Meets the Thing, 2.81
Darlene, 2.82
My Mom Travels a Lot, 2.83
Now One Foot, Now the Other, 2.84

Daddy and Ben Together, 2.85
The Balancing Girl, 2.87
A Chair for My Mother, 2.88
Animals Should Definitely *Not* Wear Clothing, 3.2
Ira Sleeps Over, 3.7
Mandy and the Flying Map, 3.14
Coleen the Question Girl, 3.16
The Silver Whistle, 3.17
Carlotta and the Scientist, 3.20
Eliza's Daddy, 3.21
The Dragon and the Doctor, 3.22
Blueberries for Sal, 3.24
A Train for Jane, 3.28
William's Doll, 3.33
Sumi's Prize, 3.34
Don't Forget Tom, 3.49
A Book about Us, 3.50
Maria Teresa, 3.62
What Will I Be?, 3.63
My Mother and I Are Growing Strong, 3.64
The Girl Who Loved Wild Horses, 3.66
Three Days on a River in a Red Canoe, 3.70
Hiroshima No Pika, 3.72
Jo, Flo and Yolanda, 4.1ˣ
My Doctor, 4.2ˣ
A Little Lion, 4.4ˣ
Penelope and the Mussels, 4.9
Liza Lou and the Yeller Belly Swamp, 4.10
I Climb Mountains, 4.11
ABC Workbook, 4.12ˣ
Rafiki, 4.18ˣ
Tommy and Sarah Dress Up, 4.20ˣ
What Can She Be? A Veterinarian, 4.21
Rosie and Michael, 4.24
What Can She Be? A Lawyer, 4.28
Fannie Lou Hamer, 4.30ˣ
The Story of Ferdinand, 4.33ˣ
Along Sandy Trails, 4.34
My Mother the Mail Carrier, 4.35
Firegirl, 4.47
Andrea Jaeger Tennis Champion, 4.62
Window Wishing, 4.69ˣ
Self Portrait: Margot Zemach, 4.81
Lordy, Aunt Hattie, 5.1ˣ
The Country Bunny and the Little Golden Shoes, 5.2ˣ
Amy and the Cloud Basket, 5.5
The Man Who Didn't Wash His Dishes, 5.7ˣ
The Terrible Thing that Happened at Our House, 5.10ˣ
The Sunflower Garden, 5.11ˣ
First Snow, 5.12ˣ
Annie and the Old One, 5.13
The Magic Hat, 5.14ˣ
Phoebe's Revolt, 5.15
Martin's Father, 5.17ˣ
What Can She Be? A Farmer, 5.43
Some Things You Just Can't Do by Yourself, 5.49

Don't Put Vinegar in the Copper, 5.56ˣ
Did You Ever?, 6.12ˣ
Women at Their Work, 6.15
The Squire's Bride, 6.18ˣ
This Time, Tempe Wick?, 6.22ˣ
My Little Book of Cats, 6.83ˣ
Daddy Is a Monster...Sometimes X6.94
"I Am Cherry Alive," the Little Girl Sang, 6.95ˣ
Doctor Mary's Animals, 7.7ˣ
Fresh Fish...and Chips, 7.8ˣ
Three Stalks of Corn, 7.9ˣ
Nothing but a Dog, 7.60ˣ
Song of Sedna, 7.69ˣ

# RELIGION/ MYTHOLOGY

A Promise Is a Promise, 3.15ˣ
Ikwa of the Temple Mounds, 3.18
Mixed Marriage Daughter, 3.43ˣ
Are You There God? It's Me, Margaret, 4.7
The Preacher's Kid, 4.13
A Year in the Life of Rosie Bernard, 4.40
Bitter Herbs and Honey, 5.35
Dorothy Day: Friend of the Poor, 6.64
The Golda Meir Story, 6.92
Rose Kennedy: No Time for Tears, 7.58
Breakthrough: Women in Religion, 8.36
Daughters of the Earth, 9.9
The Jewish Woman: New Perspectives, 11.6

# SCIENCE/TECHNOLOGY

Rachel Carson: Who Loved the Sea, 2.21
Plants in Winter, 2.27
Carlotta and the Scientist, 3.20
Frankie and the Fawn, 3.26ˣ
Listen to Your Kitten Purr, 3.85
My Doctor, 4.2ˣ
What Can She Be? A Veterinarian, 4.21
Going to the Sun, 5.55
Mary's Monster, 6.17ˣ
Miss Hickory, 6.20
America's First Woman Astronomer: Maria Mitchell, 6.42
Science Experiments You Can Eat, 6.69
America's First Woman Chemist: Ellen Richards, 6.77

Doctor Mary's Animals, 7.7ˣ
What Can She Be? A Geologist, 7.64
The Cancer Lady: Maud Slye and Her Heredity Studies, 8.23
Marie Curie, 8.25
Careers in Conservation, 8.27
Sea and Earth: The Life of Rachel Carson, 8.30
Wild Animals, Gentle Women, 8.35
New Women in Medicine, 8.42
Watching the Wild Apes: The Primate Studies of Goodall, Fossey and Galdikas, 9.16
Math Equals: Biographies of Women + Related Activities, 9.20
What Can She Be? A Computer Scientist, 9.22ˣ
Contemporary Women Scientist of America, 10.11
ChemistryCareers, 11.10
Witches, Midwives and Nurses: A History of Women Healers, 12.2
Looking Forward to a Career: Veterinary Medicine, 12.4ˣ
Contraception, Abortion, Pregnancy, 12.5

# SCIENCE FICTION

Star Ka'ats and the Plant People, 3.56
Notes on the Hauter Experiment: A Journey through the Inner World of Evelyn B. Chestnut, 4.45
Maria Looney and the Remarkable Robot, 4.59
This Time of Darkness, 5.51
A Wrinkle in Time, 6.29
Women of Wonder: Science Fiction Stories by Women about Women, 8.10
Enchantress from the Stars, 8.16

# SPORTS

Max, 2.2
Wonder Women of Sports, 3.69
Flat on My Face, 4.5
Chris Evert: Tennis Pro, 4.37
Andrea Jaeger Tennis Champion, 4.62
Billie Jean King: Queen of the Courts, 4.65
I Am the Running Girl, 4.72
She Shoots, She Scores!, 6.1
I Always Wanted to Be Somebody, 6.70

Girl Sports, 6.72
Zanballer, 7.6
Contributions of Women: Sports, 7.26
Famous Modern American Women Athletes, 7.27
Billie Jean, 7.41
Women in Sports: Swimming, 7.68
Women Who Win, 8.6
American Women in Sports, 8.7
100 Greatest Women in Sports, 9.7
Sports for the Handicapped, 9.31
Self-Defense and Assault Prevention for Girls and Women, 11.8

# WOMEN'S STUDIES

Never Jam Today, 3.39ˣ
Child of the Dark: The Diary of Carolina Maria de Jesus, 3.45ˣ
Memoirs of an Ex-Prom Queen, 4.50ˣ
The Sexes: Male/Female Roles and Relationships, 4.58ˣ
Stories for Free Children, 4.84
Pioneer Women: Voices from the Kansas Frontier, 5.62ˣ
Women of the West, 6.24
Nectar in a Sieve, 6.49
Daughter of Earth, 6.50ˣ
Ariel: Poems by Sylvia Plath, 6.52
Tell Me a Riddle, 6.58
Feminine Plural: Stories by Women about Growing Up, 6.59
Childtimes: A Three Generation Memoir, 6.61
Lady for the Defense: A Biography of Belva Lockwood, 6.63
Plays by and about Women, 6.66ˣ
By and about Women: An Anthology of Short Fiction, 6.74
Chief Sarah: Sarah Winnemucca's Fight for Indian Rights, 6.76
Margaret Sanger: Pioneer of Birth Control, 6.84
Women of Crises: Lives of Struggle and Hope, 6.89ˣ
Contributions of Women: Labor, 6.96
Cowgirls: Women of the American West, 6.102ˣ
The Wife of Martin Guerre, 7.33
Other Choices for Becoming a Woman, 7.38
Women's Rights, 7.39
Women in Television, 7.40
Crazy Salad: Some Things about Women, 7.47
Women Working: An Anthology of Short Stories and Poems, 7.49
Women and Fiction: Short Stories by and about Women, 7.52
I Love Myself When I Am Laughing, 7.55

Women Who Shaped History, 7.57
From Parlor to Prison, 7.60
Motherlove: Stories by Women about Motherhood, 7.61
Why Am I So Miserable If These Are the Best Years of My Life?, 8.8
Youngand Female, 8.9
Women of Wonder: Science Fiction Stories by Women about Women, 8.10
A Room of One's Own, 8.17
The Yellow Wallpaper, 8.18
And All Her Paths Were Peace, 8.20
The Gender Trap: A Closer Look at Sex Roles (Book 1: Education and Work), 8.24
Bella Abzug, 8.29
Breakthrough: Women in Religion, 8.36
Against Rape, 8.38
In Her Own Image: Women Working in Arts, 8.41
New Women in Medicine, 8.42
New Women in Entertainment, 8.43
Saturday's Child, 8.44
The Young Woman's Guide to Liberation, 9.8
Daughters of the Earth, 9.9
The Feminine Mystique, 9.10
Blackberry Winter: My Earlier Years, 9.14
Enterprising Women, 9.15
I'm Running Away from Home but I'm Not Allowed to Cross the Street, 9.17
A Pictorial History of Women in America, 9.18
Black Foremothers: Three Lives, 9.23
Blue Collar Jobs for Women, 9.24
Famous American Women, 9.25
Breakthrough: Women in Writing, 9.29
I Am the Fire of Time, 9.30
Portraits of Chinese Women in Revolution, 9.32
Our Hidden Heritage: Five Centuries of Women Artists, 10.3
New Women in Politics, 10.5
Root of Bitterness, 10.6
Margaret Mead, 10.7
Feminism: The Essential Historical Writings, 10.8
Women See Women, 10.9
Contemporary Women Scientists of America, 10.11
Mirror Mirror: Images of Women Reflected in Popular Culture, 11.1
Popcorn Venus, 11.2
Single and Pregnant, 11.3
Psychology and the New Woman, 11.4
Women Artists: Recognition and Reappraisal from the Early Middle

Ages to the Twentieth Century, 11.5

The Jewish Woman: New Perspectives, 11.6

Beautiful, Also, Are the Souls of My Black Sisters, 11.7

What Are Little Girls Made Of? The Roots of Feminine Stereotypes, 11.9

Masculine/Feminine: Readings in Sexual Mythology and the Liberation of Women, 12.1

Witches, Midwives and Nurses: A History of Women Healers, 12.2

Man's World, Woman's Place: A Study in Social Mythology, 12.6

Women and Womanhood in America, 12.7

Rights and Wrongs: Women's Struggle for Equality, 12.9